Partners in Pleasure

Prologue: The Legend of the *Naupaka*

This Hawaiian *mo`olelo* (legend) of expressed love between a lovely maiden and her handsome suitor speaks not only of love, but of love's unity beyond time and space. Seeking blessing from a high priest *(kahuna)*, the couple was saddened when told that their union could not be sanctified and were heavyhearted when the verdict was to be absolute separation, he sent to the mountains, she to remain at the side of the sea. Mournfully, they obeyed. But the Hawaiian lovers' hearts and minds were *kakou*—united forever in *aloha*. Not even the *kahuna*'s curse could divide them into two "I"s *(o wau)*. To symbolize their lasting love, the maiden removed a flower from her hair, and, tearing it in half, she gave her now lost love half of the blossom. The other half she kept. Both halves were moistened by her tears.

Today, in the mountains of Hawai`i, the *naupaka* flower grows hardily with a beautiful half-blossom that seems to lean down toward the sea. At the ocean, the other half of the *naupaka* flower seems to lean up toward the mountains. If one looks very carefully at these white half-blossoms, faint purple tear stains can be seen. Never to be physically together again, apart, the *aloha* of the Hawaiian lovers still blooms and remains today and forever.

Other Books by Dr. Paul Pearsall

Super Immunity: Master Your Emotions and Improve Your Health
Super Marital Sex: Loving for Life
Super Joy: Learning to Celebrate Everyday Life
The Power of the Family: Strength, Comfort, Healing
Making Miracles: Finding Meaning in Life's Chaos
The Ten Laws of Lasting Love
A Healing Intimacy: The Power of Loving Connections
The Pleasure Prescription: To Love, To Work, To Play—Life in the Balance
Write Your Own Pleasure Prescription: 60 Ways to Create Balance and Joy in Your Life
The Heart's Code: Tapping the Wisdom and Power of Our Heart Energy
Wishing Well: Making Your Every Wish Come True

Ordering

Trade bookstores in the U.S. and Canada, please contact:
Publishers Group West
1700 Fourth Street, Berkeley CA 94710
Phone: (800) 788-3123   Fax: (510) 528-3444

Hunter House books are available at bulk discounts for textbook course adoptions; to qualifying community, health care, and government organizations; and for special promotions and fundraising. For details please contact:

Special Sales Department
Hunter House Inc., PO Box 2914, Alameda CA 94501-0914
Phone: (510) 865-5282   Fax: (510) 865-4295
E-mail: ordering@hunterhouse.com

Individuals can order our books from most bookstores or by calling toll-free:
(800) 266-5592

JUL 0 2001

PARTNERS IN PLEASURE

Sharing Success, Creating Joy, Fulfilling Dreams — Together

Paul Pearsall, Ph.D.

Hunter House
PUBLISHERS

Hunter House Inc., Publishers
PO Box 2914
Alameda CA 94501-0914

Library of Congress Cataloging-in-Publication Data

Pearsall, Paul.
Partners in pleasure : sharing success, creating joy, fulfilling dreams—together / Paul Pearsall.—1st ed.
p. cm.
Includes bibliographical references and index.
ISBN 0-89793-323-0 (pbk.) — 0-89793-324-9 (cl.)
1. Pleasure. 2. Couples—Psychology. 3. Conduct of life. I. Title.

BF515 .P317 2001

646.7'8—dc21   2001016617

Project Credits

Cover Design: Hunter House/Jil Weil
Cover Illustration: Damien Friesz
Book Production: Hunter House
Developmental Editors: Kiran S. Rana and Kelley Blewster
Line and Copy Editor: Kelley Blewster
Proofreader: Lee Rappold
Indexer: Kathy Talley-Jones
Graphics Assistance: Ariel Parker
Acquisitions Editor: Jeanne Brondino
Associate Editor: Alexandra Mummery
Publicity Manager: Sarah Frederick
Marketing Assistant: Earlita Chenault
Customer Service Manager: Christina Sverdrup
Order Fulfillment: Joel Irons
Administrator: Theresa Nelson
Computer Support: Peter Eichelberger
Publisher: Kiran S. Rana

Printed and Bound by Publishers Press, Salt Lake City, Utah
Manufactured in the United States of America

9 8 7 6 5 4 3 2 1   First Edition   01 02 03 04 05

Table of Contents

Contents (cont'd)

`Olelo Ho`omaika`i (Words of Acknowledgement)

E ho`omau Ka Ha Hawai`i

To perpetuate the culture of Hawai`i.

—Kumu Kawaikapuokalani Hewett

This book came through me, not from me. Any mistakes are mine, but all of its truths were inspired and guided by the *na`auao* (wisdom) and *aloha* (love) of the *lahui kanaka*, the culture of the past and present people of Hawai`i. My extended *`ohana* (family) of Kuhai Halau O Kawaikapuokalani Pa `Olapa Kahiko continues to patiently teach and show me the profound Hawaiian knowledge of a balanced, aligned, and totally connected way of living. Kumu Kawaikapuokalani has long been my spiritual teacher, and Mapuana Ringler, Carmen Kanei, Nalani Badua, Pat Gooch, and the rest of the *halau* help me share his wisdom when they *pule* (pray), *mele* (sing), *oli* (chant), and *hula* (dance) with me as I speak to those who would learn more of the amazing grit and grace of the cultural lessons of Hawai`i. *Mahalo* also to Kaulu Amaral, who has traveled the world to teach with me through her unique body-prayer *hula*.

For the Hawaiian lessons that appear throughout this book, I owe a tremendous debt to my own *kumu*, Frank Kawaikapuokalani Hewett, and his *halau* (*hula* group), Kuhai Halau o Kawaikapuokalani Pa `Olapa Kahiko, for continuing to share their *mana`o* (wisdom) and their *ahonui* (patience) with my continental scientist's mind. All of the credit for the ideas expressed here goes to these people. I express my most sincere *kala mai ia`u* (apologies) for any errors or oversimplifications. They are due to my overeagerness to share the sacred treasures of Hawai`i with as wide an audience as possible.

My humble knowledge of *kakou*, of "we" thinking, has been a life-saving gift from my wife, Celest Kalalani. When I write of *kakou* throughout this book, I share as best I can her total "we" orientation to life as confirmed and lived by Ka Ha Naupaka, a group of Hawaiian couples of which my wife and I are deeply honored to be members. Together, the members of Ka Ha Naupaka have more than two thousand years of marital life and experience in sharing the delight and despair of the necessary chaos of living. My most sincere *mahalo* to this group, including Jack and Betty Jenkins, Kawa`o and Nappy Durante, Mary and David Peters, Analu and Halani Berard, Napu and Richard Kong, Sophie and Jessie Makainai, Janice and Joshua Akana, Tina and Tom Van-Culin, Pupu and Pat Mattson, Amber and Milton Smith, Nina and Charles Maxell, Alma and Roland Ahuna, Charles and Wahine-hookae, Philip Kekaku, Napua and Gabriel Makuakane, Tutu Mama Ellis, and all of our *aumakua* (ancestors), whose *aloha* resonates within us not only as a blessing but as a responsibility.

Heroes do not always have to be one courageous individual. The marriage between my mother, Carol, and my deceased father, Frank, continues to serve as an inspiration and model of love's enduring healing power to transcend time and space. *Mahalo* also to my publisher, Kiran Rana, and the `ohana at Hunter House Publishers for helping this book to be created as a *makana* (gift) from the heroes mentioned above to those who would seek to live *kakou* style—together forever.

Foreword: A Naupaka Marriage

By "Aunty Betty" Kawohiokalani Ellis-Jenkins

Told and retold, love stories never grow old. Told and retold, the *aloha* of pleasurable relationships creates bonds that last forever. Told and retold, the memories made in a *naupaka* marriage of lasting love surface in mutual admiration unhampered by the pressures of the modern world. Such is the nature of man and woman . . . such is the nature of love in its truest form. Hawaiians call this *kakou*, the all-inclusive "we."

The Hawaiian *moʻolelo* (legend) of the *naupaka* represents a loving pleasure bond. It speaks of realizing our half-ness and our endless yearning for the true pleasure and contentment we experience when we join our heart, mind, body, and soul with those of our other loving half. There are many versions of the *naupaka moʻolelo*, and the one told by Dr. Pearsall, the one you will encounter later in this book, speaks of the goddess Pele's interference in love and how spiteful selfishness, deceit, and jealous meanness from any source can tear at a loving bond. The version in the prologue depicts characters without negative behavior but still united forever in *aloha kakou*, inseparable love. The main lesson is the same in all versions of the *naupaka moʻolelo*. It tells us, as Dr. Pearsall says, that seeking self-fulfillment only leaves us unfulfilled and grieving for someone with whom we can share the pleasure of the gift of life. We are all half happy without the full and unconditional love of another.

Despite the many riches of the modern world, many still seem unable to find peaceful pleasure and gentle contentment in their daily lives. This is because they too often seek and think of these things as individuals—as an *o wau* ("I") instead of as *kakou* ("we"). The *naupaka* plant lives on, one at the mountain and the other at the sea, an enduring symbol and constant reminder of our sacred need for a partner in pleasure.

My partner in pleasure, Jack, and I met through mutual friends—I an island woman, he a North Carolinian Tarheel in the Navy. We spoke often about our "platonic" relationship. After a Hawai`i-style courtship followed by a separation imposed by distance and obligations, a flow of letters and telephone calls canceled the platonic relationship and gave birth to a long-distance romance that included an engagement via the U.S. mail. After permission from my father, we *naupaka* distant halves became partners in pleasure forever.

After a marriage of forty-six years, three children, and nine grandchildren, we are now retired. Our refection time is much more *kakou* then it was at the beginning, except now the joyful voices of our grandchildren remind us of the power of *naupaka aloha* to create more love. Together we are `ohana (family), with our roots deeply planted in the larger family of our ancestors. As we are never separate from our ancestors, time and space can never separate us—even when one of us seems up on the mountain and the other down at the sea.

Like the *naupaka* that blooms in Hawai`i's mountains and at her seashores, our love remains strong, enduring, and everlasting. Even after floating on ocean waves for long periods or being stranded on open soil, *naupaka* seeds breed new life. *Naupaka* leaves are a snorkeler's delight; they rub their goggles with them and their vision is made clear. Such are the gifts, as well, of a *naupaka* marriage: endurance of a common spirit; strength of shared purpose; sympathetic love that transcends time and space; mutual commitment to life lived as one no matter the pressures wanting to pull it apart; a clear vision of the meaning of a successful and joyful life.

With a modern mind, Polynesian soul, and Hawaiian heart, Dr. Pearsall asks us to take our eyes off our personal goals and gaze together reflectively up toward the mountains and down toward the sea, where the two *naupaka* halves beckon us to remember our own halfness and to anticipate the joy of loving joined with our other half. He shows us how to rediscover the timeless connection of the *naupaka* lovers, who always know that their other half waits for them and is with them in spirit forever. Offering to show us the path of lovers who are *pa'a* (grounded) and *pono* (right), *Partners in Pleasure* revisits the times of honor, promise, duty, courage, patience, spiritual connection, and respect that make our *pu`uwai* (hearts) one.

Dr. Pearsall, better known to us as Ka`ikena, and his dear *naupaka* partner, his wife, Celest Kalalani, share one heart that beats with the acknowledgment that we are forever `ohana. What goes by and through us, likewise, goes to and within Ka`ikena and Kalalani. Their Hawaiian names, gifted to them by my mother, Tutu Mama, our ninety-six-year-old Hawaiian matriarch, bonds us as family forever. The name Kalalani refers to being of the heavens. The name Ka`ikena refers to a person of vision with the responsibility to share that vision. Ka`ikena was given an awesome trust from Tutu Mama and Hawai`i, and his book honors that trust. Together as `ohana, we embrace *aloha* (love) and *lokahi* (unity and harmony), the results of hearing the *naupaka* halves as they constantly echo their love song between the mountains and the sea.

Partners in Pleasure alerts one to listen more carefully to *naupaka's* song. At the end of the book, where Tutu adds her *mana`o* (wisdom) as a parting gift, you will read the words of this song as best we could capture it. The song alerts us all to feel our half-ness more openly, to understand it more acceptingly, to know it more wisely, and to realize that perhaps it is the *o wau*, the "I-ness" of the modern world, that is preventing so many from finding the pleasure they seek. *Partners in Pleasure* helps us remember that "we-style" love, *aloha kakou*, is a many splendored thing!

Hauoli ke like na mea male

Happy is marriage, shared

`Olelo no`eau (Hawaiian proverb) by
Tutu Mama Ellis, offered in honor of Ka`ikena,
Kalalani, and *Partners in Pleasure*

Dedication

For Ka Ha Naupaka (Breath of the Naupaka)

Mahalo ia `oe for sharing the breath of life and the
healing power of *aloha*

Introduction

Rediscovering the Miracle of "Us"

"Awaiaulu ke aloha"

Love made fast by tying together. [1]

The *Naupaka* Principle: We are all "half" happy without a loving partner. Healthy success and enduring pleasure require two partners in love, both acknowledging and behaving daily in terms of their incompleteness without the other.

A Loving Outlook

You fall in lust, but you choose to love. Deep, joyful, lasting love results not from gazing longingly into your lover's eyes but from learning to look out at the world together through the same eyes, one heart, and a shared soul. Contrary to what we may believe, this sort of love does not mean succumbing to an irresistible force that causes lovesick giddiness, a racing heart, and a hormonal surge. Rather, it involves an intentional change of mind about the meaning of life, what constitutes success and happiness, and a sweet surrender of self-consciousness in favor of co-consciousness. It is a decision to think now and forever from the perspective of two, and it means adopting an automatic "dyad default mode," a co-consciousness so pervasive that each lover instinctively thinks "what about us" rather than "what is in this for me."

Partners in Pleasure: Sharing Success, Creating Joy, Fulfilling Dreams—Together tells you how to build this kind of love. It is offered as an antidote for the self-fulfillment addiction that has evolved over the last decades. It is about changing your mind to think totally and exclusively from the perspective of two. It is about developing a lover's mindset, a connective consciousness to replace individualistic self-consciousness. This book is not a marriage or sex manual with steps to making a better marriage or relationship. It does not present a set of communication rules or explain better ways to understand your partner or to understand the differences between genders that are assumed to have come from different planets.

This book suggests that a more mutual definition of what constitutes success and joy is what brings the ultimate pleasure, that the greatest joy is that which is created together, and that learning to share and fulfill dreams results in the most comforting and enduring delight. It shows how forging a partnership in pleasure is possible and even essential at this time, when years of self-help and "doing one's own thing," the appearance of hundreds of relationship guides, the seeking of personal power, and a pervasive and dominating sense of self-entitlement seem to have left so many still feeling unsatisfied and as though there must be more to life.

Partners in Pleasure tells you how to find success and happiness through your loving relationship, rather than how to find a partner who will go along with you as you seek your own goals and rewards. You will learn about the importance and comforting bliss of losing your "self" rather than celebrating it. You will see how paying more attention to your mature inner elder than to your selfish inner child can help you commit to someone on all levels—to think, feel, and dream together forever.

Unlike falling in love, choosing the perspective of a loving partnership is not easy or automatic. Our genes' drive to perpetuate themselves is strong, as is nature's biological romantic reward system of quick lust and intense physical attraction to draw us together to reproduce. Likewise, passionate love is the opiate of the selfish brain. It grows from the brain's own desire to perpetuate itself. It is intense, fast, immediately satisfying, and makes the individuals involved feel wonderfully daffy and individually fulfilled—at least for a while. By contrast, an enduring and creative love that seems to become even more wonderful over time despite the most challenging crises requires learning to think, dream, pray, and play as one inseparable unit—a true spiritual, physical, mental, and emotional partnership. It requires an "us" rather than a "me" mindset that causes us to experience and remember everything in terms of two. I offer this book with the hope that its lessons will help you and your partner follow and enjoy your biological imperatives while going to the next, more difficult, but ultimately much more rewarding and pleasurable step of learning to think in terms of two.

As a clinical psychologist, I have worked with couples for almost thirty years. I directed a marital clinic at the Sinai Hospital of Detroit and have published many books and research papers about intimate relationships. I have seen the physical, mental, and spiritual devastation caused by selfish love, but I have also witnessed the rarer delightful bliss of partnerships in pleasure. I have been the "expert" on television talk shows where the word *love* was so easily and disrespectfully bandied about that it lost any real meaning. From my Hawaiian perspective, I have observed what the rampant self-entitlement of the recent decades has done to those less selfish in their orientation, and what the devastation of the all-consuming self has done to the world. But I have also seen the miraculous spiritual hardiness enjoyed by two people of one mind who are committed to seeing and experiencing life together. This book shares what I have seen and learned.

Discovering Our Eighth Sense

I think one reason why my book *The Pleasure Prescription* became a best-seller was because it offered proof of what most of us knew and sensed all along: what feels good is good for us. It showed how regular doses of daily delight are at least as important as exercise, diet, and stress reduction. It discussed how and why we seem to be so prewired for pleasure that our forefathers wrote the right to its pursuit into our Constitution. But after *The Pleasure Prescription* gained popularity, my Hawaiian family and teachers reminded me that I had not placed sufficient emphasis on what they and their ancestors have always seen as the key component and prerequisite of pleasure, what they call *mahele*—sharing.

In *The Pleasure Prescription*, I discussed how our drive for pleasure seems to function as our "seventh" sense, directing us toward whatever makes us healthier and happier. I described how it is the sense that makes our other six senses (touching, tasting, hearing, seeing, smelling, and even our "psychic" sixth sense) more intense and gratifying. It also guides us to adopting attitudes and behaviors that result in a longer and much more pleasing life. I have written this sequel to *The Pleasure Prescription* because my Hawaiian background and clinical research clearly show that our seventh sense is accompanied by what might be seen as our eighth sense: our need for shared pleasure with someone we love.

Think of the most pleasurable experiences you have had in your life. Perhaps these include the first cry of your newborn baby, an amazing golden sunset, some sudden and surprising good fortune, or just a sweet-smelling, gentle rain. Were any of these events made more pleasurable because they were shared with someone you love, or even by just thinking about what that person would feel if he or she were there with you sharing the pleasure? Has even the most wonderful event been somehow diminished in its pleasure because your partner was not there with you to enjoy it? Perhaps our eighth sense is love, our deep and profound longing to reach out and share life with another person.

The Pleasure Paradox

We live in a world that values independence over interdependence, competition for a piece of the pie over making a new pie together, one that devalues and even diagnoses "codependence" as "dysfunctional," and views "needing someone to be happy" as immature. Our selfish brain has learned more and more to take its pleasure from a singular perspective. We wake up thinking, "What do I have to do?" rather than "How are we today?" Still, despite the dominance of selfish thinking in America, something deep inside each of us seems to constantly nag us that we need someone else in order to feel whole. I suggest that even if we think we have *found* the "right" partner, the real challenge is to work harder to *be* the right partner, to grow into someone willing to change his or her mind from "me" to "us" regarding all of life and love.

The paradox that led me to write this book says that the more personally successful we feel, the more lonely and afraid we also feel. We sense that, in our hurry to get all that our brain thinks we really want, we might be losing what we know in our heart we truly need. Most of us have much more of the basic comforts of life than our grandparents did, but can we truly say we are much happier than they were? I suggest that a pleasurable life is one that happens when we totally embrace and are embraced by another person.

When I was dying of cancer, I cried at night not so much from the pain but because the disease caused me to dread the possible loss of what I knew more than ever was the ultimate source of joy in my life: my relationship with my wife. Each time Celest Kalalani came to my bedside, I felt joy despite my physical suffering. Although my wife and I see many divorces or "might-as-well-be" divorces all around us, although we have witnessed the early deaths of three of our four parents, raising two impaired children and suffering together through my cancer seem to have only made our partnership more joyful. I was never sure I could be cured, but I knew I would be healed—made whole— because my *naupaka* other half was with me always in my heart.

My fellow cancer patients agreed that their greatest fear was not of leaving this world but of never being fully connected to someone else while they were still in it. We did not dread impending death so much as we dreaded our disease's causing us to feel alone and unloved in the world now. You will read that we are never really alone unless our individualist and selfish brain causes us to suffer from the division delusion. By learning to be less self-conscious and more co-conscious, it is possible to experience love across time and space and beyond the limits of our mortality. You will see that it is our selfish brain that is often too love-blind to see and know that it is safe to give up the self for the sake of a loving two.

Talk to any parent waiting for a phone call from a busy child or to a widow sitting alone in a nursing home. Ask them what would bring them the most pleasure. In their answer, you will hear a soul crying out not to be left alone, one yearning for the simple pleasure of loving connection. Although this book focuses on intimate male and female relationships, the drive to connect deeply with another in any form is a vital part of being human and of feeling fully alive. No matter how many tangible things we give to others or receive from them, no matter how personally pleasured and successful we may feel, the ultimate pleasure is derived from feeling seen, heard, touched, and understood by someone. The ultimate joy is sharing the same loving point of view.

I will challenge much of what you have been taught about how to be successful, happy, healthy, and in love. I will ask you to try intentionally to become creatively codependent with another person. The cliche "you must love yourself before you can love someone else" is not only wrong but one of the leading causes of personal misery and failed relationships. Endeavoring to love one's self "first" detracts from one's availability to join fully and without reservation with another person to from a true union of spirits. The resulting loneliness and isolation eventually weakens the immune system and increases vulnerability to illness. The model of the first loving unit is a two-person union: that of mother with child in her womb. The feeling of a self full of love is a consequence, an internal spiritual reward for being open and willing to experience a profound caring relationship with another person. We do not love someone because we like them or they like us; we love them because they *are* us. In the context of *kakou*, self-love is an oxymoron.

I will offer you a two-thousand-year-old Polynesian path, supported by new research-based insights, to a pleasurable loving relationship that literally lasts forever. In Part One, you will read about the leading cause of failed relationships: the "self-fulfillment" fallacy that often dominates modern life. You will learn about one of the most important decisions you will ever make: whether to look at life from a personal perspective or from a partner perspective, and whether to seek to *be* happy or to *share* happiness. In Part Two, you will be offered the chance to try eight paired pleasure prescriptions. These prescriptions are based on current research blended with ancient Hawaiian teachings about *aloha* (love) that these "new" findings substantiate. Throughout the book, I have freely used Hawaiian words and phrases. These are defined when they first appear in the text, and the most important of them can also be found in a convenient glossary—which contains a pronunciation guide—located at the back of the book.

Living *Aloha*

In my home in Hawai`i exists a culture based exclusively on *aloha*. *Aloha* has many meanings, but it most often refers to love. This love goes beyond romantic lust and passion to the root meaning of the word *aloha*—to share the sacred breath of life. I have blended my clinical work with the *aloha* teachings of my Hawaiian elders (*kupuna*) because the Polynesian way of thinking offers much we moderns can learn about connecting on the deepest level.

The Polynesian islands, in the South Pacific, surround an area that covers almost one-third of the earth's surface. United by a common culture and similar languages, the lands came to be known collectively in the West as Oceania. Hundreds of years before inhabitants of Europe even learned to sail, the Polynesians had already sailed the vast Pacific Ocean by learning from it and joyfully accepting its mysteries. Living so interconnected with the world's greatest body of water gave the indigenous inhabitants of these islands a special perspective, a "third way" of living life and of regarding the world that is distinct from the traditions of both East and West. I call this mindset the oceanic way of thinking. In the oceanic mindset, there are no barriers. A water-like logic causes one to think "us" (*kakou*) first. By contrast, in the way of "rock logic," what I call the continental mindset, one rock plus one rock equals two separate rocks.[2] In oceanic thought, water added to water is still a mixture of water. This ancient Hawaiian "us" (*kakou*) orientation to life accounts in large measure for the relaxed joy and celebration of life so commonly noticed by visitors to our islands.

By showing you how to embrace this perspective, I hope to help you avoid two common romantic errors that prevent the evolution of a Polynesian-style partnership in pleasure. The first mistake is to marry because you think you have "fallen in love," rather than deciding together that you have "chosen to learn to love" by coming to understand life and love from one shared perspective forever. The second error is to end a relationship because you feel you have "fallen out of love."

Despite conventional wisdom, decades of research clearly show that even a "bad" marriage is better for the spouses and their children than a so-called "good divorce."[3] The negative effects of divorce include health risks for both spouses and children, deep and long-term emotional problems, and difficulties for the children of divorce in forming their own loving relationships.[4] While the stigma of a failed relationship has been largely erased by the current emphasis on self-pleasure, the dangerous side effects of what sociologist Judith Wallerstein calls "the powerful ghosts" of frenzied parents too selfishly busy to love and to model a loving relationship continue to haunt survivors of divorce.[5]

Dealing with the complex issues of divorce is beyond the scope of this book. The point I want to emphasize is that how we have come to think about life, love, and the role of intimate relationships bears profound and widespread influences. So long as we feel compelled to take advantage of our Constitutional right to the pursuit of individual happiness at all costs, we stand in danger of continuing to extend that same consumer orientation to our intimate relationships, using them but neglecting them.

Almost three of every four divorces occur in what researchers call "low-conflict" marriages and in marriages that seem relatively happy.[6] Three-quarters of couples who divorce say they do not quarrel or even disagree very often. These relationships seem to end due to failure to establish the "dyad default" mode I mentioned earlier. One or both partners seem unwilling to learn to think in terms of "us" instead of "me" when going through love's necessary growing pains.

Many such spouses seem to be searching for individual pleasure and happiness and have not yet learned to think about joy from the perspective of the Hawaiian *kakou* way of one loving mind. They fail to demonstrate toward each other the five components of *aloha* that were described in *The Pleasure Prescription* (about which you will read more in chapter 1):

▼ When patience and forgiveness (*ahonui*) could comfort, there is resentment.

▼ When harmonious connection (*lokahi*) could soothe, there is withdrawal and self-protection.

▼ When agreeableness and pleasantness (`*olu*`*olu*) could lead to composure, there is combativeness and anger.

▼ When humble modesty (*ha*`*aha*`*a*) could lead to serenity, there is self-assertion and arrogant certainty.

▼ When gentle tenderness and kindness (*akahai*) could lead to bliss, there is curtness, sarcasm, and blame.

Instead of choosing peace, such spouses choose instead to give each other a "piece of their mind" and to defend their personal turf. Where there could be pride in the maintenance of a loving pair, there is the drive for change and newness preferred by the selfish brain.

By contrast, in the pleasure partnership I describe in this book, a mutual effort is made to remember a key component of a marriage of minds: if one is seeking to have it all, it may be wise to look with *aloha* at the person you love to remember that you already do. If one adopts the "marital mindset" of Hawaiian *kakou* that I am suggesting in this book and commits to an "us" point of view even at the worst of times, something interesting happens. Research shows that, in nine of ten marriages whose partners said their marriage was "bad" but who still "stuck it out," both spouses reported five years later that their marriages were much happier. Six of ten of those spouses said their marriage had become "very happy."[7] This book shows you how to overcome the natural partner pessimism that appears at times in every relationship and to cling to the *kakou* view.

Lessons from Oceanic Lovers

To fairly consider and try some of the ideas and behaviors presented in the following pages, you will have to be willing to go along with the metaphors, tests, unusual exercises, and teasing inherent in the teaching stories of the *kupuna* (Hawaiian elders) who are members of Ka Ha Naupaka (breath of the *naupaka*). Ka Ha Naupaka is a group of long-married Hawaiian couples of which my wife and I are members. It was

formed and named by Aunty Betty Jenkins who, along with her partner
in pleasure, Uncle Jack, generously provided the foreword for this book.

Aunty Betty was inspired to start Ka Ha Naupaka when she noted
that in perpetuating the cultural lessons of Hawai`i, teachers had often
neglected one of the most significant resources of that culture—the
model of lasting bonds based on *aloha* and at the root of the sacred
`ohana*, or family, that is the center of Hawaiian culture—in favor of
other important but more individual issues. My wife and I were invited
to join Ka Ha Naupaka because of our deep respect for those lessons
and because of our own thirty-five years of marriage based on the principles of *aloha kakou*, loving as two. Ka Ha Naupaka members meet to
support one another in their commitment to lasting loving unions and
to learn more about their evolving couple wisdom. We share not thera-
peutically or just as a support group but as couples continuing to learn
what it truly means to be together forever. We "talk story"—converse
informally—about how we met and developed our enduring love. We
share stories of the good and bad times and what our ancestors taught
us about *aloha*. In typical Hawaiian style, we *mele* (sing), *hula*, and create and recite proverbs, jokes, and poems that keep the spirit of *kakou*,
known to our ancestors, alive in our hearts today.

To learn from the *kupuna* of Ka Ha Naupaka, you will have to try
to be open to seeing the loving *naupaka* half-flower symbolism you read
about in the book's prologue and foreword as it may apply to your relationship. You will have to be willing to allow the wisdom contained in
this legend to flow through your loving.

In the spirit of the trickster found in so many indigenous cultures,
you will have to be willing to play with gimmicks, tests, codes, catch-
phrases, and other ways of learning that may at first seem silly to your
Western mind. The image of the trickster often takes the form of clown,
jester, demigod, or other spirit; its purpose is to subtly get our attention
about what should really matter most just when we are paying the least
attention to these things. The trickster asserts its presence and wisdom
by teasing and hassling us via little interferences with our best-laid
plans. When we think and act as if we are important and in control,
that is the time the trickster will cause us to fail to notice a little piece
of lunch dangling from our lip for all to see at an important business
meeting. When we are sure we can go it alone, that may be when the

trickster causes the tire on our car to go flat with no one around to help, or gives us a cold that makes us long for comfort and care from another person. At times, I have used a trickster approach in this book. I hope you will not take these elements too seriously—while still trying to take from them some wisdom about how your loving might be made more *kakou* before you discover your need for such connection when you can least afford the reminder.

Whenever I use the word "marry" or "spouse" in this book, I am not just referring to a man and woman in legal wedlock. I am not arguing for a sugary-sweet illusion of two lovers who cannot bear to be apart for one second, or for a return to an ultra-conservative view of staying married forever for dogmatic reasons. I am not arguing for a puritanical, rigid, austere view of marriage dictated by a religious code, or for sexist roles of husband and wife. I am offering for your consideration the oceanic view of marriage, a unique way of seeing and experiencing the world two by two that brings a level of pleasure beyond any possible for one person alone.

To assess whether the material you are about to read has relevance and meaning for your relationship, be willing to risk losing your continental mind and finding your oceanic heart. In the Polynesian-style pairing I am suggesting as a model for a partnership in pleasure, the connection between two lovers becomes so profound that there can be no rock-like individualistic distinction within the relationship's thinking, feeling, and behaving. To a degree that may seem too childishly dependent and over-reliant to the continental mind, there is little "I" or `o wau` in the oceanic marital mind. Instead, there is a complete merging of minds regarding what makes for fulfilling work, lasting love, and renewing play.

The first thing that comes to mind when a partner in pleasure alone sees a lovely rainbow forming is to regret that the partner is not there to share its beauty. The power of this *kakou* thinking is illustrated by one *kupuna* in the Ka Ha Naupkaka group. "I can't really see all the fullness of a rainbow unless Nalani is with me. Whenever I see one, I think of how much we would enjoy seeing it together. Nalani died twelve years ago, but she is always with me. I feel her presence the most when I see rainbows, because they are there, gone, and there again. You just have to be patient and wait and they will always be there."

Weaving a *Lei* of Love

The oceanic model of paired pleasure is represented by a floral *lei*. If you have ever been to Hawai`i, you have seen these gorgeous-smelling necklaces of flowers. For Hawaiians, the *lei* is not just a string of individual flowers to be thrown over a visitor's head. The flowers represent *aloha*, love. Their arrangement in a circle represents the never-ending connection of true love, and they are to be given with gentleness and respect.

Hawaiians know that a neglected *lei* withers and dies too soon. They teach that we should always cherish and protect that which is precious, and the *lei* of love is a cherished symbol that love's beauty rests in its connection—the word *lokahi* in Hawaiian. When one flower seems to dominate or stand out too much or any of the flowers are treated with disrespect, some of the *lei*'s magic, beauty, and significance is diminished.

I invite you now to begin to weave your *lei* of love together forever. I invite you to cherish and protect that which is most precious to you: the privilege and opportunity to share love, to *aloha kakou*. I offer you some "new old" ideas about forming a partnership in pleasure so that you can join more fully with someone to reduce the suffering of life's stormy times, someone with whom to look for the rainbows after the rain.

Me Ke Aloha Pumehana (with warm *aloha*),

Paul Ka`ikena Pearsall, Ph.D.
Honolulu, Hawai`i, 2001

Part One

*Firmly Together, First
and Forever*

Chapter One

*Love Lessons
from Paradise*

Ho`i mai kaua e pili

Come. Let us be together.

Beginning the Voyage

What is the first thing that comes to your mind when you awaken in the morning? Are your first thoughts about you, or about your relationship? Do you think first about what you and your partner will be doing together to make this a wonderful today, or about what you have to do yourself to make it through another busy day? How you answer these questions indicates whether you embrace an "I" and "me" orientation in your thinking about life (`o wau` in Hawaiian) or the "us" and "we" orientation of partners in pleasure (*kakou*).

The ways of thinking needed to understand the *kakou* orientation are related to the *aloha* concepts described in *The Pleasure Prescription*. In that book, I used the lessons of the Hawaiian *aloha* chant created by Pilahi Paki to illustrate the balanced way to personal pleasure. Here is a review of these concepts as they apply to forming a loving partnership in pleasure—what Hawaiians call *aloha kakou*:

A—Ahonui: **Persistent patience.** As you read about the partner way of thinking, try to be patient with yourself and your partner. Trying to follow specific steps or communication suggestions is easier than making a complete mental shift to partner-based thinking, so take your time, reflect, and let the ideas sink in. Persistent patience, tolerance, and forbearance are also essential to forming and protecting a pleasure partnership, so start practicing *ahonui* now as your read this book. Remember, you are trying to love someone who is a flawed person, and your partner is trying to love someone (you!) who is also not always a true joy to live with. Patiently try to fit the "new old" ideas about loving into your thinking and relationship. Wait until the end of the book before making your final decision as to whether you want to fully embrace the concept of a total partnership approach to loving.

L—Lokahi: **Harmonious unity.** This concept is the centerpiece of becoming partners in pleasure. You are being asked to change your mind and how you pay attention to the world from a self-oriented to an us-oriented perspective, and to see everything from the outlook that "we" always comes before "me." Even after reading only this far in this book, are you thinking, "I wonder what I think and how I feel about all this?" or "I wonder how my partner and I might consider, reflect on, and feel about these ideas together and as one?"

O—`Olu `Olu: Pleasant agreeableness. Retain your good humor as you approach this material. For now, avoid looking for flaws or reasons why *aloha kakou* cannot work in your day-to-day modern world. Suspend cynicism and comparing the *naupaka* approach with other theories you may have read about loving. Simply try some of the ideas on for size. Avoid mentally debating them from a continental mindset; instead, give them a fair hearing in your heart. Go along for the fun of it, and see if your relationship might not be strengthened and invigorated by some of the lessons of *aloha*. You may feel criticized for how you are loving, but that is not my intent. You may think that the prescriptions are weird, silly, and even stupid. I ask you to go along for the cruise, roll with the waves, and give *aloha kakou* a chance.

H—Ha`aha`a: Humble modesty. You may feel you have "heard and read it all" when it comes to advice about love and relationships, but I hope you will open your mind. Many of the things you have read and heard about love and relationships stem from the self-fulfillment orientation, more a $1 + 1 = 2$ approach than the $1 + 1 = 1$ *kakou* idea.[1] Modern motivationalists are seldom asked if they are outstanding husbands and wives, and even relationship gurus are not often held accountable for their own relationship history. Listen carefully to their advice, and you may hear the "rock" logic of two individuals trying to connect by maintaining each of their own unique points of view and styles of loving. Promotions at work and rewards for most endeavors in today's world have little to do with whether or not someone is a joy to live and love with at home. Society emphasizes "thinking for yourself" more than "thinking as us."

I offer the material you will be reading with *ha`aha`a*. I am not at all sure I am entirely right in what I am suggesting about the partner way to pleasure, but I am sure I have carefully researched everything I present here and have done my best to convey the lessons my Hawaiian *kumu* (teachers) have taught me about *aloha kakou*. I know that the prescriptions presented in Part Two have been tried by thousands of persons around the world with wonderful results. I know that my wife,

Celest Kalalani, and I have been partners in pleasure for forty years and married for thirty-six years. I know we try to live our love by these prescriptions. I know that the members of the Ka Ha Naupaka group of Hawaiian couples have, as their ancestors before them did, led their lives by the *kakou* principle for decades, totaling well over two thousand married years for the group collectively. I ask only that you humbly consider the possibility that, no matter how loving your relationship is now or how firmly you believe in maintaining and protecting your individuality, your relationship may have at least some room to become a little more *aloha kakou*.

***A—Akahai*: Tender kindness.** As you take the journey to a pleasure partnership, be gentle with yourself and your partner. No one is ever loved exactly the way he or she wants to be, and no one loves totally in keeping with the concepts you will be learning. They are invitations, not laws or rules. You may want to think of them as buoys in the ocean, reminders of where the most safe and enjoyable sailing may be.

Imagine a lover who showed the above characteristics of *aloha* every day. Imagine:

▼ A partner who was patient with you even when you acted like an insensitive fool.

▼ Living with someone with whom you felt so connected that you never felt alone, even when that person was physically absent.

▼ A partner who was so pleasant and agreeable every day that it was a true joy to wake up with that person every morning.

▼ A partner who showed such humble modesty that you never felt unimportant, left out, or taken for granted.

▼ A partner who was so kind and tender that you could always count on feeling heard, embraced, held, comforted, and sensually fulfilled every moment of your life.

Of course no such partner exists, but simply being willing to consider a mindset less "I" (`*o wau*) and more "we" (*kakou*) can lead to a more pleasurable life for everyone touched by your partnership.

The *Naupaka* Principle

At the beginning of this book, you read a brief version of the legend (*mo'olelo*) of the *naupaka*. The full legend is more sinister and is designed to warn of the dangers of selfishness, even when that selfishness seems to be initiated from outside the relationship. It is reflective of the outside pressures on today's relationships. It teaches what happens when lovers allow themselves to be separated by outside pressures and by one of the partner's short-sighted, selfish passion and love-blindness.

The legend tells of a beautiful but selfish woman who came to a village and fell in love with a young man who was already in love with another woman. The visitor decided that she wanted the young man for herself. She was so beautiful and irresistible that the youth impulsively turned from his commitment to his sweetheart to fulfill his own immediate selfish needs. As always happens when the immediacy of passion fades, he eventually tired of the new woman and tried to return to his sweetheart. Her selfish pride hurt, the scorned woman followed him and tore him away from his former sweetheart.

She blazed so with anger that all Hawaiians knew only the goddess Pele could be so beautiful, powerful, and self-demanding. It had been the ever-demanding goddess of the volcano who had taken the man from his love, and now she jealously pursued him into the mountains and threw lava after him. But the other gods took pity on him and transformed him into a half-flower before Pele could catch him. That flower is now called the *naupaka kuahiwi*, the male *naupaka* half-flower that grows in the mountains of Hawai'i.

Unable to exact her vengeance on the young man, Pele shrieked in jealous rage. She fled on a river of lava down to the ocean where she overtook the young man's sweetheart. She wanted to turn her to stone with lava, but the gods had already intervened for her as well. They had turned her into what is now the female *naupaka* half-flower, called the *naupaka kahakai*, which grows at the beach. Even though the lovers had experienced devastating stress and challenges, the half-flower of the young man on the mountain and the half-flower of the sweetheart at the beach have blossomed forever—an enduring symbol of the timeless, insistent yearning of two persons incomplete without one another's love.

Even if you have a "brown" or "black" thumb, you can grow *naupaka*. It is a very hardy plant—perhaps, *kupuna* (Hawaiian elders) say, because of what it had to endure in its encounter with Pele. Hawaiians say you must be aware of and honor the partnership and infinite connection of the two half-flowers if you are to benefit from *naupaka's* power. They say that one half-flower will not bloom without the other also blooming, symbolic of the fact that no matter how successful or happy we are as individuals, we all remain half-flowers until we reawaken to our dependence on our other half for true pleasure.

The Case for *Kakou* (Coupling)

Recognizing our "half-ness" and then deciding to pursue pleasure and life *kakou*-style—as a "we" instead of as a "me"—has been shown to be one of the most powerful healing acts. Our bodies respond differently and with more healthy balance when they feel connected to another body, and this represents a distinguishing feature of a partnership in pleasure. Research now shows that living and thinking *kakou*-style:

- ▼ Helps keep our immune system in balance and our cardiovascular system less stressed.[2]

- ▼ Helps us develop a kind of "bond buffer" against illness, a unique, couple-generated physiological hardiness related to having a constant partner in whom we can confide completely.[3]

- ▼ Helps us be more physically resilient and to heal and recuperate better and faster than those who are not in such a relationship.[4]

- ▼ Allows us to avoid the illness-causing stress of putting all of our emotional eggs in one basket by allowing us to live the multiple roles of spouse and parent not available to those who elect to go it alone.[5]

- ▼ Provides the "helper's high immune boost" experienced by those who lovingly give time to another person.[6]

An ancient Hawaiian proverb says, *"O ke aloha ka mea i ho`ola ai"*—

compassion is the healer. It seems that ancient Hawaiians knew millennia ago what modern researchers are just discovering. But there is another recognizable benefit of a pleasure partnership: the pure enjoyment it provides both partners.

The *Aloha Kakou* Test

One of the most consistent findings regarding what constitutes happiness is its link to being in a lasting and mutually pleasing relationship.[7] I suggest that it might significantly enhance health if joggers would get off the road, gym-goers would turn off their treadmills, and self-help-seminar participants would leave their support groups to go home to their partners and start seeking their pleasure, power, health, and sense of well-being there.

More than ten years of research has shown that people in lasting relationships are significantly happier than single people, even when other variables such as age and income are statistically controlled. When we ask and strive to answer the question "Am I happy?" we are looking only at the *naupaka* flower located at mountain or seaside. When we ask and learn to answer the question "Are *we* happy?" our feelings of success and joy can take full bloom as our *naupaka* flower is made complete.

To get ready to form your own partnership in pleasure, review the following ten questions. They make up the *Aloha Kakou* (Loving as One) Test, similar to the *Aloha* Test in my book *The Pleasure Prescription*. How you answer the questions will help to determine how far along the journey to paired pleasure you have already come. I suggest you take this test now, with someone with whom you may want to form a pleasure partnership, and then take it again after you have completed the pleasure partnership program, as described in chapter 3.

The *Aloha Kakou* (Loving as One) Test

1. Are you a true joy to live with?

2. Would you want to be married to you?

3. Do you love as intensely as you work?

4. Is your relationship as successful as you are?

5. Are you sure you are not giving up too much of what you really need to get what you think you want?

6. Do you relish the simple pleasures of everyday life with your partner?

7. Do you think you and your partner share the same definition of a successful life?

8. Do you think you share the same view of what it takes to be happy?

9. Do you think you both have faith that you will be together forever?

10. No matter what happens or what opportunities arise, will you chose "us" over "me"?

The more *yes* answers you have to the above questions, the more your relationship is living and loving by the *naupaka* principle. It is to those who answered with a few *no*'s and who wish to increase their number of *yes*es that I offer this book with *aloha nui*, much love.

Mid-Love Crisis and Mutual "PMS"

When the selfish brain encounters the demands of love, it often suffers from what I call PMS—post-marital shock—a kind of spousehood surprise that one or both partners might experience at different times and with different levels of intensity. You may experience a little PMS as you begin to change "your" mind to "our" mind and start following the pleasure prescriptions in Part Two. Remember *ahonui*, persistent patience. The symptoms will pass as the love grows.

Based on my clinical work with couples, here are the symptoms of Post-Marital Shock:

▼ *An increasing number of "lovers' spats" over unimportant and often very silly things.* One PMS sufferer said, "We made love on our wedding night, and afterward he turned on the hockey game.

It shocked me. For some reason, I started to cry. He seemed confused and said, 'What's that all about?' I felt hurt about how he said the words, and I turned my back to him. He turned off the game and stared at the ceiling. We both sulked, he finally took my hand, and we made up. But I never forgot it. That whole night I thought about calling the whole thing off. We didn't and we've been married twenty-two years. He still turns on the game, I still don't like it, but we go with it. We don't get in spats over it. We save that for more important things."

▼ *Sudden bursts of tears.* Another said, "Hey, I'm a man. I don't cry easily. But after it hit me that I would be with her forever and ever and no one else, I just started to cry. I sort of went into my private little shock. It wasn't her, it was me. I felt sad and overwhelmed that I had lost my independence, but I still wanted to be with her."

▼ *Secret calls to parents and friends for support.* A PMS sufferer said, "It was like my first weeks at college. I kept sneaking away to call my dad and mom and my best friend. I kept asking them if they felt like I felt about realizing the finality of it all and how I was finding stuff wrong with him right away."

▼ *Headaches, nausea, and digestive and bowel upset poorly matched to the romantic image of the honeymoon.* Another woman said, "I wasn't sexually aroused at all. I know it was our honeymoon and all and we had always had great sex, but I just wasn't into it. I felt like I had morning sickness all day and night. I kept popping aspirin and stuff for diarrhea. I tried to hide it, but I felt seasick and we weren't even on a boat. I started to be afraid I was allergic to Sam and that he made me sick."

▼ *Wanting to be alone just when you're expected to want to be always together.* A newlywed said, "Here I am on the perfect honeymoon with the perfect woman, and I just wanted to be alone. She kept hanging onto me, but I wanted some space. It really scared me. I got past it and knew it was just a phase, but it did shock me when I wanted to get away from the woman I had wanted to marry all my life."

▼ *Noticing and fixating on a spouse's disgusting or annoying habit.* A PMS sufferer said, "He picked his nose. I couldn't believe it. A college dean, no less, and he does that. He was always so clean and perfect and a total gentlemen, and suddenly he does that. He would try to sneak a pick, but I couldn't help it. I began watching for it as if to convince myself that I could never stay with a nose picker. I have, though, and he has either learned to sneak his picks or I've stopped looking for them."

▼ *Periodic feelings of dread for having made a disastrous and life-ruining mistake.* Another man said, "It became sheer terror. I had night sweats. I kept asking myself how I could have been so dumb. Other times I was fine and really loved and wanted to be with her. I felt sure she was the one for me. Then, suddenly, I'd think, 'Oh no, what have I done? There might be a better one.'"

All of these symptoms happen in varying degrees to partners in most newly forming intimate relationships. They can also happen to those who try to develop a marital mind after loving for so long from the "me" perspective. They are manifestations of our dependence dread—reactions to the gravity of getting drawn deeper and deeper into an intense interdependent relationship.

I've listed these symptoms because they are so obvious and blatant. Most partners experience lovers' PMS less intensely and more indolently. However, if both are serious about their commitment to living as partners in pleasure, the occurrence of PMS is actually a good sign. It means that both partners are becoming sincerely aware of the power, significance, and awesome responsibilities of going through life with another person in a profoundly connected *naupaka* partnership.

Entering Voluntary Spousal Slavery

Perhaps surprisingly, one remedy for PMS is to resist the fearful brain's insistence on its independence. Instead, submit to the very thing that may be upsetting and even frightening you: the *lokahi* (harmonious unity) that can forever bond two persons together as one. In the face of your brain's fear of losing your independence, allow your heart to lead you ever deeper into the interdependence that—if given a chance and plenty of time—ultimately will calm and soothe your soul.

In his *Devil's Dictionary*, author Ambrose Bierce defines marriage as "the state or condition of a community consisting of a master, a mistress and two slaves, making, in all, two."[8] The partnership in pleasure proposed in this book requires a gentle voluntary enslavement to the relationship rather than to the selfish ego. It is not slavery to your lover but to the loving relationship. In a society so intent on self-fulfillment, most lovers do not go gently into joint slavery.

A *kupuna* from the Ka Ha Naupaka group heard my discussion about the voluntary servitude that characterizes *naupaka* partnerships. She said, "I think we are all slaves to something. We can be slaves to our work, to our vices, even to our children. We have chosen together to be slaves to our relationship."

What is required to develop the skill of being a servant to our relationship without feeling that we exist in servitude? Perhaps paradoxically, you will need a bigger ego, not a smaller one. You will have to be strong enough as an individual not to have to assert your individuality. You will need an ego large and inclusive enough to allow itself to be totally entangled with another ego while remaining free of the fear or even resentment of a perceived loss of boundaries. The principles and exercises in this book can offer practical help. And following them can soothe a brain reluctant to drop its guard, can let it know that it is not only safe but joyful to become self-less.

The Magic of the *Menehune* Factor

There is a Hawaiian proverb that says, *"Na`e`epa o Waolani."* It translates as "the extraordinary ones of Waolani on the island of O`ahu." Waolani is said to be the home of the *menehune* and other legendary beings that could do things beyond our everyday comprehension. The proverb refers to the magical ways that are often incomprehensible to the modern mind but that can make big things happen from what may seem to be only small gestures. The eight pleasure prescriptions in Part Two may seem like "little things," but they can work marital magic.

The *menehune* were a legendary race of small people said to work at night to accomplish miraculous things in an amazingly short time. I am writing this book on the edge of Kuapa Pond, one of many fish ponds some say were built by the *menehune*. Some people say that the *menehune* were real people of small stature who settled in Hawai`i before the first Hawaiians came, but that theory has been strongly refuted. Whatever its source, *menehune* magic can be seen and felt all over Hawai`i, and it serves as a lesson about the magic of creating pleasure partnerships.

As a clinician who has worked with over two thousand couples in crisis, I know that it is almost always the *menehune* factor—the little things—that does the relationship in or makes it strong. The words *please* and *thank you*, a gentle sincere compliment, a smile and a hug at just the right time, hearing that your partner was bragging about you to someone else—each of these can create an ecology of daily delight within your relationship that a special candlelight dinner with strolling minstrels cannot match.

Discussing the importance of the little things, psychologist Carl Jung wrote about the myths of the "little people," the elves and gnomes who did remarkable things. As Mother Teresa put it, doing great things is less important than doing small things with great love. And psychologist William James wrote, "I am done with big things and great things, and I am for those tiny, invisible, molecular forces that creep from individual to individual like so many rootlets, or like the capillary action of water." Becoming partners in pleasure means becoming absorbed in enjoying the little things in life together, and being aware of this *menehune* factor is a key step in beginning to form a pleasure partnership.

Overcoming Popeye's Pride

"You can't change a man," said the wife. "Even if I could, the only person who would appreciate it would be his next wife." The audience laughed at her joke, but it contained a message about relationships that can prevent them from becoming pleasure partnerships. We have come to think we cannot or should not change for anyone and to accept the over 50 percent failure rate of the modern marriage. I was startled by the cavalier way one of my medical students was viewing his pending marriage. He joked, "Are you and your wife coming to the wedding for my starter marriage?"

If you are going to try the partnership path to pleasure, you are going to have to decide that your relationship is not simply *a* priority but *the* priority in your life. This is not a choice everyone will want to make, but for those who do, there are immense mental, spiritual, and physical benefits. It is a choice that requires taking an oceanic point of view about what you have been told is self-fulfillment. It requires a willingness to allow yourself to be "couple converted," transformed to embracing a less selfish and more connected view of well-being that goes against the philosophy of the cartoon character Popeye the Sailor: "I y'am what I y'am and that's all that I y'am."

Why Gurus Make Lousy Husbands and Wives

Reliance on another person for the pursuit of a successful and enlightened life has long been seen as a sign of weakness and an obstacle to the highest personal attainment of bliss. Can you name one great mystic, guru, or religious figure who wrote extensively of treasuring a wife or husband above all and who taught from that perspective? There may be some, but I could not find them.

An implicit assumption states that whether it is called enlightenment, satori, personal power, the path of the heart, or developing various chakras, the path to bliss and extreme well-being is primarily a personal one. Gurus may love the world, but they often seem to fail miserably at two-person intimacy. When intense personal relationships are mentioned in most inspirational works or descriptions of sages, they generally occur between teacher and pupil. Most gurus are much better at loving the entire cosmos than they are at getting along with a spouse. Writings about such figures seldom refer to a spouse or intimate lifemate whom the guru or sage needs desperately, learns and studies with, and is committed to loving forever.[9]

Enlightenment is often seen as a solo pursuit, but I suggest that a partnership in pleasure can lead to a depth of experience and knowledge that transcends that of one person alone. If you are going to be a partner in pleasure, you are going to have to come down from the mountain, go home, do the laundry, clean up the dog poop, and sit down and listen to and learn with your spouse.

Wired for "We"

Even the "tickle response" takes two. Try it and see for yourself. Try tickling your own underarms, ribs, or feet. No matter how many different ways you try to tickle yourself, you won't succeed and you will probably become irritated in the process. In similar fashion, we are prewired to live, love, and be thrilled two by two. We can sit alone looking in awe at a gorgeous sunset, but we savor it most deeply when we sit with someone we love and gaze together at the orange glow. We chuckle when we see something funny, but we guffaw when we experience it with someone who matters in our life. We feel personal satisfaction and pride when we experience high levels of success or joy, but we feel validated and valued most when our success and delight is accomplished, appreciated, and shared with another person. No matter how high you've climbed, it means very little when there is no one around to celebrate with when you reach the summit. It seems that God saw to it that we would enjoy life more together by making things funnier, sadder, more beautiful, and more fun when we share (*mahele*) experiences.

The six-year-old daughter of a couple who had decided to divorce was sitting in my office. She was telling me about her feelings as the bond that had created her was dying. Her eyes were red from crying, and she kicked her little legs back and forth as she looked down at the floor. I sat and listened as she twisted her hair between two fingers and looked up at the ceiling as if to prevent tears from falling out of her eyes. After several moments she said, "You know, Dr. Pearsall, I guess there's isn't anything wrong with being alone except that you don't have anyone to share it with."

As we talked further and I offered assurances of her parents' continued love and support for her even after they went their separate ways, she spoke of her fears not for herself but for her parents. "I don't see how they can be happy apart. I don't think they tried hard enough to be happy together. I think they will be very disappointed that they don't have each other, and I think they will have to get back together then." Her enduring childish hope, characteristic of so many children of failed marriages, reflected the longing we all have for a stable *naupaka*-style connection. Despite my own and her parents' assurances, the little one could not be fooled. She was less concerned about the pending divorce than she was about the spiritual disconnection she sensed between her parents and their forgetting of the *naupaka* principle. She knew something more than a legal marriage was ending and that she would lose at least for now the pleasure of *aloha kakou*, a "we" love from her parents together.

While divorce or ending an intimate relationship is sometimes necessary for the ultimate safety and good of all concerned, you read in the introduction that it is not a terrible marriage but a selfish brain that is usually at the root of failed relationships. Ending a relationship is never easy on any of those involved, and until we learn to work harder at forging new and stronger partnerships in pleasure and at seeing success, happiness, and our dreams as "ours" rather than "mine," more and more of us will end up like the little girl trying to hold the tears in her eyes. No matter how happy we become over time, we won't have anyone to share it with through and beyond time.

As you prepare to read the remaining chapters, be mindful of an Old English proverb that summarizes what you have read in the introduction and in this chapter about the self-fulfillment fallacy that limits the evolution of more loving and lasting relationships. I hope you will keep it on your mind and in your heart as you consider the eight paired pleasure prescriptions. It says, "The best way to see the divine light is to put out your own little candle."

Chapter Two

Together Through It All

Ku a `aha lua

Standing together in twos.[1]

Refers to the power of facing life with comradeship and
cooperation rather than alone.

Love Hardiness

Couples who suffer together stay together. In working with couples for over thirty years, I have observed that couples who have endured crises together are often those who seem to share the most pleasure. Relationships in which partners have nurtured their impaired children, worked together to help an ailing parent, or coped with one of their own serious illnesses or other life setbacks often seem happier and more joyful than couples who have not yet had their turn at the down side of life.

My wife, Celest, and I often feel that we have had the worst of lives and yet the best of lives. We have a son with cerebral palsy and another son with severe learning disabilities. Not long after we were married, both of our fathers died suddenly and much too young, my wife's mother suffered a severe stroke that left her alert but speechless and unable to walk, and my mother developed a disabling lung disease. We continue to endure discrimination and insensitivity toward our impaired sons. At the peak of my career, I was diagnosed with Stage IV lymphoma, underwent a bone marrow transplant, chemotherapy, and whole-body radiation, and nearly died several times. Through it all we have suffered greatly, but somehow, during the rare quiet times, we've noticed that we seemed strangely happier than many couples who have not gone through so many life challenges together.

When I was in the cancer and bone-marrow-transplant unit, I noticed the same shared joy and happiness among many of the couples we met. While certainly this is not always the case, it seems that times of misery can be great times for finding meaning together. When your body is being torn apart, there seems to occur an intensifying of the drive for connection with the person who matters most in your life.

When you adopt the *kakou* orientation to thinking about life, death, joy, and pain, a kind of couple coherence can develop—a sense of mutually established and shared comprehensibility, manageability, and meaningfulness in reaction to what seems to be the unfair and unequal dispersal of life's challenges. A relationship resistance factor seems to evolve for couples who view every aspect of life as "our" opportunity or problem. Couples who have yet to experience "pleasure through the pain" may have yet to fully test and flex their relationship muscles. They may have yet to grow fully aware of the *naupaka* principle that paradoxical pleasure and a unique life energy are gained by going through hell together.

My cancer and the pain and suffering of our sons seemed somehow more *comprehensible* when my wife and I talked for hours into the night about "why us" instead of "why me." Our problems seemed more *manageable* with our constant mutual assurance that, somehow and in some way, we would manage these problems together and things would work out. We were able to find *meaning* in the chaos and to find an energizing challenge in what I am sure neither of us could have handled as well alone. The essence of *aloha kakou* is what psychologist Aaron Antonovsky calls "a sense of coherence": that life's setbacks can be better understood, handled, and made positively significant when two persons of one mind decide to cope with them together.[2]

Depression Display: The Strange Attractor

When we experience life's setbacks and feel down, something strange happens. In a kind of relationship reflex, our body automatically begins to send signals to attract loving care from another person. Our eyelids droop, our gaze turns downward, our shoulders slouch, and our face seems to say, "Doesn't anyone see how sad I am? Doesn't anyone want to help me?" Conversely, something within us causes us to be attracted to those who seem in distress and who are flashing their depression display. We may respond by saying, "Are you okay?" or "You look like you're carrying the burdens of the world on your back," or "You look like you could use a shoulder to lean on." As though we were a wilted and drooping *naupaka* half-flower, our sadness signals are received by our other half-flower, our partner who is so *kakou* with us that he or she is strangely attracted by our message.

We flash this almost universal signal automatically. You often must work to put on a happy face, but sad faces can occur all by themselves. Sometimes we are not even aware that we are depression flashing until our *naupaka* other half lets us know about it by saying, "You look like you're feeling down."

As I discuss more thoroughly in chapter 12, to fully understand the idea of paired pleasure and to follow the eight pleasure prescriptions in Part Two of this book, it is helpful to understand that joy is not restricted only to the wonderful times in our life. Partners in pleasure do not always wear cheerful smiles. Something miraculously beautiful and significant can happen to us when we join with someone we love to face adversity together. It is at such times that we often most realize that we were never intended to experience life's ups and downs alone. We were created as *naupaka* flowers to blossom as two halves and make one strong whole.

The Benefit of Failure and the Threat of Success

One aspect of continental consciousness differs considerably from Hawaiian or oceanic consciousness: many people think they are most at risk when they are weak. They assume that when things are not going well and when they are not personally "successful," they are vulnerable to all sorts of further difficulties. They forget that there is a reverse gravity to the down side of life that tends to pull us up—in the same way that the down side can pull us back from our extreme highs.

Hawaiians knew and current research shows that our weakest periods can serve as a time for spiritual aerobics. They can lead to a strengthening and deepening of spirit, and the same holds true for relationships in which both persons are willing to conceive of life, love, health, and happiness from the perspective of two.

If your relationship is going through problems now, just wait. Things will get better if you are committed to the *kakou* orientation. If things seem fine now, watch out. It is during the very, very good times—when we are experiencing high levels of individual success and happiness and when our time is more and more invested elsewhere—that our attention can be drawn away from out relationship. We can become love lazy and seduced into `o wau* thinking, only to forget the *kakou*.

The paradox that we can become stronger when we are at our "weakest" challenges the continental mind that has been taught to be strong. But if you reflect a moment, you will see that the Hawaiians may have it right. Life can offer its best opportunities to feel most fully alive and in love when our love hardiness is being tested. There seems to be nothing we need more when we are suffering than another person to love us and go through our challenge with us.

Almost anyone can stay in love at the best of times. It is at the worst of times when the depth of love is challenged and the two halves of the *naupaka* can blossom together. It is during the bad times when our spirit and love are being extended and exercised more fully. If we think *kakou*, disasters can serve as catalysts for renewed and deepening love.

They're Always with Us

To more fully appreciate how *kakou aloha* can outlast any setback, it is helpful to understand the Hawaiian belief that our *aumakua* (revered ancestors) are always with us and guiding us to love this way. Where the continental mind sees a loved one, the Hawaiian mind sees not only the partner but every one of the loved one's ancestors. Loving one person is loving and honoring all those who have gone before that person. Harming a partner in any way is seen as harming every one of that person's ancestors.

The power of *naupaka*-style love derives from the combined spiritual power of every person who is part of a lover's ancestry. Hawaiian *aloha* (loving) involves being constantly aware of the subtle but immense power (Hawaiian call it *mana* or spiritual energy) of the eternal spiritual presence of every single great-great-great-etc.-grandpa and grandma and uncle and aunty who ever lived. In times of need, this *mana* or loving energy can work miracles, but if we think `o wau and forget that we also are manifestations of our own ancestors, interacting with our lover's ancestors, we may miss out on the power of this connective love.

In the introduction I discussed the idea of the trickster and its role in helping us remember with humility where our priorities lie. Hawaiians believe that when we forget to live with *aloha* by getting too cocky, too self-assured, too selfish, or too egocentric (`o wau), or when we forget the *naupaka* principle by thinking we can suffer or thrive alone, it is our *aumakua* who will get our attention so as to teach us differently. We are vulnerable to their remindful discipline and spiritual nudgings and scoldings when we feel most personally successful and when we are pursuing life as if we were alone in a world made for us to use and abuse. The next time you spill gravy on your tie at an important function, or get a paper cut from hurrying too fast through your piles and files, think of it as a little love bite from your ancestors reminding you to slow down and be a little less self-assured.

Mahele: **We Share**

As we sat circled together, talking about what it means to be Hawaiian, a *kupuna wahine* (old Hawaiian women) struggled to her feet. Her voice was soft but firm. She had listened quietly and smiled as different people discussed lessons of living they had been taught by their *makua* (parents) and *kupuna* (grandparents). As she cleared her throat, the room fell silent in the tradition of deferring to the oldest voice. She raised her walking stick and said as loud as her frail voice would allow, "*Mahele*—we share!"

The group of Hawaiian couples listening to the woman's simple message was Ka Ha Naupaka. The members responded with tears in their eyes, saying "`*Ae* (yes)!" over and over until it sounded like a song. "That's it. That's Hawaiian. We share! `*Ae!*"

For Hawaiians, sharing goes far beyond the continental idea of dividing and allocating as a means of distributing the fruits of one's labor. It is a core value upon which all life in the islands is based, a different mental set from the continental mind. It emphasizes a profound and infinite connection without boundaries of any kind.

One can witness *mahele* not only when the fishermen share their catch and families bring gifts and food to one another's homes as if every visit were the first and a true housewarming. You also see it in the "go ahead" and "thank you" gestures in traffic, in the view that honking your car's horn is very rude, and in the custom of "zippering" or taking turns as cars merge together when a traffic lane ends or construction is encountered.

Hawaiians are no more perfect in their practice of *kakou* than anyone else. The pressures of modern life have taken their toll, and it would be blind romanticism to suggest that Hawaiians or those who live in the islands are models of a totally unselfish, loving, connected lifestyle. But those who have spent their life in Hawai`i and who remain sensitive to the ancient principles upon which the host culture is based can feel the subtle urgings of the ways of *aloha kakou*. I am not asking you to abandon your own cultural heritage and its unique lessons of love but rather to consider adding some of the Hawaiian ways of *aloha* to your most intimate relationship.

Nor am I suggesting that the concepts of *aloha, kakou*, and *mahele* are exclusive to Hawai`i or Polynesia. Similar concepts are embraced by many spiritual traditions throughout the world and particularly by indigenous peoples. For example, the idea of *kakou* (us) over `*o wau* (me) is the essence of Advaita Hinduism, in which *advaita* means "non-dual" or "not two." One of the most important Buddhist texts, the Lankavatara Sutra, expresses the *naupaka* principle this way: "Conditions of existence are not of mutually exclusive character; in essence things are not two but one." According to the Gospel of St. Thomas, Jesus said, "When you make the male and the female into a single one, then you shall enter the Kingdom." The idea of purely romantic love sought to soothe the desires of the individual ego is a relatively modern concept, and like many more rock-logic, continental-mind orientations, I am suggesting that it lies at the root of our increasing sense of lack of fulfillment even with all of our wealth and conveniences.

Finally, in the spirit of *mahele*, it is important to recognize the contributions of the continental way of thinking. It has led to miraculous developments and great personal and societal advancements. Its respect for individual rights and its faith in the power of the person to accomplish almost anything have contributed to one of the most productive, creative, and effective cultures in history. The oceanic way of thinking has sometimes suffered from its lack of faith in and even distrust of the assertive, confident, self-sufficient individual. I am asking you to balance both of these points of view about life and, because most Westerners have more experience with the individualistic way of thinking, to consider a very different way of dealing with the world. The competitive, self-assertive, often adversarial ways of continental thinking have their place, but when this thinking filters into a loving relationship, less pleasure can be the result.

A Lesson from Tutu's *Papale*

My wife, Celest, learned the value of sharing in a most embarrassing way. She noticed a gorgeous handmade *papale* (hat) on the head of Tutu

Mama, a ninety-six-year-old Hawaiian woman who is a revered and cherished member of our Hawaiian `ohana (family). She is the mother of Aunty Betty Jenkins, and her wisdom guides us in our striving for a *naupaka aloha*. Some of her *mana`o* (great wisdom) will be shared in the epilogue.

Tutu always wears things of beauty and spiritual significance associated with the `aina (land), and this hat was no exception. It was plaited beautifully and tightly with strands of *lau hala* leaves from the pandanus tree, and everyone noticed it. My wife complimented Tutu on it, saying, "My, Tutu, your *papale* is so very, very *nani* (beautiful)." Tutu smiled, removed her hat, and handed it to my wife. Blushing, Celest tried to hand it back, saying, "Oh no, Tutu, I really couldn't." She stopped when Tutu's eyes focused on hers in grandmotherly fashion to remind her of the important protocol that represents Hawaiian sharing. "Hush, now," said Tutu. "You know, we share. You can wear it now. It's not mine or yours. It is ours. Nothing belongs to one person, most especially beautiful things like the *lau hala* leaf that comes from the `aina." To have returned Tutu's hat would have been a serious insult to Tutu and to *pono*, the way things are supposed to be.

Chasing or Waiting for Rainbows

In our modern world, we often feel frazzled and harried, with too little time to *mahele* the joys of life with the person who can help us more fully experience and relish them. Consequently, the colors of our life fail to seem as rich and deep as they might, as if we were taking pictures and then removing them from the photo-developing solution too soon for the depth of their hues to coalesce. I learned this lesson not only from the couples in my clinic who aborted their relationships before they had a chance to flourish but also from a Hawaiian fisherman as we sat watching a fresh rainbow that arched over the Koholau Mountains behind my home.

"See that," he said. "Watch and see how life is. Watch how the rainbow forms, becomes very bright, and then slowly fades away. Most people have never really seen a rainbow. They see it coming or going because they are always busy bodies constantly coming or going themselves. They might catch a glimpse, but they don't catch the rainbow.

You have to stay for the rainbow. You have to really commit to it and let it happen to and with you. You have to let the brilliance sparkle. Sometimes you will think you see two rainbows, but they are really one big rainbow like two lovers dancing together across the sky. The space between them is actually a part of them. It all depends on how you look at rainbows." Being partners in pleasure resembles patient rainbow-waiting. It requires a commitment to remain and share the entire experience.

Assessing Your Pronoun Propensity

One way to gain insight into the degree of *mahele* that exists within your relationship is to count your pronouns. In our clinic, we asked couples to leave a tape recorder running during dinnertime. We asked them to collect one tape a week for one month, and then to spend about one hour together playing the tapes back. We were not interested for the time being in the topic or tone of the conversations. We asked only that the couples write the words "I, me, mine" and "we, us, ours" in two columns at the top of a page, and then place a tally mark in the respective column whenever one of those words was used. We randomly selected five couples each from two sets: those who were discussing divorce or separation in their marital therapy sessions and those who were coming to the clinic not for marital help but for family therapy to deal together with a problem with a child, parent, or relative.

The results of our little study are not statistically valid, but they do provide some insight into the level of connection between partners as reflected in their conversations. Because dinner length varied greatly, the actual number of pronouns was not as important as the difference between the number of times personal versus collective pronouns were used. As expected, the couples thinking about ending their relationship tallied over five times the number of personal pronouns as the family-therapy couples. Of course, persons in conflict would be expected to use more personal and adversarial language because they believe in boundaries and have drawn their respective lines in the sand. We could not be sure which came first—the conflict or the personal orientations of the partners. Whatever the case, pronoun preference reveals much about the "me" (`o wau`) or "us" (*kakou*) ecology of a relationship.

Partners in Health

I have also conducted the pronoun-propensity test in my work with heart patients. Among patients treated for various forms of arterial disease and blockage, stress has been shown to be a major risk factor.[3] Feeling stressed is associated with feeling alone and helpless. As expected, the personal-pronoun count for the heart-patient group exceeded that for a comparison group of patients coming for routine physicals by more than three to one. The relationship between disconnection and lack of intimacy and heart disease is being studied as an important variable in cardiovascular health.[4]

You read in chapter 1 about some of the health benefits of living life *kakou*-style. These benefits are compounded by the loving care mutually bestowed upon each other by partners in a *mahele* marriage. When I want to assess the healing potential of my patients, I often look at the patient as he or she sits in the waiting room with his or her spouse. I also observe how the spouse shows caring for the wife or husband in the coronary care unit or intensive care unit.

After "our" battle with "my" cancer, I was dying and was rushed to the intensive care unit. My treatment for cancer had weakened me to the level of total exhaustion, and a simple virus was causing my lungs to fail. My partner in pleasure, my wife, Celest, was by my side for hours on end. She would leave only when total fatigue or near starvation made her return home, but she always quickly returned to sit next to me as I lay unconscious. Nurses trying to enforce rules about visiting hours were afraid to approach her. They said, "She's like a lioness guarding her cub." I felt her presence and it helped save my life. We often wondered where the partners of my fellow patients were, because so few seemed to have the healing benefit of the constant loving vigil of a partner sharing, learning, and seeking meaning together through their suffering.

Another indication of the role of connection and health is the impact of physical intimacy on the heart. More than half of heart attack victims have one thing in common, and it is not a poor diet or lack of exercise. It is their report of the lack of any sexual activity with their spouse for the entire year preceding their heart attack.[5] Pleasure-partner deprivation can have devastating effects not only on our emotional well-being but also on our physical health.[6]

There is danger in trying to "go it alone." Cardiologist Dean Ornish writes, "Anything which promotes a sense of isolation often leads to illness and suffering. Anything that promotes a sense of love and intimacy . . . is healing."[7] The data show that the self-success route to happiness can affect our health several ways.

▼ *The Couple Compliance Factor*: Because it lacks the benefit of mutual monitoring afforded by a caring couple, the solo success approach increases the chances that we will engage in behaviors that are not good for our health. With no one around who really cares enough to nag us about our diet and lack of exercise, we are more likely to slack off in our health program.

▼ *The Mutual Motivation Factor*: Going it alone decreases the chances that we will make lifestyle changes that are essential for our well-being. The high level of connection in a committed partnership can double our motivation to do and try things that can enhance our life but that we may not think of, do, or stick with when we try to make changes on our own.

▼ *The Love and Longevity Factor*: Research shows that people who go it alone are 200 percent to 500 percent more likely to suffer from serious illness and to die prematurely from all causes, independent of whether or not they engage in other life-threatening behaviors. Why this is so is not clear, but there is something very significant and even magical about forming a partnership in pleasure that transcends two people in a relationship designed to enhance the success and pleasure of separate individuals.

▼ *The Half Happiness Factor*: The best short definition of a pleasure partnership I have been able to come up with is: "Two persons irrationally committed to one another's welfare." By modern, rational-thinking standards, two people giving up much of their individualism to join together in creating one joyful life seems illogical. I wanted to write this book more than twenty years ago, but publishers at the time said the idea seemed "just too far out" and "too absurd" as a way to think about loving relationships. They told me that they were interested in books that talked about how individuals can be happy and that explained the "well-known" idea that we must love ourselves before we can love anyone else. Oceanic *naupaka aloha* asserts the exact opposite. Happiness depends first and foremost upon a deep sense of connection. Oceanic thinking does not understand how anyone could possibly love himself or herself, because no one exists separately. As one *kupuna* put it, "Love is a collective verb, not an individual feeling."

▼ *The Lifeguard Factor*: After years of working in hospitals and after months of undergoing chemotherapy, radiation, and surgery as a cancer patient, I know only too well that hospitals can kill you as well as save you. Every patient needs a lifeguard while in the hospital or seeking any medical treatment. The input of a partner who is deeply concerned and well-versed in our health, our body, and what seems to work and not work for us when we are sick can save our life.

▼ *The Loving Lifeline Factor*: Faith has long told us and modern research now documents that prayer works.[8] Healing by focused, even distant intent has been shown to bear positive effects on our immune system.[9] The kind of partnership in pleasure I am proposing offers a unique spiritual source of healing between partners on a level that transcends time and space.

▼ *The Humor Factor*: Laughter heals.[10] Just as you read in chapter 1 about how tickling requires two people, the hardiest and most healing laughter tends to occur when we have someone with whom we can laugh very hard at the same things at the same time. When we have a partner in pleasure, they know what tickles our funny bone, because their funny bone is tickled by the same thing.

The evidence is in. No matter how many miles you jog, how much fiber you eat, or how much personal power you achieve, no matter how many self-improvement books you read, self-help tapes you listen to, and self-development seminars you attend, seeking health and happiness through *aloha kakou* is ultimately the most meaningful and fulfilling way to live. As Reverend Ghris Williamson pointed out, those who wish to make quick spiritual progress don't retire to monasteries; they get into relationships.[11]

Profile of a Partner in Pleasure

To help you focus on the destination of your voyage to pleasure partnership, here is a profile of someone who is *kakou* and *mahele* in his or her thinking, feeling, and behaving. These are characteristics I derived from thousands of interviews of highly successful couples over more than three decades. They may sound unrealistic and idealistic, but I assure you that there are many partners who think and behave in the ways listed below. No one shows all of these traits all of the time, but persons who seem to have found a partnership in pleasure tend to practice most of them most of the time. You may want to put a check mark by the ones you think characterize your partner or yourself.

You or your partner embodies the characteristics of a partner in pleasure if you or that person:

▼ Always seems to have time to listen to you.

▼ Brags about you more than about himself or herself.

▼ Compliments you constantly.

▼ Easily says no to more obligations and busyness that may detract from the *naupaka* gifts of attention and time for the relationship.

▼ Puts your relationship above all else in deed and not just words.

▼ Seems very proud of you and lets others know it.

▼ Never corrects you in front of others.

▼ Seems legitimately excited when you tell of one of your successes.

▼ Seems to feel sad when you are down and happy when you are up.

▼ Would sooner be with you than with work colleagues and friends.

▼ Truly values your input and acts on it.

▼ Highly values your opinion regarding his or her work.

▼ Easily admits being wrong.

▼ Shows respect for your intelligence.

▼ Understands, gets, and appreciates your sense of humor.

▼ Will drop everything when you need her or him.

▼ Is not totally self-assured and often asks, "What do you think?"

▼ Avoids ranting and raving about others and telling "work war stories" at home.

▼ Includes you in plans about work and will make major changes based on your input.

▼ Calls you often when he or she is not at home.

▼ Behaves in the privacy of your home exactly as he or she does in public.

▼ Uses "we, us, ours" instead of "I, me, mine" when talking about your home, family, or her or his success.

▼ Cannot be really happy unless you are.

▼ Cannot enjoy a movie, music, or television show if you absolutely hate it.

▼ Never makes you feel reluctant to "bother" him or her with the little things and problems of daily living.

▼ Seems to have plenty of energy for your relationship.

▼ Monitors and takes responsibility for the relationship and does not leave that to you.

▼ Does not seem to take you for granted.

▼ Seems to know that he or she really needs you, shows it, and says it.

▼ Keeps "time promises" regarding when he or she will be home.

▼ Does not speak with sarcasm or cynicism about you or your relationship.

▼ Uses a kind and gentle voice with you.

▼ When opportunities come up, thinks first about the two of you instead of just herself or himself.

▼ Checks in regularly with how you are doing and feeling.

▼ Is very sensitive to your giving him or her "the look" when you want to get his or her attention.

▼ Remembers what you said, keeps appointments with you, and remembers birthdays and anniversaries without hints.

▼ Will try hard to change a behavior that annoys you.

▼ Can comfortably sit and do nothing with you.

If this list seems long and the criteria for being a partner in pleasure much too stringent, this is because we have become such an individualistic society that many of the above behaviors seem impractical, impossible, or just too good to be true. You may find the pleasure partner list wistfully nostalgic and not something that can really be practiced in today's world. However, if we are to be healthy and to help our children survive and thrive, it is important that we at least try to lose some of our continental `o wau or egocentric mind and become *kakou* with another.

Chapter Three

Two Paddlers, One Canoe

Ho`okahi ka `ilau like ana

Refers to wielding the paddles of the canoe together as one.[1]

Learning to Paddle

"Paddles ready!" yelled the Hawaiian paddler behind me. We all rested our paddles straight across our laps and looked ahead. We sat together in the orange glow of the setting sun and felt the canoe gently rock us. We first had to connect before paddling forward. As I learned to paddle the long outrigger canoe, I thought about the lessons of how the ancient Hawaiians guided their canoes with a wonderful balance of grit and grace. I thought of how they worked navigational miracles long before Western exploration began—not by setting out to conquer but by sailing to connect. I could sense how they must have felt gliding as one—not so much *on* the ocean but as part of it, and I thought their way of paddling might be of help to those choosing to learn the art of *kakou,* of thinking totally connectively about life and love. Hawaiian paddling is symbolic of how such lovers live in their relationship—as two paddlers in one canoe.

As you prepare to follow the eight paired pleasure prescriptions in Part Two, here is a physical exercise you can try with a partner. (If you do not yet have a life partner, consider doing the exercise and working through the eight prescriptions by yourself to the extent possible. This will help you reach a *kakou* or partner frame of mind.)

The Partner Paddling Exercise

Paddle Position One: *Ahonui* (Persistent Patience)

Sit straight in a chair, close your eyes, and imagine you are sitting with someone you love in a wooden canoe on the ocean at sunset. If you have a partner, you might want to sit one behind the other (taking turns in the front and back positions) as if you were in a canoe together. Imagine that the gentle trade winds are blowing against your face and that you can smell the sweet odors of the many flowers on shore. Imagine that you are holding a wooden paddle in both hands with palms down and fingers curled around it. Hold it gently and very straight on your lap. Sit patiently and feel the canoe become one with you and the ocean.

To get the most benefit from the eight prescriptions in Part Two, you will have to learn to sit, wait, and be persistently patient. If you become impatient with yourself or your partner and start paddling too fast or too much as an individual, the canoe will not slide easily with the ocean. Sit for a few minutes, take several deep *ha* or breaths, lower your shoulders, and relax. Think of some of the ideas you have read about, but do not try to remember, memorize, debate, or absorb them all. Just reflect on one or two of the ideas that may have drawn your interest or attention. Commit to being *ahonui*, persistently patient with yourself and your partner in your voyage toward lasting love.

Paddle Position Two: *Lokahi* (Harmonious Unity)

After relaxing for awhile, slowly raise your paddle with both hands high and straight above your head. This position is symbolic of connection and respectful unity not only with your partner but also with your own and your partner's ancestors, whose energy or *mana* is a part of your loving partnership. Imagine you are reaching out and up to them to show that your love will take them into account and will honor their dignity and the love they have shown to both you and your partner. Commit to being *lokahi*, more connected with your partner and all of those who have made your partner and yourself the persons you are.

Paddle Position Three: `Olu`olu (Agreeable Pleasantness)

From time to time, it is essential that paddlers change the side of the canoe on which they are paddling. If they do not, the canoe will only go in circles and never progress. With your hands still holding the paddle above your head, parallel to the ground (that is, the surface of the water), and after honoring *lokahi* or connection with your partner and the ancestors, slowly turn your upper torso and shoulders to either your right or left. The paddle, still overhead, will turn as well.

To be an agreeable and pleasant paddler, you must realize and remember that you do not always know the correct or perfect side on which to paddle. Sometimes it is to the left, sometimes the right; sometimes you paddle one side and your partner paddles on the other; sometimes you paddle together on the same side. These decisions must be worked out together, or your paddles will clash and the direction and joy of paddling will be lost. Try to let the decision about which side your respective paddles are turned to "just happen" and fall into synch together naturally without one person dominating. With practice, you will be surprised to see that, without saying a word and by committing to a pleasant agreeableness, you can fall into synch. As you will read in chapter 11, you will seem to "psi" together, or experience psychic connection. If one or the other of you is too single-minded or too compliant, you will have more trouble coordinating your paddling. This step takes a lot of practice, but it can be a wonderfully pleasurable feeling when you fall into *kakou* paddling.

Paddle Position Four: *Ha`aha`a* (Humble Modesty)

Next, you are ready to *kommo mai kau mapuna hoe*, put the tip of your paddle to the water. The lesson here is not to dip too aggressively or to put your paddle in the water faster or harder than your partner does. You must be a humble paddler, willing to join with your partner to dip together at the same time, over and over again rhythmically. Let your paddle touch but not yet break the water's surface, a symbolic gesture of humbly asking the ocean's permission to pull your paddle through her body.

So far, you have held your paddle in your lap, moved it above your head, turned it to one side, and touched its tip to the water's surface. Now, slowly but firmly move your paddle down with both hands and imagine it dipping in the water with hardly any splash. Do not pull the paddle yet; just gently dip it into the surface of the water. Practice all of the four paddle positions, and think of what they mean for forming a loving partnership of patience, connection, pleasantness, and humbleness.

Paddle Position Five: *Akahai* (Tender Kindness)

Now that your paddle is slightly dipped into the water, bend slowly forward while pulling your paddle alongside the canoe in one pendulum-like swing, then back up with both hands to about head level, then slowly down again to pull through the water. Imagine moving *with* the ocean rather than just *on* it. The idea of *akahai* is to paddle with as little disruption to the sea as possible. Think of your paddling as a gentle request for help and energy from the ocean, joining more than driving, as dipping into the energy of the water without asking too much from it or stirring things up. Think of your paddle as tenderly caressing the water, rather than cutting through it.

Paddle a few times on one side of your imaginary canoe, and then switch to the other side. Imagine and feel yourself falling into a rhythm with your partner as you move along the orange path of the setting sun. Remember that the sun is not actually setting. What the continental mind calls a sunset is for the oceanic mind a horizon rising, symbolic of new beginnings for your loving partnership.

From time to time, go for a paddle together with your partner or in your own imagination. Be sure each time that you think of yourself always paddling *with* your partner rather than alone. Go through the five *aloha* positions as a mutual meditation exercise or when you are alone and missing your partner. As with *hula*, Hawaiian paddling is a form of body prayer. Paddling together with *aloha* can be a form of praying together.

A Couple Commitment: Eight Paired Pleasure Prescriptions

As you begin your pleasure partnership program, I suggest you think in terms of a one-year commitment. A sample time line for implementing the program appears later in this chapter. Living *aloha kakou* can be a noble lifetime endeavor, so decide with your partner that you will give your partnership plenty of time to grow and develop.

The eight paired pleasure prescriptions that appear in Part Two are briefly introduced here. To help you understand each one, I have included comments from some of the partners who participated in my clinical research to illustrate their implementation of the prescriptions.

Paired Pleasure Prescription One—Discovering a Mutual Vision: *Remember what you need and decide together where you are going.*

Personal mission statements have been popular for years. Stephen Covey, author of the smash bestseller *The 7 Habits of Highly Effective People*, suggests that your personal statement focus on what you want to be, do, and achieve.[2] The first paired pleasure prescription describes the importance of a mutually developed couple's mission statement and of determining together what "we" want to be, do, and achieve.

Comments from Paired-Pleasure Partners: "I never really thought of a marriage mission statement. I've created dozens of work vision statements, but none for us. Just talking about it made me realize what I'd been missing between us. It really drew me back to her."

"We have our couple's mission statement posted on our refrigerator now. We see it every day, and people who visit see it. We were embarrassed at first, and then we felt proud."

Paired Pleasure Prescription Two—Thinking with One Mind: *Think less for yourself and more for "us."*

Particularly important in making a partnership in pleasure is learning how to think alike. The second prescription has to do with combining cognitive styles, our general way of thinking about the world and how we react to and process life events. The chapter compares and contrasts oceanic and continental minds—or "tortoise mind" and "hare brain."[3] It shows how cognitive styles can fall into synchronization through reading the same books and going to movies, plays, and watching television programs—not "for" but with your partner—and then taking time to talk about these activities with the intent of coming to one mind rather than debating two views.

Comment from a Paired-Pleasure Partner: "When we first married, we saw things very differently. It was a clash of minds, but we have worked hard to become of one mind about a lot of things. People think that sounds boring, but we assure you it is stimulating and creative and really helps you solve problems."

Paired Pleasure Prescription Three—Connecting Heart to Heart: *Listen to what your hearts are saying to one another.*

This prescription builds on the finding that our heart is more than just a pump. It is a thinking, feeling organ that can connect with other hearts. Partners can literally join and synchronize their hearts. By doing so, they can communicate on a level beyond the brain's comprehension.

The chapter introduces the cardio-synchronization technique, which allows partners to experience their two hearts energetically connected.

Comment from a Paired-Pleasure Partner: "I have felt it in my heart. Not just romantically. I mean I have felt my partner's heart reaching out to mine. I can't do it when I'm rushed or thinking about all I have to do, but I can connect with Jerry heart to heart by focusing on my heart instead of my head. That's when my heart goes out to his."

Paired Pleasure Prescription Four—Praying from the Same Soul: *Live your prayers together.*

Couples who pray together stay together. This principle is not related to a specific religion or dogma but to research findings that confirm what most of us already know: prayer is powerful and effective. The fourth prescription shows you how pleasure partners learn the art of shared prayer and how to "live" a prayerful life together.

Comment from a Paired-Pleasure Partner: "I'm not a particularly religious man. I never go to church, and I'm not sure I really believe in God the way most people say they do. But I do pray, and I've learned to do it with my wife. Something spiritual happens when we pray together, and we both say how it seems to make us more connected. We pray together before every meal and before bed. Maybe it's just a ritual, but it has become very important to us."

Paired Pleasure Prescription Five—Dancing to the Same Beat: *Take the time to pay attention.*

This prescription deals with one of the biggest obstacles to forming a partnership in pleasure, the issue of time. It shows partners one of the most important skills for their relationship: the ability to have less, do less, and say no.

Comment from a Paired-Pleasure Partner: "We never had enough time. It was as if time wasn't under our control. Everyone and everything was taking up our time, and we spent very little of it together. We were saying yes to everything except our own relationship. We just couldn't give each other the two gifts of time and attention. Then we learned the three time tips of having less, doing less, saying no. It has really made a big difference."

Paired Pleasure Prescription Six—Singing the Same Song:
Speak as if your relationship were a vulnerable child.

Philosopher Nisaradatta wrote, "The ideas of 'me' and 'mine' are at the root of all conflict." This prescription deals with the psychological principle that we become what we say. Our words have tremendous power, and learning to speak gently, politely, and in complimentary fashion helps to bond our relationships. Another part of this prescription is the importance of mutually shared silence.

Comment from a Paired-Pleasure Partner: "It amazes us how people talk to one another. We seem most rude and feel free to take the most liberties with those whose feelings we should really be caring most about. We have learned to create a pleasing and pleasurable marital ecology by simply watching our mouths. Another thing we've done is learn to sit quietly together in the dark for a few minutes every day. Not in bed, because we fall asleep. I mean we just sit in silence, and we feel very connected that way."

Paired Pleasure Prescription Seven—Becoming One Body:
Hold each other each time as if it were the last time.

Researchers have observed that women living or working together for a prolonged period of time experience synchronization of their menstrual periods. My work with couples indicates that partners in a committed, intimate shared-pleasure relationship also experience a matching of their immune systems and cardiovascular systems. The sexual experience of partners in pleasure seems to be one way in which they fall into synch physically, emotionally, and spiritually. This prescription shows how couples can constructively combine their innate resistances to disease and their natural healing powers.

Comment from a Paired-Pleasure Partner: "People say we have started to look alike. I think I can see it, too. I know we can sense how one another feels and take strength from one another when we are sick. We even are starting to walk at the same pace, whereas before, I always dragged behind. I've speeded up and he's slowed down, and that's the secret of our success."

Paired Pleasure Prescription Eight—Sharing a Sixth Sense: *"Psi" together.*

This is perhaps the most controversial and challenging of all of the eight paired pleasure prescriptions. It presents ways for couples to connect using "psi" (meaning psychic phenomena or a "sixth sense") through dreams and across space and time, no matter where the partners may be. You may really have to open your mind and heart to implement this last prescription, because it deals with issues of clairvoyance, telepathy, psychokinesis, and "presponding," that is, hunches lovers have about one another across time and space.

The prescription also offers an exercise for sharing the same dream while sleeping. The possibility of mutual lucid dreaming—of connecting with your partner through dreams—is perhaps hard to believe, but research supports it.[4]

Comments from Paired-Pleasure Partners: "I just know when he is going to call and when he needs me, and he says he has the same feeling. We don't tell many people about it, but we can connect anywhere, anytime. We have become very sixth-sense sensitive to one another."

"We don't dream about each other, we dream together. Many times we see ourselves together side by side in our dreams, and we can send each other our dreams. We know what the other has dreamed because we dreamed it together. If we are apart, we can actually communicate through our dreams. Many people don't believe us, but that doesn't matter. We know. It's in our mutual mission statement to work on our shared dreams."

One Year for Us: A Suggested Pleasure Partnership Program

Here is a suggested program for implementing the eight pleasure prescriptions. It is only a suggestion and one way to begin the challenging task of changing "your" mind to "our" mind—of moving from `o wau to *kakou*. Gently remind yourself when necessary to approach your program from an oceanic orientation; think of your attempts to follow the prescriptions not as steps in a marital manual but as two paddlers dipping their oars in the water together, pushing them through the water, pulling them out of the water, and then repeating the cycle. As with paddling, your efforts eventually will result in movement.

In this book, I have offered the Hawaiian way of shared living and loving, but every culture has its own unique and valuable versions of most of these ideas. If you notice similarities within your own cultural wisdom, see if there are ways to modify this program to fit your ancestral heritage. Remember, your ancestors are watching and are with you in this whole process!

First Two Months

Read *Partners in Pleasure* and take the tests together. Discuss the test results and concepts. Also discuss the paired pleasure prescriptions and how you might begin to implement them. Practice the paddling exercise alone and together.

Next Four Months

Dedicate one month each to the first four prescriptions.

Seventh Month

Take a vacation from the program to allow some of the prescriptions to work. As with any prescription, it will take time for each one to get into your marital system.

Next Four Months

Dedicate one month each to the final four prescriptions.

Twelfth Month

Celebrate and review. Retake the *Aloha Kakou* Test from chapter 1 to assess your partnership progress, and then decide which prescription(s) may need to be taken again. Pick a month you will designate as your "partnership in pleasure month" each year. Most couples pick the month of their wedding anniversary or when they first committed to love together forever. Dedicate that month to renewing your pleasure partnership by redoing some of the prescriptions.

Following the eight prescriptions will require more than just doing exercises together. You have read that reaching *aloha kakou* requires learning to think differently about love and about your relationship. You will be asked to make some difficult choices about what life and love mean to you and about whether or not you really want to try to experience *naupaka aloha*. Discovering a mutual vision is the first prescription because it helps you and your partner form a couple's mission statement; from there you can begin to decide if you want to work together toward *kakou, lokahi, mahele,* and *naupaka aloha*.

I invite you to *hoe kakou*, to paddle through life together. I hope the prescriptions you are about to take will help you become of one heart and will change your mind from "mine" to "ours."

Part Two

Paddling Together Through Life: Eight Prescriptions for Paired Pleasure

Chapter Four

Discovering a Mutual Vision

Paired Pleasure Prescription One: Remember what you need and decide together where you are going.

`Uo `ia i ka manai ho`okahi

Strung on the same lei needle, to be married.[1]

Refers to the idea that we are strongest and happiest when we are mutually weaving one *lei* of love. We find contentment and joy when we are connected by the same "thread" tying us together at the center of our being.

A Mysterious Current

The first prescription relates to sharing the same wishes, aspirations, goals, and vision. This can be achieved through the realization and discovery of a couple's mission statement.

Marriage researcher John Gottman refers to a "mysterious current" that seems to be dragging our marriages apart. He writes, "It's as though some powerful, subterranean current takes hold of you both and leads you down a path of negative thinking, destructive feeling, painful action and reaction, drifting toward isolation and loneliness."[2] Pleasure partners are aware of this current that can constantly tug at their relationship. They try to protect the relationship's integrity by discovering a mutual vision in the way described in this chapter.

How to Weave a Lovers' *Lei*

You read in the introduction about the significance of the floral *lei* in Hawaiian culture. The *lei* represents *kakou*, a lovers' alliance joined by a common thread. Discovering a shared vision means working together to find the common thread of your relationship.

Hawaiians say, "*E lei no au i ko aloha*," meaning, "I will cherish your love as a beautiful adornment."[3] One reason intimate relationships fail is that we have become much better at making our own individual *lei* than at jointly weaving a *lei* with another person. To learn the first paired pleasure prescription, you must begin to see your relationship as a constant process of weaving a wonderful, vulnerable, but resilient *lei* that both of you find beautiful and value highly.[4]

Below, I pose two *lei*-making questions that I ask of my workshop couples seeking to practice the first prescription.

How is Your *Lei* of Love?

▼   If your relationship were a floral *lei*, imagine how it would look so far. Is it pleasing to contemplate? Is it clearly endowed with mutual hard work and the gifts of time and attention? Or does it appear neglected or lopsided—riddled with gaps, components (i.e., blossoms) that need replacing, signs of stress, and imbalances?

▼   Are you both weaving the *lei*, or does it seem that one of you
is doing most of the work? Are you both protecting and nurturing the *lei*? Do you seem equally invested in the project, or
are you weaving separate *leis*?

Answering and discussing these questions together provides a starting point for learning the *naupaka* principle of two becoming one. In our
selfish society, we often seem to be solo *lei* makers. While the particular energy or *mana* of the individual certainly goes into a couple's *lei*,
partners in pleasure decide to combine their *mana* into a shared *lei*
of love.

The Vision Compatibility Test

Before creating a couple's mission statement, take and discuss the
Vision Compatibility Test. This will help you assess where you are now.
Following the test are some guidelines for discussion. Allow plenty of
time and give your full attention to this test and its discussion, as if you
were weaving a *lei* together while sitting in the shade of a palm tree near
the ocean.

The Vision Compatibility Test

If possible, take the test together. Score your relationship on the following scale:

$$0 — 1 — 2 — 3 — 4 — 5 — 6 — 7 — 8 — 9 — 10$$

NOT AT ALL — — — OFTEN — — — ALWAYS

1. Do you and your partner place the same meaning on the
importance of work and career, even if only one of you works
outside of the home?

2. Are you in agreement about how much time you should invest
in family activities?

3. Are you in agreement about having children, the number of
children to have, and the way in which they should be raised?

4. Are you in agreement about whether one of you should stay home while the other goes to work, and, if so, about who should fill each role, and how?

5. Do you agree on the importance of money and how to spend it?

6. Do you agree on the obligation of caring for your parents?

7. Do you and your partner approach the world with similar cognitive styles; that is, do you both tend to be rational/logical/analytical or intuitive/impulsive/emotional?

8. Are you in agreement about taking risks?

9. Are you in agreement about the meaning of retirement and about your plans for its time, place, and activities?

10. Do you both define success and happiness the same way?

Total _____

The closer your score is to 100, the more you already share the same vision.

Discussing Test Item 1:
Are We Working As Hard for Us As We Are at Work?

To help you discuss item 1, I have provided below a scale of "isolation versus intimacy". Each of you should score yourselves somewhere along the scale, then score your partner. Next, get together and score yourselves as a pair. Now, take plenty of time to discuss the various scores, looking for differences and similarities among them.

Remember to try to tune into your oceanic mind as you discuss this test and the others that follow. Don't let your continental brain rush you. The *naupaka* gifts of time and attention will be required. Equally important, remember to approach this discussion (and all of the others you will encounter in the book) bearing in mind the principles of *aloha* you read about in chapter 1. If your partner's scoring of you on the isolation versus intimacy scale makes you want to jump to the defensive, try instead to slow down, think *kakou* rather than `o wau, and focus on responding to him or her with *lokahi*, harmonious unity. If your scoring of yourself compared to your partner tempts in you feelings of smugness and superiority, remember *ha`aha`a*, humble modesty. In any of these exercises—in fact, in all interactions with your partner—try to practice staying open to hearing what your partner has to say by assuming that he or she is at least partly right. (The next prescription, Thinking with One Mind, discusses these ideas in more detail.)

Isolation (Hard at Work) — — — . . .
. . . — — — Intimacy (Working Hard at Love)

$$0 — 1 — 2 — 3 — 4 — 5 — 6 — 7 — 8 — 9 — 10$$

Psychologist Erik H. Erikson considered what he called "intimacy versus isolation" to be one of the key life-development challenges. He defined it as a passage wherein the individual is challenged to transcend individual happiness and connect with another person to find joy and well-being. He noted the importance of finding a balance between loving and working. Erikson wrote, "Freud was once asked what he felt a normal person should be able to do well. The questioner probably expected a complicated answer. But Freud, in the curt acerbity of his old days, is reported to have said: 'Lieben und arbeiten (to love and to work).'"[5]

The challenge in discussing the first item on the Vision Compatibility Test is to examine how much of your shared life together should be work time and how much should be love time. It is not important to come up with a decision. What matters is taking the time to discuss where your relationship falls on the isolation versus intimacy scale, and whether you are both happy with that location.

Discussing Test Item 2: How Much Time Is There for Us?

If your day were represented by a pie, how big a piece would represent couple time? I ask couples in my seminars to draw a pie representing their marriage, and then to divide it into wedges representing time spent doing various activities—such as working at their jobs, housework, childcare, sleeping, preparing and eating meals, and time spent alone as a couple. Is your relationship getting a big enough piece of the pie? Is the piece the size both of you want it to be? How does the relationship piece compare with the size of the other pieces? How could it be a little bigger without cutting too deeply into other obligations?

Discussing Test Item 3: What About the Kids?

Research indicates that discussions and decisions about children and about trying to raise children are the leading cause of stress and conflict in most marriages. In at least one study, dealing with kids was far and away the biggest stressor for couples who had children.[6] Whether or not to have children was also sometimes a source of long unresolved and often covert conflict.

One *kupuna* joked about the frustrations of parenthood, "I think grandchildren are God's reward for not having killed your own children." The older children get, the more they challenge their parents' long-established ways of seeing the world, and the more this triggers potential marital struggle over what constitutes appropriate fatherly and motherly behavior.[7]

Here are two questions to discuss related to item 3 on the vision test. The first is "Would I want to be raised by me?" There is no doubt that our children's physical and emotional future is determined in large measure by who and how we are as their parents.[8] Particularly important is how parents display their love for one another.

The second question is "Are we sharing the hassles and happiness of child-rearing together?" Single-parent homes do not occur only after divorce or separation. They can occur by default when one spouse's busyness or psychological absenteeism in effect renders the other spouse the only real parent. When this happens, the benefits of having two involved, loving parents—which have been shown as fundamental to a healthy childhood and a functional later life—can be lost.

Discussing Test Item 4:
Who Keeps the House and Makes the Home?

Men, who still earn more money than women for doing the same work, have long been accused of using the power of their income to require their wives to perform a disproportionate number of the everyday tasks involved in the running of a home and the caring for children.[9] Many men, it seems, feel hassled when they believe they are being expected to go beyond doing what they consider "men's work." They tend to feel that delivering the paycheck is more important than giving of themselves to the relationship and parenting. To discuss this issue about your shared marital vision, it helps to examine together three basic homemaking rules.[10]

▼ First, talk about the *tradition principle.* Discuss whether either or both of you have fallen into the trap of holding preconceived notions about what constitutes "men's work" or "women's work."

▼ Second, question the *helping-out principle.* Discuss whether one or both of you believe that certain tasks belong exclusively to one partner while the other partner may, on rare occasions or in an emergency, try to "help out." A Hawaiian principle of work is *kokua*, meaning to help always. This means that one's work is not done if someone else is still working. As one wife in our seminar put it, "I wish my husband would stop waiting to be invited to help out and would start digging in. No one invites me. I don't need a helper, I need a coworker. I don't want to be the supervisor. I want a colleague, not an apprentice."

▼ The third homemaking rule to question is the *equity principle.* This principle says that the work of taking care of the house should be divided fifty-fifty at all times. Discuss whether the rather rigid fifty-fifty housework rule is something you want to embrace in your relationship. Is it realistic in terms of outside obligations? What about days when one or the other of you simply needs a break? What about the factor of enjoyment and who likes to do what? And finally, what about doing tasks together—that is, actually enjoying working as a pair on the little things?

While abandoning the fifty-fifty housework rule may seem on the surface to contradict what you've concluded in discussing the preceding two principles, if you take time to consider this idea at a deeper level, you may realize that it reflects an *aloha* approach to your home life. Forgoing a strict adherence to equity in housework actually demonstrates shared flexibility and compassion. Constantly negotiating tit-for-tat compromise can lead to keeping score, and who wants to be married to someone who keeps score? If you try to think *kakou* rather than `*o wau*—if, that is, you bear in mind the goal of becoming one with your partner, even when it comes to life's mundane details—you may surprise one another. You may find yourself cheerfully volunteering to do most of the evening chores on days when you notice your spouse is especially tired or careworn, or by anticipating your partner's wishes about how to prioritize the weekend's "to do" list. (Read more about the idea of transcending the need to force compromise later in this chapter, under the heading "The *Waena* (Middle) Way.")

Pleasure partnerships tend to contain two full-time homemakers free of the limits of tradition, assigned obligations, and a negotiated fifty-fifty approach to daily living. Remember, these are goals to work toward, so be easy on yourself and your partner—practice *ahonui*: patience and forgiveness.

Discussing Test Item 5: Is Time Money?

The question to discuss here is whether the two of your agree with the modern-day philosophy that time is money. If you adhere to this belief, you are almost guaranteeing that you will be under considerable daily stress and that your partnership will sooner or later experience a serious lack of the gifts of attention and time.

Swedish economist Stephen Linder points out that, under this philosophy, as income increases, the value of one's time spent earning that money also increases. It then begins to seem less and less rational to spend time doing anything other than making money.[11] Eventually, whenever we are "wasting" time "just" playing with our children, reading a book, or sitting with our spouse, we will experience what Linder calls the "opportunity costs" of lost time that could be spent working for money. The cost of these leisure activities begins to feel too high. One of my patients, noting this concept, said, "When we finally got to be the leisure class, we discovered we didn't have any leisure."

Ask yourselves whether you and your partner want to give your time and attention to earning more money and accumulating more things. Or would you rather bestow these gifts on each other and on your relationship?

Discussing Test Item 6: Who Will Parent Our Parents?

The good news is that one or both of your parents is probably going to live a longer life than their own parents did. The bad news is, just when you and your spouse feel ready to start leading your life and flourishing in an empty nest, one or all four of your parents are probably going to need a nest. They are going to require considerable investments of your mental resources, help, money, and time. How are the two of you going to manage your emotional, financial, physical, and spiritual resources for this challenge? How much mutual obligation and caring do you feel for your respective in-laws? You probably will not be able to resolve this challenging issue right away, but talking about it now can help you be better prepared to face it later with *lokahi*: harmonious unity.

Discussing Test Item 7: Head or Heart?

Where do you and your partner each fall on the following scale?

Head (Rational, Logical, Analytical) — — — . . .
. . . — — — Heart (Intuitive, Impulsive, Feeling)

$$0 — 1 — 2 — 3 — 4 — 5 — 6 — 7 — 8 — 9 — 10$$

Does one of you seem to be a "head" person and the other more of a "heart" person? Do you tend to be more rationally oriented, or do you like to go with your gut? How about your partner?

Discussing the head-heart orientation can help you identify similarities and differences in your "pleasure temperament": the way in which and the degree to which you react to events that influence your relationship. Chapter 5 will address the issue of learning to think with one mind, and chapter 6 will examine in more detail the issue of heart-to-heart connection, but first discussing item 7 on the vision test will help you both realize and understand your respective rational or intuitive styles. A strong contrast in styles can leave both partners wondering, "Why can't my partner see things the way I do?" A sense of loneliness can result when partners feel that what constitutes real pleasure and pain for them is not really understood by their partner.

Differences on the head-heart scale may show themselves clearly when you reach the eighth prescription (chapter 11), which concerns connecting psychically. Dreamers or heart/intuitive people are generally happy to try such an exercise, but realists or head/rational people may resist, mock, and even become angry when psi or psychic connections such as those presented in chapter 11 are discussed.

During your discussions of this item, try to come up with a couple identity in terms of the head-heart continuum. If you find yourself at opposite ends of the scale, see if you can both agree to move at least a little more toward the middle, the "non-two" or *kakou* orientation of the pleasure partnership.

Discussing Test Item 8: How Much Risk Should We Take?

Place yourselves on the following scale.

Risk (Don't Wait; Just Do It) — — — . . .
. . . — — — Reluctance (Wait; Be Careful)

$$0 - 1 - 2 - 3 - 4 - 5 - 6 - 7 - 8 - 9 - 10$$

Imagine that the two of you are running toward the ocean. Who will go faster and jump in first? Who will splash water on the other while the one being splashed protests, runs away, and perhaps even becomes a little angry? Would both of you jump in together, or would one of you have to be teased and goaded into the water? Is one of you the risk taker and the other the worrywart? Pleasure partners manage to move together toward a common orientation regarding taking risks versus playing it safe.

Discussing Test Item 9: What Does Retirement Mean, and How, When, and Where Will We Do It?

Psychologist Erik Erikson identified the later life-development challenge of "ego integrity versus despair." He was referring to feeling integrated toward the end of life, or content with how you have put it all together, rather than wishing you had a life to live all over again. As the two of you contemplate the autumn of your life together, how do you envision those years? I am not asking you here to talk about financial plans and life insurance, although they are also important issues. I am inviting you to discuss your respective views of what should constitute a healthy, happy retirement—which might better be called your mutual transition to another phase of your spiritual development.

When they discussed this item, most couples in our clinic decided that they would not "retire" in the conventional sense of the word. While one or both may plan to leave their jobs, most couples preferred the phrase "later life transition" to "retirement." They looked forward to more of what Aunty Betty said in the foreword that she now shares with Uncle Jack: *kakou* or "we" time together. Consequently, the couples seemed to begin right away to give each other more of the gifts of attention and time.

An uncomfortable but necessary element must be addressed in the discussion of this item. As you will read in the last chapter of this book, couples—like individuals—go through developmental stages. Most partnerships ultimately end with one partner living alone due to the other's death. Take some time to talk about this issue and how you both feel about it. Creating a partnership in pleasure does not mean gleefully wandering through life together in denial. It is a union in which the partners learn to embrace one another more fully now in order to fix their memories in both of their hearts as spiritual reserves to be drawn on later, during the time of eventual physical separation. The *naupaka* principle says that partners in pleasure are together forever, each feeling the love of the other across the divide between the physical and spiritual planes.

One of the wives in my seminar identified this. She said, "It's really strange, but we both hope that one of us ends up alone. If not, we would have to be killed suddenly at the same time together. Somehow, knowing that one of us will miss the other terribly makes us connect even more strongly now and treasure our moments."

Discussing Test Item 10: Do We Agree on What Constitutes Success and True Happiness?

Discussing item 10 of the vision test helps serve as a transition to the task of creating a couple's mission statement. Each partner should write down a short and clear definition of success. As you discuss your definitions, see how much of those definitions are "me" (`o wau`) as opposed to "we" (*kakou*) oriented. Are you each on your own mission, or do you share a common vision?

On a Mutual Mission: Creating a Couple's Vision Statement

Now that you have discussed your shared-vision status, putting the first paired pleasure prescription into practice and implementing the next seven prescriptions require a couple's mission statement. Based on my clinical work and seminars with couples around the world, here are the steps in creating yours.

1. *First, write your own individual life-mission statements.* Psychiatrist Victor Frankl writes, "Everyone has his own specific vocation or mission in life. . . . Therein he cannot be replaced, nor can his life be repeated. Thus, everyone's task is as unique as is his specific opportunity to implement it."[12]

    The personal mission statement has a long history, and there are many books that show you how to write your own. You may have gone through this exercise before, but take time to update and review your statement before moving on to the mutual mission statement.

    For the purposes of this assignment, keep it brief. Ask yourself the following three questions: What is my life for? Who do I want to be? What do I want to accomplish? Write clear and concise answers on an index card.

2   *Exchange your individual mission cards, and review your partner's in private for a few days.* By now, you are seeing that becoming partners in pleasure requires a lot of time and attention. It cannot be rushed.

3. *Schedule a time when you can both focus on constructing a mutual mission statement.* Together, begin to write your mutual mission statement on one card. Do this by answering as a couple the same three questions you answered as individuals, modified slightly: What is our life together for? How do we want to be together? What do we want to accomplish together?

The challenge is to avoid trying to *make up* a couple's mission statement; instead, as Frankl suggests for individual statements, *discover* it. Let it come to you rather than chasing after it. Talk about all ten items on the Vision Compatibility Test, and see if elements of a mutual vision begin to come to your shared mind. It may take many meetings, but the effort will pay off in much bliss.

What If We Can't Do It?

If you run into trouble creating your marital mission statement, calm down together. You are just beginning your journey to forming a pleasure partnership, and extra time spent on the first prescription will make the following seven prescriptions much easier to follow.

Here is a suggestion to get things going if you find yourself stuck at this step. It is a learning game that comes from the clinical work of marital therapist John Gottman.[13] I use a version of Dr. Gottman's game in my own clinical work and couple's seminars. I call it the Mutual Mission to Pluto. (I deliberately didn't pick the planet Mars or Venus because a popular psychology has sprung from the idea that the two genders symbolically originate from these environmentally contrary planets.) Write on another index card the numbers one through ten. Working together, come up with a list of items you both agree you would need for the very long trip to Pluto. Put them in order from most to least important.

Once you have completed your list, together review how you came up with your list. The list itself is not important; what's important is the way in which you decided as a pair what would and would not be included on it. What were your individual styles for solving this problem? Was one person dominant? What is the difference in the nature of the items each of you came up with, and how do they reflect the mental and emotional styles of each partner? Once you have examined your respective styles of making your Pluto survivor's list, you might understand more about the styles you each bring to writing your mutual mission statement. Try to move a little more toward each other's style as you work on your couple's mission statement.

The *Waena* (Middle) Way

In Hawaiian myth, the *po'o* (head) of the fish represents the past. This is because it has already gone ahead. The *hi'u* (tail) of the fish represents the future, for it has yet to come through the water. The *waena* (middle) of the fish represents the now. Hawaiian legend says that the healthy and happy person is one who finds the middle way, not through forced compromise or by someone's having to give in, but through mutual humble awareness of the challenges to come in our respective futures and a reverent respect for our pasts.[14] Anxiety is born of concerns for the future, and depression stems from being stuck in the past. A creative couple's mission statement is like the middle of the fish, aware of the future and the past but focused on the present.

Discovering your mutual mission statement is easier if you consider what Hawaiian and Buddhist philosophies call "the middle way." In Buddhism, *middle* does not mean "compromise" but rather a higher way, different from but somehow better and more constructive and creative than each of your individual ways. Draw an equilateral triangle with each of your names on opposite corners of the base. The apex or top of the triangle represents the *kakou* (the us, or non-two), a more constructive, rich, shared way—a higher way—to look at your mission statement. If your couple's statement comes out looking too much like either of your individual mission statements, keep working for the middle way.[15]

The following is one example of a couple's mutual mission statement. "It's not much, it's not right yet, but it's ours," said the wife who helped discover it. Her husband said, "It would never work in business and I don't even know if it will work in our own life, but in a way it is working already. Just doing this thing really brought us much more together, and the trip to Pluto was a lot of fun and really helped."

One Couple's Mission Statement

What is our life together for? "Our life is for love. Nothing takes precedence over our showing our love for one another. If either of us has a choice to make, the first consideration will be 'What will this do to our love time?'"

How do we want to be together? "We want to be calm together. When either of us feels rushed, we will ask for the two gifts of paired pleasure partnership: time and attention. We will just sit down, shut up, hold hands, and be together."

What do we want to accomplish together? "We want to feel that our life together has been our own and not controlled or taken from us by other people or other obligations. We will remember that our most important time together is now, our most important gift is our attention, and we will say no more often to those opportunities that diminish either of these things."

▼ ▼ ▼

Author Jack Kornfield identifies the ultimate goal of the couple's mutual mission statement. It is a theme that runs through most couple's statements, and I am recommending this view as fundamental to the first paired pleasure prescription. He writes, "The element of nonidentification with a limited self seems to be central to [the] experience of the world. Out of this expanded or unified experience comes naturally . . . equanimity, contentment, joy, and profound love."[16] Instead of shaping your life's vision primarily from an `o wau orientation—what Kornfield calls a "limited self"—consider the rich benefits of a life purpose grounded in the "unified experience" of a kakou orientation.

Chapter Five

Thinking with One Mind

Paired Pleasure Prescription Two:
Think less for yourself and more for "us."

E pupukahi

Be united in thought.[1]

We become wiser when we try to see and think about the world through the eyes of others. We can be happier if we learn how to put "our" mind rather than "my" mind to it.

Are You Out of Your Mind?

"When I think 'maybe,' he thinks 'obviously,'" said the wife in my couples seminar. "When I'm thinking, 'Let's think this over,' he's thinking, 'Let's just do it.' When I want to reflect about a question and just kind of mull it over in my mind, he rushes me and asks, 'What's there to think about?' He can read maps, but I can't even fold them. He laughs at me when I keep turning the map around to match it up with the direction we're going in the car. I remember every little thing, but he can't seem to remember anything except work stuff. He focuses on something and has tunnel vision, and I'm easily distracted because I can see everything and every possibility. That's why I like to shop and he just goes to get something specific. He can't understand why I get so upset at some of the things he says to me, but I can 'hear' much more than he thinks he's saying. Sometimes we get frustrated and ask each other, 'Are you out of your mind?'"

Professor Henry Higgins asks in *My Fair Lady*, "Why can't a woman be more like a man?" He should have also asked, "Why can't a man be more like a woman?" The answer is because it's almost impossible and would take most of the pleasure out of our partnerships.

Despite the popular gender politics of the last few decades, emphasizing the lack of differences between men and women, the fact is they do tend to exhibit different interpretive and thinking styles.[2] American neurologist Richard Restak writes, "It seems unrealistic to deny any longer the existence of male and female brain differences. Just as there are physical dissimilarities between males and females . . . there are equally dramatic differences in brain functioning."[3]

The genders are equal as members of the same human species, but there is a wonderful—and potentially complementary—difference between how they think about the world. Neither the woman whose comments appear at the beginning of this chapter nor her husband is out of their mind. In fact, science tends to support one of the very examples she mentioned: research shows that most men can read maps better than women, but women tend to read character much better than men.[4] The idea of the second paired pleasure prescription is not to help women think more like men or men more like women. Learning to be of one mind is learning how each of you thinks and then figuring out how to combine both styles into one—to find the higher and more creative middle way of thinking.

Life would be more boring and less pleasurable if we were partnered with a person who thought just as we did. Geneticist Anne Moir and author David Jessel write, "The best argument for the acknowledgement of differences [in brain structure and function between men and women] is that doing so would probably make us happy. . . . Men and women could live more happily, understand and love each other better, organize the world to better effect, if we acknowledge our differences. We could then build our lives on the twin pillars of our distinct sexual identities."[5] We would be happier because instead of spending so much time trying to figure out how our partner thinks and why, we could start using both styles to create a more complete and interesting life together. *Different* does not imply *better*, and the pressure on men to try to be more "feminine" in their thinking and on women to be "as good as the next man" only leads to stress and conflict. Trying to find a way to capitalize on the brilliance of both genders is the path to the second paired pleasure prescription.

Men Are from Earth, Women Are from Earth

The problem of gender conflict and misunderstanding is not due, as a popular psychologist suggests, to men being from one planet and women from another. Both genders have elements of the supposedly more warlike Mars and the more gentle, loving Venus—and of all the other planets as well—in their intellectual repertoire. They possess an array of ways of thinking and expression that change as they develop through life. To divide the genders as coming from one or another planet and then to attempt to teach them to speak the language of the "other" planet can make us more alien to one another or cause us to try to love in a style that is not truly from the heart. The pop-psychology planetary divide may unnecessarily assign characteristics to one or the other gender that can become self-fulfilling prophecies or even excuses for failure to try to become of one heart and mind.

Rather, the challenge to partners occurs when they each think from the continental, rock-logic perspective and then express that view in their respective gender-related ways. Partners who embrace the oceanic view, by contrast, understand that the different cognitive styles of men and women are not separate "rocks" (or planets) sitting next to one another. Their respective thought processes flow back and forth to influence, inspire, annoy, aggravate, and intellectually invigorate one another. Each style is the *naupaka* half of the other, but it still forms part of one style unique to each couple. Recognizing this, partners can begin communicating not from the perspective of two different planets but as two halves of the same flower.

One of my *naupaka* seminar participants pointed out the benefits of thinking with one mind. She said, "My husband can get us to the party, but I have to get us through it. He finds the place, and I find the people that are worth partying with. We're a team that way. If it were up to me, we'd never find the place. If it were up to him, we'd never enjoy the party. We're one brain. I think I might be the right hemisphere or half of the *naupaka* flower, and he's the left side. We really blossom when we see our differences that way. When we don't, we're just like two rocks trying to change each other."

Alpha and Beta Styles

So, what are these differences in male and female cognitive styles, and how do they originate? While cultural and other learning factors certainly play a role, a general template is laid out while we are still in the uterus. You could say that our minds are almost entirely made up before we are born. The template is not permanent, but it seems to provide a starting point for how we will process the events of our life, a kind of love-map that we can modify. I use the term *alpha* to mean the more typically masculine mental makeup, and the term *beta* to indicate the more typically feminine mindset. At about six or seven weeks after conception, the fetus's brain begins to make up its mind whether it will develop along the alpha or beta template. Almost always, alpha-thinking males and beta-thinking females come through this short window of mental opportunity.

At this time, the genetically male fetus (meaning it has the chromosome combination XY; alternatively, it may have started out as an

XX, with one of the X chromosomes lacking a tail on the right bottom side, resulting in a "broken" X, as some women suspect who are frustrated with the male way of thinking) develops special cells that produce the male hormones called androgens. The main androgen is testosterone. While both genders have testosterone, most men have more of it than most women. If the embryo is genetically female (XX), nothing much happens at the sixth week; the biological default mode for mental development seems to be female.[6] Whatever the genetic constitution of the embryo, the fetus will only develop a male physiology if testosterone, the male hormone, is present at this crucial stage of development. A female physiology will develop only if testosterone is absent or at least present in a much smaller amount.

Accordingly, testosterone seems to lead to the alpha cognitive style, while less testosterone is related to the beta orientation. As one woman frustrated with the difference between her husband's and her own thinking styles said, "I think he got testosterone poisoning and it affected his brain." In a way, she was right. Testosterone is a mind-altering substance that contributes greatly to the alpha way men think, feel, relate, and communicate. The lack of this hormone leads to a different brain chemistry—and therefore to different ways of thinking, feeling, and relating—in women. Of course, various mixtures emerge; no one person is all alpha or beta.[7]

The Alpha/Beta Brain Test

To help partners begin to understand their respective cognitive styles, I developed the following Alpha/Beta Brain Test. It is intended to promote discussion and a more creative approach to how "we" can learn to think together—rather than staying focused on how "you" think versus how "I" think.

Circle the items that most closely reflect how you think and feel about people, places, things, and events. Resist the temptation to view the qualities in either column as right and good or wrong and bad. All of the characteristics under both columns are essential to a full and joyful approach to life. No one is a total alpha or beta; the items are intentionally broad and simplistic to promote more discussion between partners attempting to learn the second prescription.

BETA MIND STYLE	ALPHA MIND STYLE
1. Vulnerable	Callous
2. Acquiescent	Antagonistic
3. Can't forget	Poor memory
4. Flowers and plants	Cell phones and techno-toys
5. Worrier	Denier
6. Compassionate	Numb
7. Reads faces	Doesn't "see" emotions
8. Can't find TV remote	Dominates TV remote
9. Ruminator	Forgetter
10. Selfless	Selfish
11. Accommodating	Resistant
12. Good listener	Poor listener
13. Flatterer	Takes things for granted
14. Naive	Cynical
15. Sensual	Sexual
16. Smiler	Frowner
17. Cries easily	Masks tears
18. Enjoys being there	Loves going places
19. Picky taste buds	Numb taste buds
20. Eco- or world-oriented	Ego- or self-oriented
21. Pushover	Fighter
22. Patient	Impatient
23. Delayed, subtle revenge	Immediate reactive strike
24. Wants to talk it over	Wants to get over it
25. Consider it	Solve it
26. Compliments	Criticizes
27. Never sure	Always right
28. Tired out	Stressed out
29. Resident nurturer	Resident
30. Others are basically nice	Others are basically dopes
31. Fears independence	Fears interdependence
32. Cooperates	Competes
33. Not sure of intelligence	Unappreciated genius
34. Just go along	Stand up and resist
35. Strong sense of smell	Numb sense of smell
36. Few body noises	Many body noises

BETA MIND STYLE	ALPHA MIND STYLE
37. Feeler	Doer
38. Congeals	Controls
39. People focus	Time focus
40. Optimist	Pessimist
41. Intuitive	Rational
42. Reflects	Executes
43. Dreamer	Realist
44. Loves shopping	Hates shopping
45. Self-doubt	Self-assured
46. Peace-loving	War-seeking
47. Drives car gently	Drives car hard
48. Detects other's marriage problems	Can't see other's marriage problems
49. Avoids tight parking place	Goes for tight parking place
50. Annoyed by dripping faucet	Can't hear dripping faucet

Total Beta Attributes____   **Total Alpha Attributes____**

Being able to joke about the traits on the test is important to forming a partnership in pleasure. Debating which style is the "right" style only accentuates differences and causes couples to miss out on developing a marriage of minds. The creative joy of a loving relationship comes from learning to celebrate and join our alpha and beta natures into one *naupaka* couple consciousness.

A Genital and Brain Match?

Now that you've taken the test, can you begin to identify the pattern of thinking in your relationship? Does your partnership consist of the typical alpha-thinking male and beta-thinking female? Or are you both more alpha or more beta? My clinical experience indicates that alphas and betas tend to find each other and marry. This may be a manifestation of the *naupaka* drive to find our other half. One of my patients said, "You've got us pegged. Our genitals match our letters. I'm the beta and he's the alpha, and we're going to try to see if ever the twain shall meet."

Role Reversal

As you consider this matter, be aware of important research that supports the finding that some men seem to "think more like a woman" (that is, they tend toward the beta cognitive style), while some women "think like a man" (they tend toward the alpha style). As you have read, hormone production before birth influences the course of the brain's development and eventually its general way of thinking. Sometimes brain production "accidents" occur that can cause the genders to take on one another's cognitive characteristics.[8]

Consider the case of Sylvia and Sam.[9] Sylvia is a lovely and graceful thirty-seven-year-old woman. She looks very feminine, like a typical beta. She is a science teacher, a doting mother of three boys, and a gourmet cook. She also loves to chop wood for the family cottage, enjoys hunting and target shooting, loves cars and repairing them, and scored thirty-seven alpha points on the test above. She describes her husband Sam as "a little too sentimental and soft." Sam looks like an alpha male. He is a muscular licensed mechanic who owns and operates his own gas station. He played football in high school and is a hockey fanatic. He also loves to shop, designs his wife's clothes, works almost every day in the garden with rare flowers, and cries easily. He says of his wife Sylvia, "She doesn't like to just sit and talk, and I do. She can be insensitive to my needs sometimes."

Sylvia and Sam are examples of an alpha wife and beta husband. When they came to the clinic, they were struggling with their different cognitive styles. During the physical examinations, medical histories, and laboratory tests we require for all of our patients, we learned that Sam's mother had experienced hormonal problems in her pregnancy that caused her estrogen levels to rise to abnormal levels. Hormonal imbalance during pregnancy can influence the developing fetus, contributing to a "female brain" in a male's body. As a little boy and despite his athletic skills, masculine physique, and role as a star athlete, Sam had often been called a sissy for his "oversensitivity" and his desire to play games that "only girls play." He said, "I really felt bad whenever I knocked the hell out of another player in football. I would say I'm sorry and ask if he was okay. I would strike up conversations with the player on the other side of the line." There was no evidence of homosexuality or confusion over gender orientation, only a strong man who thinks more like a woman.

We also learned that Sylvia had been diagnosed with a mild form of a condition called adrenogenital syndrome. This is a circumstance in which a kidney malfunction can cause an abnormal secretion of a substance chemically similar to the male hormone testosterone. If this or perhaps some form of maternal stress occurs about six to eight weeks after conception (a key time in the brain's development, as you will recall from above), it can cause a more masculine cognitive style in a female. As a little girl, Sylvia had always preferred to play with the boys. She told us, "The boys played more competitively and it was just more fun. They didn't want to talk things over. They just wanted to get down to it and play hard." As with her husband, Sylvia gave no evidence of gender-orientation confusion or homosexuality; she is simply a beautiful, feminine, and caring woman who in some ways seems to think more like a man.

Sylvia and Sam's case is an example of the exception to the alpha-beta rule. In most people, the male (alpha) and female (beta) brain orientations match their genital insignia. But Sam is clearly beta in his thinking and Sylvia is more alpha. They often struggle to understand their respective minds and become frustrated with the way the other sees things. Sam said, "We've begun to surrender to the fact that we are not from Mars and Venus but from totally different galaxies."

No matter whether the alpha and beta cognitive styles within a couple follow or swap traditional gender orientations, partners in pleasure learn to incorporate these ways of thinking into one alpha/beta mind. Just as the left blossom of the *naupaka* flower is no better or worse than the right, neither is alpha better or worse than beta—any more than the letter A is better or worse than the letter B.

Flowing Together

Thinking with one mind—that is, blending your alpha and beta styles—requires that both partners learn to flow together in the oceanic way. The good news is that oceanic thinking can serve as the bridge—or should I say river—that connects both styles.

Recall from the discussion in this book's introduction that rock logic (or continental thinking) means seeing things from the point of view that one rock plus one rock equals two rocks. In this mindset, things and ideas do not flow together, and alpha and beta styles cannot combine. They remain separate, a source for evaluation and debate. However, if we add water to water, we just have more water. The original water is in there somewhere, but it has lost its "two-ness" to become *kakou* (we).

Edward de Bono, in his groundbreaking book *I Am Right—You Are Wrong: From Rock Logic to Water Logic,* points out that there are no rigid boundaries in water-like thinking. He writes, "Water flows according to the gradient (context). It takes the form of the vessel in which it is placed (circumstance)."[10] This is the thinking of a partnership in pleasure, a consciousness so blended that it flows easily with the changing contexts and circumstances of the loving relationship.

We can turn to the original Hawaiians for examples of the oceanic cognitive style in practice. Contrary to myth, the Hawaiians did not stumble upon a paradise in the middle of the Pacific Ocean. They had to learn to survive in a sometimes harsh and unforgiving ecology. They had to think in a way that allowed them to connect with nature rather than struggle to control it. Water logic/oceanic thinking became essential to their survival. They developed a cognitive style largely free of absolutes and of rigid insistence on being seen as right. They did not rely on verbal cleverness to win arguments. They became better at perception than at cold hard logic, more skilled at listening than at speaking their minds; they saw themselves as "a part of" instead of "in charge over." They favored an intellectual style akin to floating along until an idea seemed to just come to them. They were much less "is" oriented than "to" oriented.

Here are examples of rock logic/continental thinking and water logic/oceanic thinking from two couples in my *naupaka* seminars.

Continental Dialogue: A wife, an emergency room physician, said, "Roy is just plain dead wrong. He says I'm never home because I'm always at the hospital, but I am home. How much time does he need anyway? I'm off call every three days. I'm tired when I'm home, so I need some down time alone, but he is so needy."

"She just plain doesn't see it," responded Roy, her accountant husband. "She's on the go all the time. Even when she is home, she really isn't. I work hard too. Just because I'm not saving lives doesn't mean what I do isn't tiring, but at least I'm home and try to be with her. It's pretty simple, really. She either comes home mentally or we are going to eventually have to have different homes."

Oceanic Dialogue: "I'm on the road a lot, but I think we're out of sync seasonally," said the husband, an airline pilot. "It really depends on the time of year, I guess. I think she needs me home the most when I'm the busiest, like around holidays when the kids are out of school and I'm flying. We're going to have to look at this thing again to come up with something." (Note the "to" orientation—he wants to move together with his wife toward a common solution that will work for both.)

"I think he's right and I'm right," answered his stay-at-home wife. "He is gone the most when I need him the most, but I think we have to consider moving so he's not so far from the airport. His having to drive so much takes a lot of time away from us. I have to look at my getting bored. I'm sick of being the resident nurturer in the house, so maybe we can get a smaller house and hire some help. We'll get there; we just have to be patient with each other." (Again, note the "to" orientation.)

If the second couple sounds too good to be true, it may be because relating according to the continental style of thinking is so deeply ingrained in many of us Westerners. While a competitive, survival-oriented mindset may serve us well under some circumstances, a slowness of pace, kindness of speech, and gentleness of spirit are more apropos for building a partnership in pleasure.

Is This Your Underwear on the Floor?

What are some practical hints for learning to think with one mind, for beginning to allow your alpha and beta styles to flow together? One of the most helpful suggestions relies on the fact that oceanic thinking tends to lead to the asking of questions rather than the making of statements. When my highly beta wife notices my alpha "clothes-hamper blindness," she asks good-naturedly and with a smile, "Is this your underwear on the floor?" (If it isn't mine, I certainly have some questions for her!) She is asking me to pick up after myself, but she's doing it with a graceful humor that circumvents the harshness of saying, "Do you think there's a clothes fairy that runs around picking up your stuff? How can you be so thoughtless! Pick up your clothes!"

I suggest this gentle questioning approach between partners. When you want or need something from your partner or feel an urge to criticize or complain, do it through a question. Don't be sarcastic in tone. Do it with humor if you can, because humor is always water logic. It is not based on arrogance or asserting one's argument. Instead of saying, "It's cold in here," ask, "Do you think it's cold in here?" Instead of nagging your husband to mow the lawn, wait until he's on his way out with his golf clubs, and then ask with a smile and a lighthearted tone, "Going golfing?" If you can manage humor and openness rather than sarcasm and a demanding tone, the temperature might be made more mutually comfortable, and the lawn might get cut a little sooner than later.

Another exercise you might try is to play a couple's version of twenty questions. Take turns asking questions about the relationship. Each of you is allowed ten questions. Ask about the children, one another's work, your lovemaking, emotions, the times you go to bed at night and get up in the morning, what makes you laugh or cry. Ask about "us" rather than about "you" or "it." Each question must be answered with a question. The game ends when one of you fails to answer with a question. If you end up laughing together, celebrate your newfound mutual oceanic thinking—a mindset that does not always require an immediate answer or a winner to every game, and that enjoys indecision and reflection. Be forgiving. Your *naupaka* flower is just beginning to bloom.

The Couple That Laughs Together Stays Together

This discussion leads to another practical tip: find reasons to laugh together. If there is one clear indicator of two persons engaged in a pleasure partnership and learning to think with one mind, it is a couple that laughs together often and hard. Humor does not demand facts, reality, or quickly getting to the point. To heighten your shared laughter frequency, review the following statements made by patients in my couple treatment program. Alternate reading the items aloud to one another, and see if they can make you laugh together:[11]

- ▼ Men like dogs better than they like women because a dog is happy when men leave the toilet seat up.

- ▼ Men feel that if God wanted them to use tissues, She wouldn't have given them fingers.

- ▼ Women have a lower center of gravity, which means they have better balance than men. That's why men get beer bellies: if they fall over, they have a built-in air bag.

- ▼ Men's brain are lower than women's, so when they're scratching their crotches, they're not really being gross . . . they're just thinking.

- ▼ It's a good thing men's real life isn't like their sex life. Most of them wouldn't have long to live.

- ▼ There's only one way to get a man to wear new clothes. Buy them yourself, cut off the tags, and throw them on the floor in his closet.

All of the above statements are dumb, sexist, and silly. They are designed to poke fun at the stereotypes of men and how women see them. As you read them together, was there finger-pointing and defensiveness, or good-natured laughter at the comedy of a daily life shared by two people who live and act differently? Water logic just flows with the statements, forgives their silliness, and is free of angry defensiveness.

Another good idea is to have a joke-of-the-day ritual. Each partner is responsible on alternating days for presenting a new joke to the other. Keep a joke file, and be constantly on the lookout for jokes and funny stories that you think will tickle your couple funny bone.

Give In and Forgive

Becoming of one mind requires two more important changes in how you approach your relationship. First, it requires that you begin to think outside of the competitive box that says "I'm right; you're wrong." This approach is based on psychiatrist Gerald Jampolsky's concept of "choosing peace over being right."[12] There are endless ways to view and understand life and its joys and hassles. Your way is not the right way, only one way. Everyone else thinks they are as right as you think you are, and there are plenty of people who are sure you are dead wrong. You don't have to have a hole in your head to have an open mind, so just give in. Even if you are right and even if you win, fighting for your point of view only damages your health.

The second change of mind is to learn to forgive. This can be one of the most difficult aspects of building a pleasure partnership, but it is essential to a lasting and joyful love. Forgiveness does not mean refusing to hold people responsible for their actions. It is not about giving up your sense of justice or condoning any particular act or acts. Since most arguments and conflicts are based on what has happened in the past, forgiveness is something you do to protect the pleasure of your partnership by freeing it from being trapped in the past. Forgiving your partner is giving up all hope of having had a better past.[13] The opposite of injustice is not justice; it's love.

The One Mind Test

Now you are ready to test your newly emerging one mind. On the test that follows, score yourself and your partner, and have your partner do the same. Then, together, score your relationship. Compare all five scores. The idea is to discuss the items, not simply to raise your scores. Remember the lessons of this chapter, and try to discuss each item with those principles in mind.

$$0 - 1 - 2 - 3 - 4 - 5 - 6 - 7 - 8 - 9 - 10$$

NOT AT ALL — — — OFTEN — — — ALWAYS

1. Do you "think alike"? (How do your alpha and beta styles compare?)

2. Do you view neatness and organization—or "the way things should be done"—in the same way?

3. Do you share the same politics?

4. Do you both seem to feel completely understood by one another?

5. Do you laugh at the same things?

6. Do you cry at the same things?

7. Do you seem to know what the other is thinking and/or would think about something?

8. Do you both assess and judge people the same way?

9. Do you think at the same speed, and do you reflect and contemplate to the same extent?

10. Do you tend to agree about the "fair" or "right" solution to family conflicts and about decisions regarding your extended family?

Total _____

The higher your score, the more one-minded your relationship tends to be already. To become truly of one mind requires years of practice and a lifetime of *aloha kakou*.

Do not be discouraged if you seem to be far from your destination; in this as in everything, treat yourself and your partner with *ahonui*, persistent patience. Equally important, resist feeling frustrated over the fact that no simple "exercise" exists to suddenly make your mind one with your partner's. If you begin to practice some of the individual suggestions offered in this chapter—if you operate with more awareness of your respective alpha and beta styles; if you allow yourself to embrace oceanic thinking at least a little; if you employ the benefits of asking questions and using gentle humor; if you try to move toward giving in and forgiving—you may find yourself surprised by their cumulative effects. It is helpful to forgo an insistence upon having in hand a linear, step-by-step plan for getting from *here* to *there*. Instead, remember the *menehune* factor—how the little things magically add up to create real and lasting change.

Chapter Six

Connecting Heart to Heart

Paired Pleasure Prescription Three: Listen to what your hearts are saying to one another.

Hak`i wai a ka neki

Water agitates amidst the rushes. [1]

Said of the throbbing of the hearts of those who are connected in love.

Have a Heart

Point to yourself. Where are you pointing? Most people point to the general area of their chest, where their heart is constantly beating out a loving energy. Going beyond romantic metaphor, new discoveries in science show that our heart is much more than a pump. It has its own unique intelligence as well as an ability to experience emotions and talk to other hearts with a kind of Morse code understood only heart to heart.[2]

Even `eha koni (heartache) is more than simply an experience one endures alone. The word koni means to throb, pulsate, tingle, beat, or a fluttering of the heart. The lovers who were turned into naupaka blossoms experienced `eha koni for one another, and legend says that their pu`uwai (hearts) still resonate together between mountain and sea. Once again, ancient Hawaiian wisdom anticipated what modern science would eventually learn: that the heart can literally "ache" with love and yearning for another person. The poets were right. As philosopher Blaise Pascal wrote, "The heart has its reasons, which reason does not know."

The third paired pleasure prescription is about reminding the brain that it has a heart. It is about learning the heart's code, storing its messages as cardio-memories, and understanding that `eha koni is really our heart crying out for another heart to talk to and love. This prescription shows you how to tune in to your heart's energy and wisdom, follow its craving for connection, and join hearts with your partner. While these phrases may sound hopelessly romantic and symbolic to the busy alpha brain, you will see that they are not only in keeping with ancient Hawaiian teachings but also with the new cutting-edge science of energy cardiology.[3]

There's a Brain Down There

The Hawaiian word for heart, pu`uwai, is literally translated as "lump of water." To Hawaiians, water represents loving energy and prosperity of spirit, so the heart is seen as a lump of life and love energy that is the center of our being. Unlike the rock logic that is so characteristic of the brain, the lump of water in our chest thinks with water logic. Where the brain draws boundaries, the heart's energy flows through any barriers. We tend to be "hard headed" but "soft hearted."

To learn this prescription, you have to convince your brain that there is a very wise and powerful thinking organ nearby that has its own unique intelligence well worth listening to and learning from.

`O Wau—Oh Wow!

Our brain is naturally selfish and self-protective, so it may not necessarily want to recognize that it needs not only its own body's heart but the special energetic code of another heart to achieve the highest levels of health and well-being.

The Hawaiian word for *I*, as you know, is `*o wau*, pronounced "oh wow." It means the exact opposite of *kakou*, the sacred Hawaiian "we" at the core of the *naupaka* principle. The brain is an `*o wau* organ and thinks almost exclusively in terms of the "I." The heart's intelligence, by contrast, is based on *kakou*; it is perplexed and made to ache when the brain's tunnel-vision "I"-sight causes it to feel neglected and alone.

The symbolism of `*o wau* was taught to me by a *kupuna* (elder) in the Ka Ha Naupaka group. She said, "Uncle and I can feel each other's hearts no matter where we are. We are *kakou*. But whenever one of us senses that we are not connected by our *pu`uwai* (heart), we say 'Oh wow!' This makes us remember how important it is not to be selfish but to stay *kakou* and connected heart to heart. When we say 'oh wow,' we mean we need more *kakou*."

The brain is not very good at grasping the idea of *kakou*. *Kakou* means no boundaries, no inside versus outside, no you and I. According to the book of Genesis, one of Adam's first tasks was to draw boundaries. He was charged with naming all the animals and plants. To do so, he had to think boundary rather than connection. He had to separate the animals into categories by creating mental dividing lines.[4] Our brain—particularly our alpha brain, described in chapter 5—still seems to be Adam-ized. The beta heart, on the other hand, does not think about boundaries. As one *kupuna* told me, "The *pu`uwai* [heart] is like a *pahu* [drum] inviting other hearts to come and *hula* [dance] with it; its every beat is an invitation to other hearts to come and care and talk story with it."

The human brain's primary directive is to clearly establish a battle line of defense. It sees the skin as that line, and everything outside the skin is "over the line" and must be defended against. It has become so diligent and compulsive in its efforts to maintain and protect its version of its territory that it has trouble grasping the *naupaka* principle of no boundary between mountain and sea.

Since the brain's primary imperative is to keep its body alive and stimulated, we must think with our heart and help it capture our brain's attention. The brain will have trouble getting the message, because it has little time to hear the subtle, gentle, and tender messages of connection from the peaceful heart. Unless it sees some immediately tangible physical reward, the brain is not much interested in crossing the line and going in search of another person's brain and heart with which to connect. It thinks that if it feels safe, well fed, and sexually satisfied, all is right in its walled-off world.

So how do we assist our brain in hearing the messages of the heart? The secret lies in knowing some facts about the heart's physiology and in understanding how science has begun to view the relationship between these two vital organs.

Cardio-Communication

On a purely biological level, the heart is amazing in its power and endurance. Without needing oiling or cleaning—and usually without requiring repair or replacement—it pumps from near the time of your conception until the day you die. It beats around one hundred thousand times a day with a power that could shoot water more than six feet into the air. It generates enough electrochemical power to energize the seventy-five trillion cells that make up your body. It sends well over one hundred gallons of blood per hour through a vascular system over sixty thousand miles long. In effect, each beat of your heart sends your blood a distance equivalent to two times around the circumference of the earth.[5]

Think of your heart as a pulsating pump with an electromagnetic field of 5,000 millivolts. (By contrast, the brain emits only 140 millivolts, and the Voyager space probe transmitted signals from Saturn back to the earth using only a 10-millivolt battery.) Have you ever stood near a very powerful machine buzzing with energy and felt its hum vibrating in your body? Do you think you might be able to sense or feel the energy of such a remarkable machine as the heart simply by being near it? Most people would answer yes, and, indeed, when you stand next to anther person, your heart can sense the immense power of the pump working in the body next to it. Researchers at the HeartMath Institute in California have managed to measure the heart's electromagnetic energy dozens of feet away from the body.[6] (Read more about this principle later in the chapter, under the section titled "Falling in Love and in Synch.")

The heart "talks" to the brain in two ways. The first is electromagnetically, by its powerful 5,000-millivolt electrical force field. The second is electrochemically, via a substance called ANP or atrial naturetic peptide. ANP, secreted from the heart's atrial walls, communicates to the brain from the heart through the pineal gland, where melatonin—the sleep hormone—is regulated. ANP is a kind of "mellowing hormone" that seems to be involved in keeping the body system in balance and less reactive to stress. People with coronary heart disease produce less melatonin when they sleep than people with healthy hearts. The research question being asked now is whether sad people have broken hearts, or if a "broken" heart is sending insufficient ANP and thereby keeping the heart patient awake at night.[7]

A Mind of Its Own

The heart is a pump, but it is a conscious pump. It can beat outside of the body, without the brain in our head telling it what to do. The heart has its own little "brain" called the sinoatrial (SA) node, a tiny clump of tissue located in the back wall near the top of the right upper chamber (atrium) of the heart. The SA node regulates the heartbeat. It is made up of at least forty thousand nerve cells, a number equal to the number of brain cells found in many of the subcortical or lower parts of our head brain.[8]

While the head brain and its hormones constantly send messages to the heart to hurry it up or slow it down in service of the brain's perceived needs, the heart also talks to the brain, telling it to pay attention or chill out. The same neurotransmitters found in the brain have been identified in the heart, establishing a direct neurochemical and electrochemical link between the heart and the brain.

Cells in an emotion-controlling area of the head brain called the amygdala (the area where we experience strong emotions such as rage and passion) show electrical activity that is synchronized with the heartbeat. As the heartbeat changes, the electrical activity in the cells of the brain's amygdala also changes. Our heart rate can increase even before the brain in our head could possibly have been able to "see" or "experience" something. Sometimes our heart actually "feels" before the brain in our head "knows." You may have cried without knowing why because the heart knew what the brain had not yet recognized. Or perhaps you've sometimes cried not because you felt sad, but rather have felt sad because you were crying. We say we "feel it in our heart" because our heart is literally sensitive to emotion-provoking events before the brain can register and assign them meaning. Scientists have shown that emotional reactions show up in our brain's activity before we could possibly have time to intellectually process them.[9] As poet Kahil Gibran pointed out, the heart often knows in silence what the brain cannot understand.

So, as you can see, the head brain is not always in charge. Scientists used to assume that the brain ran everything, including the heart, but research by physiologists John and Beatrice Lacey of the Fels Research Institute showed that being "heart smart" is not only good lifestyle advice but a neurophysiological fact of life.[10] They proved that the heart has its own unique logic. Like a wise and reflective sage, it sits calmly (if we let it!) and selects which brain messages it will obey. In a way, the heart is the prototype for meditation because it knows how to free itself of brain dominance. While all of the other bodily organs fall into lockstep when the brain says "alert," the heart "thinks it over." Sometimes it goes along and begins to race. Other times it slows down when the rest of the organs speed up. The healthy heart rhythm is not a slow, steady, nonreactive beat, but rather a varying rhythm that ebbs and flows with life's ups and downs.

The Laceys discovered that the heart not only uses its own brain logic to decide if it will follow the head brain's instructions. It can also talk back to the brain and tell it what and how to think and what messages it might consider sending. Our heart rate is not just an automatic rhythm marching to the orders of the head brain; it beats out a code representing an intelligent language.

If the brain is allowed to think that it alone is running things and is unaccountable to its heart, it becomes mindless. It begins to operate without the sensitive wisdom of the heart and focuses only on the strong physical signals from its body. It becomes a real go-getter but not a very good come-and-connector. Important for the third paired pleasure prescription is understanding how our heart's brain "talks" to our head brain in a constant cardio-cortical conversation. The heart-brain loop exists in a complex communication system that constitutes a triune mind made up of a strong and healing body, a brilliant brain, and a wise and loving heart. You cannot know, understand, and seek to share pleasure with your partner if you only communicate and connect with one part of her or his triune mind.

The Codependent Heart

Finally, it is important to understand one last aspect of the interdependent relationship between heart and brain. The heart is capable of withstanding decades of neglect, abuse, and exploitation by the brain. It is codependent in that it will sacrifice its needs for the imposed needs of the ever-selfish and demanding brain. This cardio-codependence can prove to be dysfunctional and potentially deadly in the long run. The heart can endure for years the clogging of its supply lines and the spurts of adrenaline shot there by the brain's anger, impatience, aggravation, and irritability, but it can eventually be beaten to death.

At the end of life, it is usually the body and brain that ultimately fail the heart. The heart muscle is unique in that, unless disease or injury occurs, it does not age like our other muscles. It takes a beating and just keeps ticking. It will gallantly keep going even when our other body systems are failing. This is why our current definition of death is "brain death." The heart will struggle to keep beating even when it is removed from the body. Despite its gentle and subtle way of communicating its wisdom to us, the heart is like the seeds of the *naupaka* that survive even in the salty sea. It is a survivor. Considering all the heart must endure, it seldom fails us. We fail it.

Tibetan, Chinese, and Ayurvedic medicine all try to pay attention to the heart's code. They consider the pulse sounds of the heart to be major keys to diagnosing disease. When we refer to illness as a "disorder," we are referring to being "out of our life rhythm." The heart keeps the time of our life, and we are wise not to rush it.

Every moment of our life, our heart is talking to us and to others. It speaks in a soft and loving voice that often cannot be heard above the noisy drone of the modern world. To learn the third paired pleasure prescription requires listening very hard and very patiently for what your heart and your partner's heart are trying to say. Remember, the heart is as shy as the brain is bold, so you will have to listen very, very carefully.

The Intuitive Heart

One of the challenges in dealing with daily stress while connecting with a partner heart to heart lies in the fact that our feelings can happen to us faster than we can think about them, as discussed above. If this is true, how can we manage our own emotions and join calmly and lovingly with our partner to more joyfully experience a shared emotional life? We would need an intuitive organ to do that, and we have one: the heart.

The word *intuition* is defined as going beyond mental analysis to gain direct perception of events independent of any reasoning (brain) process.[11] Matching the speed of emotions requires a high-powered special energetic organ that can intuit or "sense" emotions, send and receive their energy at literally the speed of light, and be quietly sensitive to the world around it. It requires an organ capable of keeping up with the pace of events that challenge us while processing them in a healthy manner. That special organ is our *pu`uwai*—the lump of energy in our chest that works at the speed of life and love.

However, before our heart can help keep our brain more composed, we have to be able to deal with the world on a heart level. Being partners in pleasure requires that we place our trust in our heart's intuition rather than in our brain's always tardy emotional reactivity. As my *kumu* (teacher) told me, "You must remember that, to find the purpose of your life, it is often necessary to lose your reasoning in order to find your reason."

An example of the heart's intuition is seen in a mother who "just knows" that her child is sick, even when the doctor can find no evidence of illness. She senses the *mana* (subtle energy) of her child's suffering deep in her heart. She may say, "My heart tells me. . . ." Business

persons often report sensing the difference between the hard, cold logic
of the brain and the equally important soft, warm intuition that results
in some of their best decisions. One of my executive patients said, "It's
a funny thing about heart intuition. Its message is almost always no. I
mean, when I want to do more, try more, and go faster, there's this feeling right here [gestures to his heart] that says no. My heart almost
always says no to more and yes to less. I don't talk much about 'knowing in my heart' at board meetings, but I do count on it a lot. The problem is that my brain still thinks it runs everything, but I think my heart
is earning some of my pay because it has led me to some of my wisest
decisions."

Heart Memories

The heart not only sends signals to your brain and to other hearts and
brains; it not only intuitively guides us in processing emotion; it also
remembers. In my book *The Heart's Code*, I discuss the research on cellular memories and the often startling stories of heart transplant recipients who report receiving the memories of their donors. I received
much support but also some criticism for my hypothesis of cellular
memories, but careful research is verifying my hypothesis and the valid-
ity of the words of Longfellow: "The heart hath its own memory like
the mind, and in it are enshrined the precious keepsakes."

Brainless, single-cell paramecia can remember how to swim, find
food, reproduce, and recognize and evade predators. These very simple
cells have a functional or working memory of what to do to stay alive.
If these retarded cells can remember, it seems likely that our more complex bodily cells can remember. In consideration of the immense
amount of electromagnetic, pulsating, and electrochemical energy surging through our cellular system, it does not seem unreasonable to conclude that the billions of cells in our heart—and not just some specific
location in our brain—might be one place where we remember.

In their book titled *The Living Energy Universe*, Drs. Gary Schwartz
and Linda Russek present a theory proposing that, from the subatomic
to the cosmic, from cells to ideas to souls and God, all dynamic systems
have memory.[12] (A dynamic system is one that is constantly changing

and adapting in relation to other systems.) They call their concept "systems memory theory" (Hawaiians might call it *kakou* theory), and it says that every thought and awareness ever generated is contained in the universe as information or memory. (As is often the case, these "new" ideas aren't really so new after all; a similar concept has existed in India and in other cultures for millennia.) The power and energy of the heart would seem to indicate that it is an organ well suited to resonating with systemic memories.

Some heart transplant recipients report receiving various degrees of memories from their donors, and Drs. Schwartz, Russek, and I have recently published new case studies of such cardio-transplant memories.[13] A heart-lung transplant recipient named Claire Sylvia describes her own surprising associations with her donor, including having preferences for the kinds of foods he liked, craving the same Chicken McNuggets that were found in his jacket at the accident scene, having dreams about him that matched his life and personality and even contained his name, and beginning to lead as a man would when dancing.[14] My own case studies support and even extend Claire Sylvia's claims.

These findings corroborate the findings of the experiment in which one beating heart cell is placed in a petri dish with another, and the two fall into synchronization and beat as one. There are also reports of treadmill experiments in which a group of biopsied heart cells taken from a patient later tested on a treadmill began to beat faster and faster as their donor ran on a treadmill several rooms away.[15] The high energy frequency of the heart, its hormonal interactions with the brain, and these case studies of its cellular memories add weight to the argument that the heart is much, much more than a pump.

Please Let Me Thank My Heart

In working with heart transplant recipients, I learned two humbling lessons about the nature of the human heart. The lessons came back to back and have changed my view of the heart forever.

I had been so "brain" oriented in my research that I'd focused on controlling the circumstances of my interviews and on getting "the facts" as best I could given the circumstances of the urgent and complex nature of transplantation. The first lesson occurred late one evening. I was interviewing a woman waiting for a heart. We had discussed the *naupaka* principle as it related to her transplant and to her relationship with a possible donor. She spoke about feeling that her donor would always be like the *naupaka* on the mountain and she the *naupaka* at the sea. As I stood up to leave, the woman touched my arm and beckoned me to her. She was short of breath and had to whisper. She said softly, "If a heart comes, I know it will come suddenly. Please tell them to give me time alone to thank the heart I've had. It has tried so hard for me. I want to tell it I love it and will always appreciate what it did for me. Please tell them to treat my heart gently and with respect. It will always be my heart, and my body will always remember it. It will always be my *naupaka*, too."

The second lesson happened about one hour later. I was interviewing the family of a donor, and they were understandably still experiencing a range of emotions. Nonetheless, they seemed anxious to talk with me about their son who had donated his heart. They, too, wanted to speak of the *naupaka* principle and how donation of their son's heart seemed to symbolize the sacred and perpetual connection that can exist between persons. They recognized me and knew of my research not only on the application of ancient Hawaiian concepts to modern life but on the heart and its memory.

The father of the donor said, "I'm a chemist and have been a scientist my whole life. I teach at the university and I demand skepticism of my students. I don't really doubt your findings about the recipients getting the memories of the donor, but I think you might have it backwards. Don't you think my son's heart received the donation of a new body? He was a recipient. It's his heart that is getting the memories of a new body. You just see it one way, but we see it as a two-way thing." When I asked my *kumu* (teacher) about this, he said, "Of course, he is right. We don't know which *naupaka* is on the mountain or at the sea, but the donor and recipient become *kakou*."

These lessons from three experts much wiser than I have caused me to rethink my views of transplant stories and the miracle of the heart's energy. I now see hearts as *naupaka* blossoms always connected to their other half. As partners in pleasure, you will be doing your own version of heart transplantation. Each of you will be donor and recipient. Each of you will be *naupaka*.

The Heart to Heart Test

The third paired pleasure prescription applies the new research on the heart in establishing the kind of heart-to-heart union that most of us long for. You now know that the heart is much more than just a ten-ounce blood-pumping muscle. It has its own nervous system that not only responds to the brain but talks to the brain and to other hearts. Cardiologist Dean Ornish sums up the research on the heart when he writes, "The heart is a pump and needs to be addressed on a physical level, but our hearts are more than just pumps. We also have an emotional heart, a psychological heart, and a spiritual heart."[16] There is a way to tune in to our heart's emotional, psychological, and spiritual natures and to use that cardio-energy to connect with other hearts. It is called the cardio-synchronization technique, and it is explained below.

To prepare to learn the cardio-synchronization technique, first take the Heart to Heart Test to provide a baseline regarding your level of cardio-connection. The test can also serve as a comparison point for your post-synchronization level of connection.

Taking the Heart to Heart Test

As with the other tests in this book, first take the test alone and score yourself and your partner. Have your partner do the same. Then take the test together, scoring yourselves as a pair. Discuss the five scores. As always, the point is more the discussion than the score, but you should see an increase in your score following several tries at the cardio-synchronization technique.

$$0 - 1 - 2 - 3 - 4 - 5 - 6 - 7 - 8 - 9 - 10$$

NOT AT ALL — — — OFTEN — — — ALWAYS

1. Can you both seem to "feel" one another in your heart?

2. Are you similar when it comes to being romantic and thoughtful, valuing anniversaries and significant times and places in your relationship, and giving and receiving little gifts?

3. Do you both feel you are "on the same wavelength" when it comes to emotional connection?

4. Do you each feel loved in the way you wish to be loved by your partner?

5. Are you free of any feelings of disgust with the behaviors of one another?

6. Are you equally emotionally intelligent and sensitive to the pain and distress you sometimes cause one another?

7. Are you equally vulnerable and disclosing regarding your feelings?

8. Do you seem equally available, able, and willing to openly express your love?

9. Do you both seem to know what lies deep in your partner's heart and what can break one another's heart?

10. Are you equal in the three dimensions of love: passion (physical attraction), commitment (decision to stay together forever), and intimacy (strong sense of deep connection on all levels)?[17]

Total _____

Falling In Love and In Synch

Cardio-synchronization is based on the established scientific principle of entrainment. This is a phenomenon found throughout nature: the tendency of separate things to fall into a common rhythm together.[18] Entrainment was first discovered more than three hundred years ago by European inventor Christian Huygens, the inventor of the pendulum clock. After making several such clocks, he was surprised one day on returning to his shop to find that all of their pendulums had begun to sway together at the same rate. He intentionally started all of the pendulums swinging at different rates again, but they soon fell back into synchronization. Although Huygens himself never solved the mystery of his synchronized pendulums, other scientists did. They learned that all systems have a tendency to fall into synch with one another.

The third prescription is based on the concept of mutually established entrainment. It is possible to literally join hearts by helping them fall into synch. Einstein said, "Our separation from each other is an optical illusion of consciousness." It is our brain that suffers most from that illusion of "I." You will read in chapter 11 about connecting telepathically with one another across space and time. All of this challenges the brain's view of the way things work in the world, but for this prescription, you will learn to perform a brain bypass to experience the kind of heart-to-heart connection that lovers have spoken about for millennia.

The heart is the largest pendulum in your body. It draws all of your bodily systems into synch with it. When we experience a state of deep appreciation and joy, our brain responds to the loving code of our heart much as an agitated baby is comforted by his mother's soothing voice. The brain resonates with the harmony of the heart and falls into what the researchers at the HeartMath Institute call a state of "heart entrainment."[19]

Caring touch heals. Despite cynical claims that there is no research to substantiate the healing benefits of touch, sufficient evidence now exists to conclude that touching someone while feeling love in our heart transmits a signal to the recipient—a heart's code—that promotes well-being and health.[20] When we hug our friends, tap their arm to make our point, or shake and hold hands, we are doing much more than just engaging in a polite social interaction. Doing these things helps connect our hearts. We just can't seem to help ourselves. Something within us (and I suggest it is our heart) wants to reach out and touch someone— and be touched in return. Research at HeartMath and at the University of Arizona has shown that when we touch someone, the electrical energy from our heart is transmitted to the other person's brain.[21] When two people are hooked up to monitors, we can see the pattern of one person's cardiac electrical signal—as observed in an ECG (electrocardiograph)—reflected in the other person's brain waves, as observed in that person's EEG (electroencephalograph). In fact, our heart's energy can be detected in our partner's brain even if we are not touching but simply standing close together.[22]

We are constantly broadcasting our heart's code. When we stand in the express lane at the grocery store and become angry as we count too many items in the cart of the person in front of us, our heart energy spills out all over everyone around us. Drs. Schwartz and Russek report that the electromagnetic energy of the heart of one of their technicians was accidentally detected in the spontaneous antennae accidentally created when an unattached lead was left floating freely during a routine electroencephalogram.[23] Even as you read these words, you are probably well within the cardio-energetic field of someone's heart. So, when you learn the cardio-synchronization technique, remember that it will not always be necessary to be physically connected with your partner to be able to join heart to heart and heart to brain.

The Cardio-Synchronization Technique

My patients and seminar participants often tease me that it takes much too long to get around to learning the cardio-synchronization technique. They say they have to endure all the scientific explanations and Hawaiian lessons before they can "get down to doing the real thing." Perhaps, but part of learning the technique is learning to practice *ahonui*: persistent patience!

Here are the steps in cardio-synchronization:

1. Select some relaxing music that you both enjoy and with which neither of you has any negative associations.

2. Play the music at a level loud enough to drown out distractions but not so loud that it is annoying to either of you. If you have a two-person headphone system, that also works very well for shutting out distractions and helping you both focus on synchronizing the music with your heart rhythm. Do a sound check before you begin the actual exercise, and then leave the music running at the mutually agreed upon comfortable level. (Just by getting to this step in the exercise, your hearts are already beginning to synchronize.)

3. Stand close together and breathe deeply. Remember, your heart energy radiates all around you and into the heart of your partner.

4. One partner places the right hand on the chest, over the heart, and the other partner places the left hand on the chest, over the heart.

5. Partners should now join their other hands, right to left. (You should be like mirror images rather than in the traditional hand-shaking position.)

6. Let the music carry you away. Close your eyes, breathe deeply, and wait until you feel an urge to gently squeeze your partner's hand. It will take some practice. Your brain may not particularly like or understand what is going on, so give it time to calm down. It may start sending out thoughts about obligations, wasting time, and why this is a dumb exercise. Simply notice any such thoughts without judgment, and allow them to easily pass through your consciousness without becoming attached to them. Let your two hearts engage in their own conversation; you are having a true heart-to-heart talk in the scientific and spiritual sense of the words.

7. Imagine the *naupaka* blossoms. Think of one of you as the mountain *naupaka* and the other as the half at the sea. It doesn't matter who is where or even if you are selecting the same image. The idea is to imagine and visualize the *naupaka* principle of *kakou* or non-two. It may help if you have both first looked at the image of the *naupaka* flowers on the cover of this book and reread the legend.

8. Take several minutes to let your hearts connect. When either of you is ready, squeeze your partner's hand more firmly. Next, one of you take the other's hand up to your own chest to signal the end of the synchronization. Your hearts will tell you when and who should end the exercise.

9. Sit down together with the music still playing and discuss what you have experienced. Don't rush it, and don't be disappointed if it didn't seem to work. As Stephen Sondheim writes, "The Heart knows, the Thought denies, is there no other way?" At the very least, you have both been willing to try a version of connecting beyond brain and body. Your thoughts about your emotions will lag behind what your hearts know about them, but if you were wired up to ECGs and EEGs, the results would be clear to your brain. Your

hearts don't need that kind of data. For science, data is the answer. For the heart, experience is the proof.

An Emerging Spirit

Many couples who have tried the cardio-synchronization technique several times report a deep feeling of spiritual merging, even those couples and alpha-type thinkers who don't usually use such words. Here is one example:

Alpha Husband: "I'm a carpenter. I believe what I see. We believe you measure twice before you cut once. I didn't want to do this thing, but Peggy was really into it. I have to say, though, that something happened. I began to cry. I really did. It was embarrassing because we were holding hands and I couldn't wipe away my tears, so she saw them when we opened our eyes. It was really a crazy kind of spiritual thing."

Beta Wife: "I knew it. I really knew it. I knew if he would only give it a chance, we could do it. I cried too. I could feel the calluses on his hands, and I cried because I felt in my heart how hard he had worked for us. I could feel his hardened hands but I also felt his soft heart. I could see him as the strong *naupaka* up there on the mountain and me down at the sea. I began to shake and I began to pray that we could love like this always."

▼▼▼

Once partners have learned to share a mutual vision, to think as one, and to join their hearts together, their spirituality seems to emerge. Author Joseph Chilton Pearce sums up the underlying lesson of the heart-to-heart prescription. He writes, "Two closely bonded people often share information across time-space, to which we attach occultic labels of various sorts, while all the time it is only our true biology, the logic of our life system, the language of the heart."[24]

Chapter Seven

Praying from the Same Soul

Paired Pleasure Prescription Four: Live your prayers together.

`I Ke Aku I Ka Lani

Let the choosing be done in the heavens.[1]

Our life is in *pono* (balance) when we create a space where God is comfortable. Prayer to *lani* (heaven) is a humble state of receptivity without selfish conscious thought, a quiet state of awareness of our ultimate connection with a Higher Power or the Absolute. Prayer is not trying to get our way; it is learning to be at peace with "the way."

A *Hula* Prayer

The audience of over one thousand executives wept as Kaulu danced in the dim spotlight. The flowers of her *lei* waved a sweet odor that filled the room, and the slow, steady heartlike beat of the *ipu* (drum) seemed to resonate through everyone in the room. Her *hula* was a *pule hana aloha*—a prayer to invoke love. It was the Hawaiian spirit in action, a sacred body *pule* (prayer) of connection and receptivity to her gods and *aumakua*, revered ancestors elevated to the status of gods. It was also a pule to Ke Akua, the Higher Power, or what Einstein and Spinoza called the "organizing principle of the universe." She never said a word, but her hands and body expressed her *pule* in honor of the source of all life and love.

Kaulu and other members of the *halau* (dance groups) have danced with me for years in my `aha mele` lecture/concerts. Together, we present our message of the *naupaka* principle. I discuss the traditional philosophies of Hawai`i and the scientific research that supports them as applicable to modern life. She brings the principles alive as the audience seems to fall into a shared *pule* with her. When we plan our performances, we speak of the sacredness of *hula* as a form of *pule* and how, if done with the utmost respect and reverence, it seems to capture the spiritual essence of Hawai`i that often brings tears to the eyes of visitors to our islands.

Aloha and *Alaha*

In the Aramaic language that Jesus used, the word that eventually became translated as "God" was originally *Alaha*, meaning an essence or life force. This definition is very close to that of the word *aloha* that is such a key part of the Hawaiian spirit. While *aloha* has many meanings, including hello, goodbye, and love, its literal translation is "to share the sacred breath" (*alo* means to give; *ha* means breath).

In the Aramaic language, the word *prayer* meant to set a trap. In a sense, to pray is to enter a state in which we grasp the essence of life, the breath of existence, and the vital force of all life and all things and places. This is what happens when the audience connects with Kaulu's *hula*. To *pule* together means becoming deeply aware of our loving connection with our partner as a manifestation on earth of our connection with the Higher Power. It is a loving *kakou* or two-person way in which we the created become one with our Creator.

The fourth paired pleasure prescription is learning to share the same breath of life, to be still together, and to communicate together with the Higher Power even beyond words.

Paired Prayer

Many excellent books are available about the power of prayer, but my focus here is on *naupaka* or shared prayer. I am speaking of what Christian mystic Joel Goldsmith calls a total absence of one's usual self-consciousness practiced by praying or "breathing" with the one we love.[2] The Vedanta sage Sri Nisargadatta Maharaj spoke of the individual mind's tendency to consider itself isolated (`o wau`) rather than infinitely connected with everything and everyone (*kakou*). He wrote, "Mind creates the abyss, the heart crosses it."[3] This may be why, as you read in chapter 6, the heart-synchronization technique so often leads to a deep sense of spirituality.

Prayer does not always involve talking to God. Oscar Wilde wrote, "I do not talk to God so as not to bore him." As Kaulu's *hula* shows, communication with the Absolute or Higher Power is clearly experienced by those willing to be still, quiet, and selfless enough to feel the *hula* in their heart. Physician Larry Dossey writes, "In its simplest form, prayer is an attitude of the heart—a matter of being, not doing."[4] Learning to pray together is not just getting down on your knees and saying a prayer at the same time. It is leading your life together as if in prayer. It is how the two of you let the Higher Power and your ancestors know what you want to say to them through your daily living and loving.

Getting Back to the Basics Together

There is an old Hawaiian proverb that says, *"Ke ho`i a`e la ka `opua i Awalau."* It is translated as "The rain clouds are returning to Awalau." Based on the clouds that usually cluster over the mountains of Hawai`i, this statement refers to being constantly aware of the importance of honoring the source of life and love and developing a low threshold of

sensitivity to the sacred signs of nature that appear all around us. To
experience the spiritual joy of praying together, your prayers should
relate to what the ancient Hawaiians saw as the basics of life. Although
these are stated in many different ways by different *kumu* (teachers),
kahuna (healer priests), and *kupuna* (elders), my *kupuna* tell me that the
basics are as follows:

▼ To *aloha* (show love and responsibility for) the `aina (the
   land), from which all life comes and to which we owe constant
   stewardship and protection.

▼ To *aloha* `ohana (family), including the *aumakua* (ancestors,
   elevated to the status of gods after their death), whom we
   constantly represent and who are ever with us, watching, helping, and warning us in all that we think, say, and do.

▼ To *aloha* Ke Akua (God or the Supreme Being), without whom
   the first two basics would not be possible, and as manifested
   in all that was, is, and will be.

Imagine for a moment that your most private thoughts about people and events were instantly translated to pictures, broadcast around
the world, and shown on large television screens next to your photo-
graph and name. Would you be proud of yourself? In a way, this international broadcast of what is on your mind and in your heart represents
a public announcement of your prayers and of how you have really
"been" in life compared to what you have said or pretended to be.

What follows is the Hawaiian test of how you have "been," of what
kind of prayers have been coming from your soul: Picture in your mind
all those you have ever known and loved, including those who have
passed on. Be sure you include your entire spiritual `ohana (family),
including grandmothers, grandfathers, parents, uncles, aunts, and
friends. Now imagine that your ancestors and all these people were able
to know exactly what you were thinking every moment, regardless of
what you were saying and doing. They might be watching you through
the eyes of a shark or of the tiny bird that seemed to take a long peek
at you this morning, but imagine that their eyes are always looking you
squarely in the heart. Now imagine that your prayer pattern, known to
your spiritual observers, will be played back to you in detail when you

die and prepare to enter heaven. Imagine that you will be asked to sit next to God and all of your deceased loved ones and friends to review and analyze your true inner life in all of its glorious detail. Hawaiians believe that this is exactly the way our spiritual life works, the way Ke Akau and our *aumakua* keep a spiritual eye on us.

Kakou praying is not just a set of words, incantations, or petitions to God; it is what is in your heart and soul as expressed in how you love. The Hawaiian belief is that you are and will be accountable for your prayerful patterns. In a spiritual way, we have Big Brother, Big Sister, Grandma, Grandpa, Uncle, Aunty, and everyone else always watching us. Learning to pray with someone you love is a good way to get back to the basics together and to help one another monitor your mutual *aloha* for the `aina, `ohana, and Ke Akua.

An Example of *Kakou* Prayer

Here is one way to begin the process of praying together. Find a quiet place, outdoors if possible. Hold hands as described in the cardio-synchronization technique (chapter 6). Slowly, calmly, and reflectively discuss the seven sacred Hawaiian principles of prayerfulness.

1. Is how we live good for the *aina*, the earth?

2. Are we protecting and taking responsibility for the earth and all of its occupants, including human and nonhuman forms?

3. Are we really "with" our family and totally present for and patient with them?

4. Do we take plenty of time to be with our elders or to at least speak regularly with them by phone or written letter and with respect for their wisdom and status?

5. Is it likely that God has faith in us?

6. Are we living daily in such a way that God and our ancestors would be extremely proud of us?

7. Does our relationship feel like a safe and calm place created by an unconditional love and a spiritual ecology in which God and our ancestors would be comfortable?

Don't debate the questions. Don't answer from an individual point of view. Instead, read the questions out loud in unison together. Try to sense in your hearts how your deceased relatives, watching and listening, might answer them about the two of you. Talking heart to heart about these issues as often as possible can be a form of prayer, defined by mystic Joel Goldsmith as a state of receptivity in which truth is realized without individual conscious thought.[5]

Saved by a Prayer

Myth scholar Joseph Campbell offers an example of prayer in action. He wrote of a story of two young policemen driving through a mountain pass in Hawai`i. Those of us who live in the islands have heard the story many times and often speak of the spiritual *mana* (energy) that seems present at the windy gorge where the events took place. There is a very large bridge there that stretches over a sprawling green valley. Tourists regularly gather on the side of the bridge to ohh and ahh at the majestic beauty of the rolling green hills below and the deep blue sea off in the distance. As the officers approached the bridge, they noticed a suicidal young man preparing to jump from the bridge to certain death on the sharp volcanic rocks below. One of the officers leapt from the car even before it had come to a complete stop and ran to grab the man. As he took hold, they both began to tumble over the railing together. The other officer arrived just in time to save both men.

When Campbell tells this story of heroism and a life saved, he points out that the officers suddenly and without thinking gave up all their wishes and hopes for their own lives. They unselfishly disregarded their own interests because of what Campbell calls their innate spiritual instinct for connection—*kakou*. They experienced an involuntary spiritual breakthrough of the truth of the non-two and the falseness of the "I" illusion.

The officers' spiritual epiphany was their prayer in action. Whether they knew it or not, they were responding to an inborn knowledge of their infinite connection with the man whose life they saved.[6]

As you learn to pray together, remember the story of the two spiritual heroes in Campbell's story. Think of times when the *naupaka* principle of *kakou* suddenly and automatically seemed to supersede everything else in your life. Share memories with your partner of times when you suddenly sensed and acted upon a profound and sudden sense of "us." When you share some of your own spiritual epiphanies—particularly about times when the experience happened to both of you together—you are praying.

Sound Strange?

If all this talk about spiritual epiphanies, body prayer, and ultimate accountability to everyone and everything sounds weird or "new agey," remember that this is a two-thousand-year-old wisdom. It is a way of conceiving of the meaning of life without boundaries, labels, and distinctions between things.

You don't have to be religious or embrace any one set of religious principles to *pule* together Hawaiian style. Nor am I diminishing the value and significance of individually verbalized prayer or firm faith in a given religious system as a context for that prayer. I am inviting you to pray together with someone you love in a way that goes beyond sharing the same words. I invite you to decide to lead a life together that is ever more alert to the seven principles of a prayerful life.

The Rabbi's Joke

A nationally known rabbi asked me to come to his temple to speak about the *naupaka* principle and the eight prescriptions for becoming partners in pleasure. Before introducing me to his congregation, he told a story he said he thought represented the message I would be sharing about the principle of praying together.

The rabbi said, "A starving beggar came to Moses' tent. Moses immediately ordered his servants to bring food, and the beggar began to stuff the food in his mouth as quickly as he could. Moses grabbed his cane and began beating the man. Just at that moment, God appeared and grabbed Moses' hand. He asked Moses, 'Why do you harm this poor man?' Moses answered, 'He began to eat without offering a prayer, Father, and that is sacrilege.' God replied, 'Perhaps it is a good thing for humanity that I am not as religious as you are.'"

Prayer Barriers

You have read that paired prayer is a way of living and loving together. Conflict and a focus on individual or separate happiness and success can be seen as obstacles to paired prayer. German philosopher Arthur Schopenhauer asserts that our individual human desires are always destined to clash. He teaches that no matter what society does to control this confrontation, two strong-willed, selfish people will always find something to fight about. He writes that, somehow and some way, they will inevitably mar one another's lives just enough to prevent each of them from ever being happy.[7] The opposite of paired prayer is clinging to and trying to impose one's own will on the partner and the relationship.

Praying together in the way I have described is not only spiritually fulfilling; it is also pleasurable. A clash of wills is never fun, and I doubt that you can name many times when you felt good after a heated conflict, even if you believed that you won. The best indicator that you are not practicing the fourth prescription is the presence in your relationship of sulking, despair, anger, and subtle vendettas against one another to "make your point." A good indicator that you are *pule kakou*, praying together, is when you both feel deeply and profoundly loved.

At the end of this book is an epilogue written by Tutu Mama Ellis, an honored Hawaiian matriarch. It is a form of shared prayer that she offered to the Ka Ha Naupaka group. It presents simple but very wise words of nonconflict, mutual caring, and deep respect that warm the hearts of those who say them. If you feel the need to *pule kakou* now, you might want to turn to the epilogue and read Tutu's "six most important words" out loud together.

In chapter 9, which deals with talking joyfully to one another, you will read about the importance of recognizing that our words have immense power. The verbal ecology in a relationship is a form of prayerful duet, the music God hears coming from the couple's loving. One *kupuna* in our Ka Ha Naupaka group issued a warning about the nature of the spiritual song you are singing together. She said, "You must be very, very careful what you say. In a way, you are always praying together. Your ancestors are listening, and Ke Akua is listening. You have to create a place in your *hale* [home] that would be comfortable for your *aumakua* and Ke Akua. So, watch your mouths together. Speak prayerfully to one another as often as you can. That is praying together, too. That is how you sing for your *aumakua* and for Ke Akua."

Praying Like a Bulldozer

Prayer is at increasing risk of being taken for granted, of being used more as etiquette and custom than to connect with the sacred in life. Too often, our expressed prayers are mere ceremony. The early missionaries who came to Hawai`i often prayed so fast and vigorously that it seemed they never needed to take a breath. Hawaiians called them *haole*, people without breath (*ha* means breath; *ole* means without). Many public prayers seem to have a breathless quality and are said in a hurried monotone in order to get on with the real business at hand.

Author Greg Easterbrook describes what he calls the torpid ceremonial prayers that accompany the opening of each session of the U.S. Congress. He writes of these prayers as "empty words delivered in a somnific monotone as members and staff shuffle about, obviously paying no attention."[8] For much of our daily life we seem to be merely going through the motions, but learning the paired praying prescription requires the *naupaka* gifts of full, caring attention and abundantly shared time.

Hawaiian scholar George Hu`eu Sanford Kanahele points out that Hawaiians never use prayer in any of its forms as "a wishing well for the whimsical."[9] His research on the evolving culture and values of the people of Hawai`i reveals that they were an extremely prayerful people. For them, he says, prayer was a way of life and a crucial part of daily activities. Hawaiians did and still do pray before almost all enterprises. Kanahele writes that, for Hawaiians, "Prayer can be likened to a spiritual bulldozer; it can clear the way through a jungle of problems."[10] Hawaiians pray much as you might clear things off your desk before starting to work. Prayer is a method of getting the wrong stuff out of the way so you can remember and focus on the important spiritual aspects of whatever you will be dealing with.

I recommend to couples learning this prescription that they join hands, take a deep breath, and just "be" together before most activities. It was pointed out to me by a doctor at a recent large medical meeting that people were staring at my wife, Celest Kalalani, our friend the *hula* dancer, Kaulu, and me as the three of us regularly joined hands and took a deep breath before almost all the activities. He said people thought we must be very religious, but we were just being Hawaiian.

Prayer Protocol

As at most Hawaiian meetings, *pule* is the centerpiece of our Ka Ha Naupaka meetings. The *kupuna* in our group have taught me certain guidelines that should be followed in any form of prayer (they call it prayer protocol). Here are the guidelines for Hawaiian-style prayer as presented to me by my `ohana. They are also the guidelines for a marital life led paired-prayer style.

▼ Prayer must never be hurried. Whether in the *hula* or in other activity or in our words, a hurried prayer is not genuine and comes not from the *pu`uwai* (heart).
   Paired Prayer Lesson: If you are going too fast, pay more time and attention to where and why you are going. Don't fit prayer into your quick-paced life; live prayerfully to slow down together.

▼ Prayer must always be sincere. The *aumakua* and Ke Akua will know if you are faking it or just saying it. *Pule* must come sincerely and honestly from the heart and not the head.
   Paired Prayer Lesson: If either of you is holding secrets or just going along with the other rather than truly being kakou, *praying together is a way to be more vulnerable together and less territorial and self-protective.*

▼ Prayer should be faultless. This means that you should not be praying about or for anything that is not in keeping with how you truly are in your own *pu`uwai*. One *kupuna* from Ka Ha Naupaka told me, "If you pray for love, you must be loving in your heart. If you pray for peace, you must be peaceful in your head. If you pray for money and things, you must be crazy. The *aumakua* and Ke Akua will not like that at all. It only shows you are not *naupaka* and that you are `o wau rather than *kakou*."
   Paired Prayer Lesson: If either of you is expecting your partner to love you more than you are loving him or her, praying together is a way to balance the naupaka *gifts of time and attention.*

▼   Prayer must be done from a state of worship. The Hawaiian word *haipule* means humility, deference, and reverence. This state is central to Hawaiian prayer. To pray with what one *kupuna* called "divine dignity," you must be in the right spiritual mood and physically in *pono* (balance). If you are not, sit down, take a deep *ha* (breath), and prepare yourself to pray. The *aumakua* and Ke Akua will look beneath your words for their *mana* (spiritual energy). Your prayer is as much about how you are as about what you say.

   Paired Prayer Lesson: Love is a choice, not a reactive emotion. A relationship of mutual humility, deference, and reverence is the ultimate form of paired prayer.

▼   Prayer must be done in the right place. There must be little noise and disturbance. As one *kupuna* put it, "Living your prayers is creating a place that is very inviting to the gods and God. You have to ask yourself if Ke Akua would want to be with you where you are."

   Paired Prayer Lesson: There is a relationship ecology that goes beyond neatness and order. Praying together can create a more gentle spiritual relationship climate.

▼   Sometimes pray informally. Not all prayer must be formal. Hawaiians speak of a more casual yet still reverent form of prayer called *kaukau*. This is a kind of laid-back talking story or conversation with the *aumakua* and Ke Akua—a loving, gentle, heart-to-heart talk. As long as the prayer models the other traditions, this *kaukau* kind of praying is perfectly acceptable. One *kupuna* told me, "Prayer is always serious, but it can also be very enjoyable."

   Paired Prayer Lesson: Prayer is always serious, but it needn't always be done somberly. One form of paired prayer is a couple laughing together or just enjoying doing a project together.

▼   Watch and listen for the prayers of Ke Akua and your *aumakua*. We tend to think of praying as a one-way communication system. Hawaiians believe that the *aumakua* and Ke Akua also send prayers to us.

   Paired Prayer Lesson: Slow down together and be alert for the

sights and sounds of sacredness. Receptive prayer is looking together
for rainbows and listening together to the sound of the wind.

God Sends a Rainbow

Because "receptive" prayer is less common than petitionary or "sending" prayer, here is a true story to help you understand this alertness and vigilance for God's and the gods' prayers.

"Look! There's a rainbow," squealed the *keiki* (child), a little girl learning the *hula* on the island of Moloka`i. She arched one hand from the other across the sky in the *hula* gesture that represents a rainbow. "That's God's prayer. It's a prayer for us. It's a promise to take care of us."

Scripture says that God sent Noah and his family a message. As they exited the ark, a splendid rainbow spread across the sky. God said, "This is the sign of the covenant that I make between me and you and every living creature that is with you for all future generations."[11] One of the most joyful spiritual states for a couple in paired pleasure is to watch together for life's rainbows, the natural signs that remind us how wonderful it is to be alive together now. This is praying together and learning to be on the lookout for God's prayers.

Wired for God

In every culture throughout time, human beings have communicated with their versions of God or the gods—or in the case of the Hawaiians, both. In addition to the credence lent by this ageless tradition of prayer, good science exists to show that we seem to be physiologically predisposed to a spiritual practice. Harvard cardiologist Herbert Benson said a few years ago that he believed research will eventually prove that the species *Homo sapiens* is "wired for God."[12] Although Benson was primarily referring to evidence that evolution favors those with strong belief systems, there is also neurological evidence that our brain is prepared for spiritual connection.

Scientists Danah Zohar and Ian Marshall write about our SQ, spiritual quotient. They say that, in addition to our intellectual quotient

(IQ) and emotional-intelligence quotient (EQ), we also have a spiritual quotient that is represented in the interactive neuronal structure of our brain. Zohar writes, "By SQ I mean the intelligence with which we address and solve problems of meaning and value, the intelligence with which we can place our actions and our lives in a wide, richer, meaning-giving context."[13]

In the early 1990s, Canadian neuropsychologist Michael Persinger at Laurentian University fitted his own head with a "transcranial magnetic stimulator," a device that sends electromagnetic energy through the skull to small areas of brain tissue. While the device is usually used to stimulate the brain so it in turn may move or twitch arms and limbs to determine which parts of the brain control which body parts, Persinger set the device to stimulate tissue in his temporal lobes (the parts of the brain just under each temple).

When he turned the device on, Dr. Persinger said, "I saw God."[14]

Researchers have known for some time that the temporal lobes of the brain are associated with experiences of "seeing the divine light" or "everything becoming crystal clear." Professor V. S. Ramachandrun at the University of California in San Diego has worked with patients prone to epileptic seizures in the temporal lobes. Many of these patients also report a greater than usual tendency to have profound spiritual experiences.[15]

Persinger's associate, Peggy Ann Wright, at Lesly College in Cambridge, Massachusetts, reports a link between heightened temporal-lobe activity and what she describes as "shamanistic experiences."[16] Persinger found that, when nonpatients are exposed to religious symbols or words or topics of conversation, their temporal lobes tend to "light up" on brain scans and show themselves through electroencephalographic activity increases.[17] This research has led neurobiologists to name the area on the temporal lobes that reacts to religious or spiritual experiences the "God Spot" or the "God Module."[18]

If you have tried the mutual vision, one mind, and one heart paired pleasure prescriptions, you can imagine the power of two "God Spots" joining up in one spiritual union between partners. If we each have a God Spot and work to join our missions, minds, and hearts, perhaps we can develop a mutual SQ, a two-person spiritual quotient that is different, distinct, and more lovingly powerful than a single SQ.

Forming a shared SQ is made possible by trying the exercises suggested in this chapter. Holding hands and taking a deep breath together and trying to lead a prayerful life in harmony with the basics and the principles presented here are ways to become more like one soul. They are ways of *pule aloha*, loving prayer, of sharing (*alo*) the sacred breath (*ha*) of life.

The Shared Prayer Test

To help you implement the fourth paired pleasure prescription, here is the Shared Prayer Test used in our Ka Ha Naupaka meetings and other seminars. Again, the scores mean much less than the value of discussing each item together. Score the test as you have the other tests in this book: first score yourself and your partner, and then take it together and score your relationship. Then give your partnership the gifts of time and attention by lovingly discussing the ten items and the five scores.

The Shared Prayer Test

0 — 1 — 2 — 3 — 4 — 5 — 6 — 7 — 8 — 9 — 10

NOT AT ALL — — — OFTEN — — — ALWAYS

1. Would God be comfortable in the home the two of you have created?

2. Would your ancestors be proud of what they see in your hearts?

3. Do you feel you are both praying for the same things?

4. Do you share the same religious convictions and belief system?

5. On a "secular-to-sacred" scale, are you both at the same place?

6. Do you pray with one another?

7. Do you spend time talking about sacred things and the meaning of life?

8. Do you place equal value on the importance of regular attendance at religious services?

9. Do you both believe and have faith to the same extent in a "higher power"?

10. Do you share the same views of life after death?

Total _____

The higher the score, the more likely it is that you and your partner are sharing the pleasures of *pule aloha kakou*, loving prayer together.

God Is Love

Learning to pray together is learning to lead a more sacred and spiritual life together every day and learning to hold in your hearts an unconditional *naupaka*-style love for one another. While it is often neglected, spiritual pleasure is important to all the other sources of pleasure more typically associated with a secular life. Without caring for our souls and trying to unite them, we are left with a lot of stuff, too little time, a busy and burdened brain, and an exhausted body that reflects our spiritual fatigue.

As timeworn as the saying may seem, the phrase "God is love" remains a powerfully instructive one, though often neglected in terms of couple behavior. Partners who live their daily life as though connected to a greater source of love experience a balanced and healing pleasure that can guide them through all the passages of paired life you will read about in this book's last chapter. The phrase comes from a brief biblical letter in the first book of John. The author of the book remains a mystery, but biblical scholars suspect he or she was probably from the second generation of those who were trying to follow the teachings of the rabbi Jesus. This spiritual love letter sums up the message of the fourth pleasure prescription. The author wrote, "God is love, and those who abide in love abide in God, and God abides in them."[19]

Chapter Eight

Dancing to the Same Beat

Paired Pleasure Prescription Five: Take the time to pay attention.

Puhalu ka ihu, nana i ke ka`ao

When the scent reaches the nose, one senses the over-ripe hala fruit fallen to the ground. [1]

One only notices the good things a person does and how meaningful someone is when it is too late to show appreciation.

Hawaiian Time

When things start late in Hawai`i, the standard joke is that "we're on Hawaiian time." This refers to a leftover, negative Western stereotype that the Hawaiians' concept of time is a reflection of their laziness. There are jokes about "Polynesian paralysis," or a tropical lethargy that results in things seldom getting done "on time," as the continental mind regards it. In fact, nothing could be further from the truth. Most Hawaiians have always worked extremely hard, but their concept of time, called *manawa*, is one that is closer to the Zen view than to the zoom orientation of modern life.

Zen Master Dogen wrote, "It is believed by most that time passes; in actual fact, it stays where it is. This idea of passing may be called time, but it is an incorrect idea, for since one sees it only as passing, one cannot understand that it stays just where it is."[2] To learn the fifth paired pleasure prescription, you have to overcome the continental "rock logic" that sees time as moving or passing you by. You have to be willing to apply a little Hawaiian oceanic "water logic," which recognizes that it is we who are moving. Time is not rushing past, but *we* are often rushing right past one of the most important aspects of life: sharing time with and giving attention to the person who matters most.

Right Here and Now

Hawaiian George Kanahele writes that the more fluid concept of *manawa* is very different from the ticking, fleeting, interval-oriented view of time as determined by a mechanical clock. *Manawa* refers to time as similar to the lingering, gentle ebb of water across a tranquil bay, flowing rather than clicking by. The word *manawa* is also used to refer to our feelings and the seat of our emotions, so it is clear that—for Hawaiians—time is not money but rather the endless experience of life right here and now.

Learning the fifth prescription requires of couples the Hawaiian orientation of *manawa `ole*—meaning enjoying life together right now, this instant. This does not mean an urgent trying to live and love only "for the moment," but rather trying together to share the joy of being *kakou* "in this moment."

Stay a While

How long is a "while"? How much time is "lost" when we are just
"whiling away our time "? The closest English-language term I could
think of to the Hawaiian *manawa* is *while*. Whatever a while is and however long it is supposed to last, we only seem to have little whiles.
Sitting down to talk for just a little while is usually alright, but whiling
away our time might get us in trouble at work. Taking more "big whiles"
with the person we love is exactly what is needed to enjoy the pleasure
that comes from the prescription for learning to dance together to the
same rhythm of life.

There is an ancient Hawaiian proverb that says, *"Ke kalukalu moe ipo
o Kapa`a."* It refers to yet another Hawaiian lesson derived from a deep
sense of oneness with nature. It speaks of the *kalukalu* plants of
Hawai`i, which make a perfect place to lie down together, cuddle, and
while away the time. Dancing to the same beat first requires mutual
agreement about your paired pace, the rhythm you both choose as the
way you will experience life together.

Canoeing Together

A Ka Ha Naupaka *kupuna* was discussing the fifth paired pleasure prescription with my wife and me. She said, "You know, everything
Hawaiians do and think has to do with the sea. When we taste the salt
of our tears, we are tasting the salt of the sea. When we sweat, we are
pouring out to the sea. When we are in our canoe, it looks as if the sea
is racing by beneath us as we paddle, but is we who are going so fast.
The sea has her own time, but it is we who choose to race over her."

From this oceanic perspective, we are the paddler and the speed of
our life is totally up to us. The oceanic thinking of this wise woman
illustrates one of the challenges couples must overcome in learning this
prescription: the continental idea that our time is not our own but is
somehow urging us on to keep up with it.

Professor Stephen Bertman used the same comparison of time to
the sea in his excellent book *Hyperculture: The Human Cost of Speed.* He
writes, "Like the ocean itself, the sea of time can be polluted. Cluttered
with the flotsam and jetsam of hurried experience, fouled by the nox-
ious effluents of haste, that each in time can poison those who swim in
its waters."[3] A hurried relationship cannot be a fully pleasurable one.

The Heart as the Couple's Clock

Finding an enjoyable paired pace in the hurried modern world is far from easy. Attempts at "time management" are almost always individual approaches to structuring minutes and hours or trying to control and get the most of what limited time seems to exist. Couples often have to scavenge for the remnants of time left over after work and other obligations have consumed the lion's share of it.

Ask most couples who care about one another and they will almost always say that they do not have enough time together. One of the major challenges for couples facing their later years free of work obligations and clock-dominated scheduling is to face the fact that they seem to suddenly have almost too much time together. "I've got to get him out of the house," said one retired teacher. "He's driving me nuts. I'm just not used to his being around this much. I guess we never had to worry about spending much time together when we were both teaching, because there never seemed to be enough time. Now, there seems to be more time, but we just don't really know how to spend it well together."

These two teachers had come to one of my *naupaka* seminars to find their pace together. They agreed that they each had been dancing to their own beat for so long that they had failed to learn how to dance together. As have many couples, they had come to see time as if it were a quantity or object, and they often referred to the "stress" of daily life that seemed to result in always feeling short of time. To become partners in pleasure, you must realize that you already have all the time you will ever have. You have to begin to embrace the Hawaiian *manawa* view of time here and now and realize that time is not racing by. You are.

So how does a couple adopt the *manawa* view? I suggest beginning this modern-day challenge by recognizing your body's inner timepiece—the heart—and learning to let it guide you in establishing a paired pace. We each have a built-in metronome right in the center of our body. Unless the brain's sense of time rushes it or urges it to race in fight or flight, the heart is constantly beating out a guiding rhythm. When you do the cardio-synchronization exercise, your hearts can help to calm each other and help you fall into a more enjoyable life pace.

The Chronologically Challenged

Hypochondriacs are people who live in a world of sick imagination and constantly fear that their life may be speeding to a premature end. Their interests and attention are limited by their narrow focus on their own body and an unrealistic overconcern about its vulnerability to disease. Someone once suggested that the best cure for hypochondria is to get the mind off its own body and on someone else's. This may also be a good idea for the "hypochroniac," someone who is constantly chronologically challenged, who feels that whatever little time there is will soon run out. Hypochroniacs are those whose lives have become so dominated by time that their mind is seldom on anything for very long and least of all is fully focused on the person to whom they should be paying the most attention if they desire a truly pleasurable life.

The Four P's of Hypochronia

To learn to dance to the same beat, talk together about the four P's of hypochronia: *polyphasia* (doing several things at once), *pleonasm* (talking a lot but saying little), *prolepsis* (rushing others' speaking, interrupting, and finishing their sentences), and *peevishness* (perverse obstinacy and becoming easily aggravated). Here are some questions to talk about as a couple:

▼ *Polyphasia:* Are we constantly trying to do many things at once? Are we thinking of what has to be done next even when we are doing something now? Are we distracted from one another because we both are often doing something else while talking together?

▼ *Pleonasm:* Are we so time pressured that we have begun to narrate our lives to foster the illusion that we are in control of them? For example, do we say things out loud to no one in particular like, "I'm going to go brush my teeth and wash my hair and then I'm going to get dressed and go to the store. Let's see, I have to get milk, bread, and there was something else but it just won't come to me. What was it . . . ?" Do we talk to other people on the phone or type e-mails in one another's presence?

▼ *Prolepsis:* Do we finish each other's sentences, rush one another when speaking, or engage in "hurry humming," wordless tunes designed to rush someone along by muttering, "uh huh, uh huh," or "yeah, yeah, yeah"? Do we feel too rushed to finish a complete thought and say "and so on and so forth," or "you know," or "yada yada yada"?

▼ *Peevishness:* Are we obstinate and sure that our hurried view is right? Are we easily upset with others who seem to think, speak, or move too slowly? Do we push the close-door button on the elevator to speed things up, or count the number of items in a person's cart in the express lane at the grocery store? Do we try to hurry other drivers along by tailgating?

In discussing these questions, try to focus more on the rhythm of your relationship than on each partner's individual characteristics. The idea is to identify the dance you are doing together and what kind of paired pace you are setting for yourselves in the combination of your two time styles.

The Value of Thumb Twiddling

There are many definitions of the word *stress*, but time usually plays a role whenever we feel stressed. A part of most people's definition of stress is the feeling that their time is running out or a deadline is approaching too quickly.

Eight of ten Americans report that they live with stress nearly every day and have "great stress" at least twice a week.[4] More than six hundred articles on the relationship between feeling stressed and feeling time pressured have appeared in the last five years, and there are currently over one thousand books in print that deal directly with the topic of stress.[5]

One of the most important buffers against the ravages of stress is to be in a lasting, loving, joyful relationship. Conversely, failure to give the gifts of time and attention to our relationship can rob us of the advantages of sitting calmly and lovingly doing nothing in particular with someone we love. There's a simple activity that can help you "do less" with your partner.

"Don't just sit there twiddling your thumbs." You have probably heard this admonition many times in your life. As strange as it may seem, and because thumb twiddling is seen as a clear form of wasting time and doing nothing, mutual thumb twiddling is a part of the fifth paired pleasure prescription. It is a silly pastime offered to elicit the two key ingredients of a partnership in pleasure: time and attention.

After talking about the four P's of what I have called hypochronia, try the two-person thumb-twiddling exercise. Here are the steps:

- Once a day, for just a few moments, sit down together side-by-side and join your outside hands (the left hand of the person on the left, and the right hand of the person on the right).

- Place your free arms around each other to draw one another closer.

- Interlock the fingers of your joined hands.

- Raise your thumbs and rotate them around each other. You may be familiar with thumb wrestling, but that's a contest. Thumb twiddling is a connection.

- Remember to share the *ha*, the breath. Take deep breaths together, slowly and from the abdomen.

- Now just while your time away. Twiddle your thumbs round and round in a slow, steady rhythm. Try to avoid thumb contact by looking at your thumbs and going slowly enough to avoid brushing them together.

- Even though this is a game, you have formed a mutual ECG (electrocardiogram) and are taking some time to be in the moment together. Joking about the exercise is fine, but be sure you are laughing together.

- Take a while to twiddle thumbs. Decide together how long you want to do this.

Whenever I ask couples to try the paired thumb-twiddling exercise, there is laughter. Some couples cannot seem to resist falling into thumb combat, and others turn the exercise into a contest to see how long they can twiddle without brushing thumbs. After a while, however, most couples relax together and just sit twiddling their thumbs.

Two Timing

Learning to dance to the same rhythm is not easy. The world is set up to reward the fastest and most time-efficient individual, not to encourage a couple courageously swimming together against the current of modern life. The continental mind is `o wau focused; to it, kakou can seem to take too much time. By learning this prescription, you can at least try to get in the same time zone.

In my naupaka seminars, I ask each partner what time it is. In almost every case, the partners' watches are not quite in synch. One partner (often the alpha-thinking partner) intentionally sets his watch fast or considers "his time" to be the "right time." The other partner's watch (often the beta's) is slow or at least "behind" according to the alpha. The alpha partner usually announces the time precisely in terms of minutes and, because he or she is more likely to have a digital watch, even in seconds. The beta partner often states the time in "abouts" and "arounds" or as "a quarter to" or "half past."

As a part of the fifth paired pleasure prescription, I ask the partners to recognize their respective styles and discuss them to see if they might be able to find a creative, middle-way solution to their differing views of time, a "two time" to which their shared life if not their respective watches will be set.

A Brief *Kakou* Interlude

Now that you are five steps into the paired pleasure prescriptions, this is a good time for a brief interlude. Consider it a rest, as in a musical score. The composition goes on, but a creative pause is included to give the music more meaning. Enjoy an interlude together to review the main ideas of the first four prescriptions and to practice taking some time together.

▼   Remind yourselves of the kakou (we) idea behind the naupaka principle and the risks of the `o wau (I) perspective.

▼ Review your couple's mission statement.

▼ Review your ideas about the alpha and beta challenge in trying to be of one mind.

▼ Repeat the cardio-synchronization technique, and assess the heart-head balance of your relationship.

▼ Ask yourselves if your life together is becoming the prayer you want to be sending.

To keep time together and dance to the same life rhythm, all of these components must become more significant parts of your relationship and your couple's vision statement.

Love Lessons from Trees

To help you reflect on your progress toward a *naupaka* partnership of shared time and attention, consider the lesson of the sugar maple tree. It is a hardy and beautiful tree with an intriguing *naupaka* characteristic: it has time and resources for more than just itself. During dry spells, sugar maple trees use their deep roots to draw up the scarce groundwater. They are very good at digging down deep and can survive in some of the most adverse conditions. But they seem to have an innate *kakou* sense of their connection with the other vegetation around them. They do not consume all the water they manage to soak up with their unique root system. Instead, in a natural example of *mahele*, they share the water by discharging some of it back into the ground near the surrounding, smaller plants, such as the goldenrod.[6] The smaller plants in turn nurture the trees with their leaves and other byproducts. This symbiotic caring represents the essence of *kakou*, a shared loving sustenance.

The social and physical sciences have often used nature's rule of survival of the fittest to explain the inevitability of humankind's competitiveness and time-protective self-assertion and control. Actually, this is a kind of unnatural selection on the part of science, because nature, as demonstrated by sugar maple trees, also shows a very loving, *naupaka*, connective side. Recent evidence from fields such as scientific ecology, ccoanthropology, and various new branches of archaeology suggests that unselfishness and cooperativeness are as natural as the predatory side of nature. Author Greg Easterbrook writes that these findings of natural cooperation "lend cause to hope that women and men will eventually learn to emulate the cooperative rather than the predatory. This, too, encourages the search for the spiritual."[7]

Caring Takes Time

The challenge of caring is that it takes a lot of time and attention. Years pass before the love affair between sugar maple and goldenrod comes to fruition. Both plants must mature and learn their roles. The failure to invest time in our relationships and to give them our full attention is at the root of the failure of most relationships. We usually understand that our children need time and attention, but we seem to assume that our marriage will flourish without much of those things from its primary caretakers—us.

Our focus on "self-health" may be extending our bodily lives, but certainly not the lives of our relationships. Nearly half of all marriages in the United States are remarriages, and the divorce rate among second marriages is more than twice that of first marriages. More than one-third of all currently married persons report that they have seriously discussed the idea of separating within the last year.[8] While there are many reasons for these dismal statistics, lack of time and attention to relationships is certainly a major factor.

Neglected and Exploited Time

My research and clinical work indicate that time-deprived partnerships tend to fall into two categories—time-neglected and time-exploitive relationships. Here are the profiles of each of these patterns.

Time-Neglected Relationships: Both partners devalue the time they give to their relationship. They assume that the relationship will take care of itself. This kind of relationship is one of individual convenience and essentially exists in a parallel pattern of "I do my thing; you do your thing." When any "free time" occurs for either partner, he or she usually chooses to spend it either working at some hobby alone; golfing, bowling, or doing other activities with friends rather than with the partner; or "just hanging out" with friends. Eventually, each partner no longer expects or feels the need for the other's time.

Time-Exploitive Relationships: In a kind of chrono-codependence, one partner surrenders his or her time to the demands of the other, who "takes the time" of the first without reciprocity or sensitivity to the time theft. One partner becomes the resident nurturer and is expected to always have the time for the relationship's daily maintenance, for doing the little things that consume so much time and energy. This partner is expected to tolerate the other's disregard for relationship time or his or her failure to show up on time for family or school events. Questions from the time taker to the time donor such as "When you get a second, could you . . . ?" and "It will only take a minute. Will you . . . ?" are common. A vital fatigue usually sets in for the time donor, while the time taker cannot seem to understand why the time-exploited partner always seems so overwhelmed, tired, and grouchy.

Proper Care

A challenge in learning to dance to the same beat is to avoid time neglect and time exploitation within the relationship by knowing the difference between healthy and unhealthy caring.[9] *Webster's Third New International Dictionary* defines "care" as a "suffering of mind" and a "burdened or disquieted state." Researchers at the HeartMath Institute call this "overcare."[10] In the context of the *naupaka* principle, overcare is really unbalanced time and attention in a relationship.

In the case of a time-neglected relationship, the overcare occurs when the partners are investing their caring—their attention and time—outside the relationship. In a time-exploitive relationship, one partner is "caring too much" by giving his or her time and attention in a disproportionate amount to the other partner. To care is to lovingly, freely, and joyfully share our time and attention. To care together *naupaka* style is to agree to give these gifts to the life of the relationship much as we would to the life of a growing child.

But how can we care together and give each other our time and attention when there seem to be so many demands on our time? The answer lies in the following four behaviors characteristic of partners in pleasure: resisting, tending, befriending, and sleeping.

Romantic Resisting: Saying a
Sensitive `A `ole (No)

The word *no* in Hawaiian is `a `ole. It is often used in the phrase `a `ole *pilikia*, meaning "no problem." The ability to say `a `ole is crucial not only to the establishment and maintenance of a pleasure partnership but also to our physical health. I ask my couples and patients who have trouble saying no to first practice saying `a `ole in Hawaiian. Because `a `ole is a new word for them and free of many of the negative connotations they associate with the word *no*, it gives them the opportunity to ease into the real "no" of setting limits for the good of their relationship.

Saying no sensitively is romantic in the true sense because it is love-saving. It is the ability to say no without feeling guilty or that you have harmed someone else. It is being comfortable saying no because you are clear about your limits of time and attention and because you know in your heart that saying yes will result in a loss of your loving energy. Romantic resistance is saying no to those demands that take too much time and attention from your loving partnership.

Psychologist Rollo May believed that life is often a challenge of trying to weather the storms and sail with the sea. But, he wrote, "It is not only sailing 'with,' it is sailing 'against' the sea and the storm winds."[11] Saying `a `ole is refusing to be whisked away by the ever surging currents of modern living. It means being able to do as Robin Hood said to his men after their battles: "Come, sit thou here beside me, and speak at thine ease."[12]

Saying no in the way suggested here means you have decided not to squander your two *naupaka* gifts of time and attention. It is not saying no just for yourself but on behalf of the good of your pleasure partnership. The "no" of sensitive resistance means being vigilant and protective of your resources of loving energy, and it means knowing when those resources need to be saved and not spent. Saying no in this way is not self-assertiveness so much as it is we-protectiveness.

There is also good scientific evidence that documents the health value of being able to say the magic word *no*. Almost twenty years ago, research by psychologist George Solomon indicated that the ability to say no was important to the status of the immune system.[13] When

Solomon and his colleague Rudolf Moos studied twenty women suffering from rheumatoid arthritis and compared them with their healthy sisters, they found that the sisters with arthritis lacked the ability to say no. They were self-sacrificing to a fault and tended to feel trapped in unpleasurable marriages or relationships. Research on persons with AIDS who were doing reasonably well for a long period of time showed that these survivors also had a distinguishing characteristic: they knew how to say no.[14]

For many people, saying no does not come easily. They seem to be afraid of rejection, letting others down, or appearing selfish. Paradoxically, refusal or reluctance to say no is actually a selfish act, because it comes from self-protection and a reticence to share with others our honest feelings and personal limitations. I tell my patients to give the gift of `a`ole, the gift of no, for the sake of love—meaning that sharing with someone else your true limits helps them to know just how far they can or should go with you in their requests of your time and attention. It also gives them permission, through your example, to say no themselves.

To implement the fifth pleasure prescription, practice saying a sensitive no to others to avoid the consequences of a neglected relationship in which you seem to have time for everyone but the one who matters most. Practice saying a sensitive no to one another to avoid the emergence of one time bandit who exploits the relationship's time resources.

Tending and Befriending: Two Ways to Cope with Stress

You have probably heard about the fight-or-flight response to stress. Psychologists have known about it for more than sixty years. But researchers have recently discovered two other ways we deal with stress. They call these "tending and befriending."[15] Both of these newly identified strategies can help your relationship, as Zorba the Greek put it, dance together in the full catastrophe of life. They can help you find pleasure even at painful and stressful times.

Because almost all studies of how we respond to stress have focused on males, they have tended to miss a key beta or female way of dealing with daily life tension. While males tend to stick to the fight-or-flight method of handling stress, research indicates that women deal with stress by becoming more nurturing. They tend to intensify their caring for themselves and their young, employing what researchers now call a "tending" response. They also respond to stress by intensifying their alliances to other people—the "befriending" response so important to a *kakou* relationship. The researchers who identified the tend-and-befriend responses are quick to point out, however, that these behaviors are not necessarily limited to women and that men can employ them as well.

Another way to look at it is that our brain has the built-in fight-or-flight mechanism—it is wired to defend itself or escape—but our heart also plays a role in how we deal with pressure; it has its own twin mechanisms of tending and befriending.

The fight-or-flight response seems to be related to a more aggressive pattern of coping with stress that is associated with the androgens, including the male hormone testosterone. The tend-and-befriend style is related to the female hormone oxytocin, a substance associated with caring, closeness, and nurturing. You read in chapter 5 that some men are less confrontational and aggressive betas, and some women are more combative and aggressive alphas. Partners in pleasure can identify these styles within their own relationship and learn to function as a stress-coping unit that maximizes the strength of each style and minimizes their individual weaknesses.

The fight-or-flight response is mediated through the body's sympathetic—or "get up and get going"—system that turns on when we are feeling hostile and defensive. The tend-and-befriend style is more reflective or "slow down and think it over" in nature.

Seen another way, alpha fight-or-flight coping employs more of a continental or rock mindset that emphasizes boundaries and separateness. The beta tend-and-befriend style, by contrast, depends on two of the key components of Hawaiian oceanic or water logic—circumstance and context. Researchers report that one of the biggest differences between the alpha and beta ways is men's tendency to withdraw under stress and women's tendency to reach out for contact and support.[16] Learning to dance together is learning to combine the best of these ways of dealing with stress. A little dose of both is probably the ideal dance to perform together when the rhythm of life accelerates to stress-inducing levels.

Here is an example of a partnership in pleasure that embodies the resisting, tending, and befriending tactics of dealing with stress. Roy, a building contractor, is about as alpha as they come. To him, all stop lights stay red too long and all pedestrians walk too slow. Cheryl, his wife, is the poster woman for betas. To her, a red light is an opportunity to check out the stores on the corner for sales or to look at what the pedestrians are wearing. When they encountered financial problems in Roy's company, this is what they said.

"I guess it's true that if something doesn't kill us, it helps us," said Roy. "I'd like to choke the SOB accountant who screwed this up [fight], and I've thought of just junking it all and selling fish bait at the cottage [flight]. I'm pissed, and the jerks who caused this are just getting away free."

"I took the kids to his mom's when I heard the company was going belly-up [tending]," said Cheryl. "I called my girlfriends and asked them to go out to lunch with me [befriending]. We talked for hours and they really helped me by giving me a shoulder to cry on."

"We do things differently, don't we," said Roy. "I strike out or run and she reaches out and starts caring for the kids. But it works. We're getting on our feet again, and we did the heart-to-heart thing. That really helped us calm down and get back together. I used to try to get myself together when things got rough, but I stole some of her style."

"I started to help out with his business finances and books," said Cheryl. "I can be a fighter too, you know. That way, I could understand more of what was going on and not let anyone take advantage of him. The one thing we both learned, though, was to say no. My husband's financial problems started when he said yes to helping everyone and not collecting on bills due him. I didn't say no enough to his working until he dropped. Now he has a smaller company, we're in it together, and we are saying no more and more to outside stuff that takes us away from one another."

Learning to say no together and using the best of the fighting, fleeing, tending, and befriending responses can help couples find the time to love. But there are several hours a day of available and important time that must also be included in this fifth paired pleasure prescription. These are the hours we can spend sleeping very well together.

Sleeping Together

Once you have begun your dance of resisting, tending, and befriending, you are ready for the next challenge in dealing with the issue of time in your relationship: sleeping together in total darkness for nine hours every day.

You will read in chapter 11 about lucid dream telepathy. The more hours you sleep together, the greater the opportunity for sending and receiving your dreams to each other.

New research indicates that our health depends on getting at least nine hours of sleep a day in quiet darkness.[17] Going to bed together when it gets dark and getting up together when the sun rises is one of the healthiest things you can do for your relationship and for your bodies.

This day/night dance is crucial to the delicate biological rhythm that controls our hormones and neurotransmitters. We are a nation of sleep-deprived and chronically tired people. We need our dose of "nine in the dark" to support the delicate systemic balance that controls our appetite and our mental and physical well-being. Failing to say no together to the glaring computer and television screens and the general lighting that has artificially extended what constitutes a full day means that we do not sleep long enough to stay well. Additionally, recent research indicates that those who don't get their daily nine are more likely to develop extra fat around their waists, the so-called love handles many people would prefer to avoid.

There is another significant benefit to sleeping heart to heart with the person you love. The two of you can spontaneously fall into cardio-synchronization and awaken not only more energized but also more in synch with each other. As contradictory as it may sound, sleeping together is one of the best forms of dancing together.

Save Your Salt

Indigenous Hawaiians usually rose with the sun, rested during the hottest daytime hours, and worked again in the glow of the setting sun. One reason missionaries and visitors to the islands thought the Hawaiians were lazy is that they rested when they would have been sweating the most. My friend, the Hawaiian healer Clay Park, talked with me about the wisdom behind this practice. He said, "As does the sea, our sweat contains salt. Salt is magical because it preserves and because it appears from nowhere when the water leaves and disappears when it returns. Salt is precious and comes from the `aina [land] as a gift shared with the sea, the salt of the earth. We should save our salt as we protect the `aina and honor the kai, the sea. Work hard, rest well, and sleep peacefully, but do so in pono or balance. Do not waste your energy working in the hot sun. Sleep when it is dark, get up with the sun, and work, rest, and work again. Saving your salt is not lazy; it is wise."

Hawaiians may have appeared laid-back to explorers who brought with them their own version of clock time and who often worked in the hot sun and late into the night by the light of their candles. When they were "up," Hawaiians were resting, playing, and having fun. Other than utilizing the oil from the kukui nut or taking advantage of a full moon, Hawaiians had little choice but to go to bed when it got dark. Unlike in the modern world, there was little ambient light filtering around. A dark night in Hawai`i is true and pure darkness, the kind that reminds us how much artificial light has begun to control our life.

Get your daily dose of darkness together. Don't go to bed and read; go to bed and hug. Turn off the light, cuddle up, and experience kakou under the comforting cover of natural darkness.

The Dancing Together Test

Here is another test to talk story about together. Score it as you have the other tests, that is, with each partner first individually scoring him/herself and his/her partner, and then with both partners getting together to score the relationship. Afterward, give the gifts of time and attention to talking about the five scores and about each item—and remember that your shared discussion is more important than your scores.

The Dancing Together Test

0 — 1 — 2 — 3 — 4 — 5 — 6 — 7 — 8 — 9 — 10

NOT AT ALL — — — OFTEN — — — ALWAYS

1. Do you both feel you spend enough time together?

2. If you have "extra free time," do you each choose to spend it together?

3. Do you both feel that your time is your own and under your own control?

4. Can you both say no, so that you don't feel rushed or as though you have too much to do in too little time?

5. Do you agree that you are spending your time on things you truly want to do?

6. Do you go to bed together and turn off the light at the same time?

7. Do you agree that you do not feel hurried by one another?

8. Are you spending nine hours a day sleeping together in complete darkness?

9. Are you both "owls" (night people) or "larks" (morning people)?

10. Can you both sit down, shut up, and just "be" quietly and calmly together without focusing on problems or falling asleep?

Total _____

The higher your score, the more likely it is that you are living and loving to a mutually established, enjoyable rhythm of life.

Morning Time

Another Hawaiian proverb is "*O ke `ehu kakahiaka no ka we loa.*" It translates as, "The time to catch anything is in the morning." It means don't wait. The time is right now. Treasure what is most precious to you now, and don't miss it by running right past the time of your life together. This prescription is an invitation to awaken in time to the joy of two. Don't be too tired to experience it.

You have now been shown your dance steps, the components of the fifth paired pleasure prescription. You have learned the importance of saying `a`ole (no.) You have learned about resisting together those influences that steal away the precious moments of your loving time. You have learned to combine your unique styles of fighting, fleeing, tending, and befriending. You have learned to sleep together in the dark for nine hours so that your hearts can have some brainless *kakou* time without interruption by the brain's `o wau. Before you embark on the sixth paired pleasure prescription about how to speak a language of love together, put this book down, turn out the light, and go to sleep. Sweet shared dreams!

Chapter Nine

Singing the Same Song

Paired Pleasure Prescription Six:
Speak as if your relationship were a vulnerable child.

"I ka `olelo no ke ola, i ka `olelo no ka make"

Words can heal, words can destroy.[1]

Hawaiians believe that words have great *mana* or spiritual and life energy. They should never be spoken carelessly or with evil intent, but speaking them with *aloha* (love) is one of the most healing and joyful ways of making a loving connection.

The Importance of Duet

The title of this chapter—and the phrasing of this prescription—refers to thinking of your communication as singing a duet. Imagine that your words to each other create a chorus of two voices that speak, acknowledge, understand, and value a quiet, gentle, humble communication. In this way of speaking, both partners are not so much making points and reacting to each other's counterpoints as they are trying to fall into a shared message. Of course I am not literally talking about singing together. Allow yourself to embrace the symbolism and underlying lessons in the metaphor of shared song. This involves a change of mind about what we say to one another and how we say it.

Speaking as a duet is a more oceanic way of talking together. As one *kupuna* put it, "When you sing the same song together, your talk is like water flowing back and forth." The continental style of conversation—"I am right; you are wrong"—resembles a tennis match. One partner serves up words and his or her own ideas; the other returns; an advantage is sought.

Singing together means trying to get into a speaking rhythm that is like a pleasing melody. Duets usually sound best when a mutual effort is made by both singers to listen carefully to one another, stay in harmony, match each other's voice and tone, and blend rather than blare their individual voices. It is also a more meaningful and enjoyable song if both singers remember, as Hawaiians do, that the duet is being listened to by an audience of the *aumakua*—revered ancestors—who tune in to our love song and listen for its sincerity and veracity.

Two Ears but One Mouth

"*Kulikuli!* Be quiet!" said the *kupuna* at a recent Ka Ha Naupaka meeting. She was scolding a young man in the audience who kept interrupting the speaker with his questions. "Please, be quiet young man," she continued. "Respect this place, these people, and their ancestors. You were given two ears and one mouth so you can listen twice as much as you speak. You put yourself and us at great risk by being so loud-voiced."

The *kupuna's* scolding reflects one of the lessons to be learned through the sixth paired pleasure prescription. Learning to sing together means learning, for one thing, an alert quietness. This is an important Hawaiian trait because it reflects a respect for *pono*, meaning balance, the right way, the way things are supposed to be. It conveys acknowledgement and reverence not only for the people present but for all of their ancestors. Shouting, interrupting, and strongly or stridently making one's point are seen as more than just rudeness; these behaviors are insulting, not only to the person being addressed but to that person's and our own *aumakua*.

Learning this prescription asks couples to imagine that all of their deceased loved ones are sitting around listening as the two partners speak together. It means learning to speak as if you were in a sacred place and trying to keep your voices down.

Singing Lessons

To learn the sixth prescription requires three skills that are often lost amidst the business of modern life. Each of them requires trying the oceanic orientation in your relationship. Of course, you will find it much easier to sing a duet together if you are sharing the same vision, thinking with one mind, connecting heart to heart, praying from the same soul, and dancing to the same beat.

▼ *Melody*: Try to speak melodiously, softly, and always with *ha`aha`a*, gentle humbleness.

▼ *Meaning:* Try to listen intently, with *ahonui* (persistent patience), and always with gracious respect for and alertness to what a person is really trying to say.

▼ *Movement:* Try to share messages not only by talking but by using your entire body to communicate your feelings.

Speaking Hawaiian Style

An ancient Hawaiian proverb says, "*`Eha ana `oe la i kamakani ku`i o ka Ulumano.*" Literally translated, it means, "You will be hurt by the sound of the Ulumano breeze." The statement is a line from a very old chant, and it refers to the damage done by words spoken with sharpness or harshness, as if with the force of the strong winds at Ulumano.

To learn the first quality of shared singing—melody—we can observe the Hawaiian manner of speaking. If you listen carefully to Hawaiians speaking, you will hear a melodic and almost singing quality to their speech. If you have struggled to try to say the multisyllabic Hawaiian phrases throughout this book, you have already begun your singing lessons because you have been trying to speak Hawaiian style. It takes patience, gentleness, calmness, and a sense of rhythm to pronounce the long strings of sounds such as the one in the paragraph above, and it is these qualities that are key to the sixth prescription. Try the phrases together as practice for the Hawaiian way of speaking.

Many Hawaiian sentences seem to end as if they were questions, with an upward lilt or inviting tone that appeals rather than declares. The words are often expressed with a slight smile on the lips and twinkle in the eye, as though the speaker is being careful not to offend anyone by appearing too arrogant or assertive.

Whenever I am with the Ka Ha Naupaka group, I notice that there is much more asking than telling and more singing than saying. Song and dance are a regular part of each meeting, not just because they are so enjoyable but because they are also a way Hawaiians communicate. A manager at the hotel where we held our last meeting told me, "I always know when you folks are gathering here. There are *ukulele* and guitar cases everywhere, and I hear a lot of happy-sounding voices. I don't hear much of that when the mainland meetings come here."

In typical American culture, speech is often accelerated to such a rate that the three qualities of melody, meaning, and movement are lost. There seems to be an increasing lack of politeness and gentleness and a reliance on vulgarity, put-downs, and shortcuts to save the time of really having to share one's feelings or listen long and carefully to someone else. We rely on phrases such as "like, you know" and "twenty-four/seven" and on an almost endless set of letter codes to prevent us from having to talk together too deeply or too long. Young people often ask but don't really wait for an answer to the question "ya know what I'm sayin'?" We have become fast talkers and lazy listeners, neither of which trait leads to a partnership in pleasure.

A *kupuna* told me, "The language of *aloha* is a slow and deeply respectful language. You should talk with your partner as you would make love to them: slowly, caringly, and with deep respect for their pleasure as well as your own self-expression." The *kupuna* laughed and added, "Now remember, in talking together you should always come together and be *le`a* [joyful]." (As you will read in chapter 10, *le`a* also means orgasm. Hawaiians, particularly the *kupuna* of Ka Ha Naupaka, often tease and joke about serious things, and sexual innuendo is a favorite way of testing to see if you are really getting the message and are comfortable enough with intimate issues to talk sensibly about them.)

Your Couple Recording

To help you begin to monitor your speech patterns, have a tape recorder sitting where you and your partner usually talk together. If you can find a voice-activated recorder, that works the best. If not, switch the recorder on every so often when you have even a casual conversation about some simple household matter. Save up a few tapes, and when you are ready to share the two *naupaka* gifts of time and attention, play them back at accelerated speed. The words will be blurred and indistinguishable, but the point is to listen for a sense of shared rhythm and pace. Listen for the *mana* or energy of the speech, not the content or topic of conversation. Do you hear water ebbing back and forth, or a Ping-Pong match in progress? Does it seem more like a sped-up tape of two people singing a duet, or a recording of the quick, harsh chatter of two individual performers trying to take center stage to sing solo?

After trying some of the suggestions in this chapter, record additional tapes and compare how they sound. In my *naupaka* seminars, couples almost always report a marked difference in their pre- and post- "singing lesson" tapes. One wife said, "I was shocked when I stopped trying to listen to *what* we were saying and just listened as if it were a recorded song. Even though we weren't arguing on the tapes, those early versions sounded like two angry rap artists. The newer ones sound more like a waltz being played fast."

Pet-Assisted Wellness

The physical, mental, and emotional benefits of the "reverse domestication" effect of animal companionship have long been established by research.[2] Data show that caring for a pet is very good for our health, cardiovascular system, immunity, and overall well-being.[3] Cats have been shown to have a favorable effect in reducing blood pressure in patients with hypertension and even in helping reduce the need for medication.[4] Interacting with our pets seems to domesticate us by calming us down and making us a little more docile.

A caretaker in a hospice in Dayton, Ohio, reported that a dog named Flapper was her "therapy dog." Every day she did her daily rounds, visiting suffering people in the last stages of terminal illnesses, and she would take Flapper with her.[5] As she reported, "I remember a man who had cancer but who was also diagnosed with Alzheimer's. He would sit in his room in silence. Flapper would climb up in the chair next to his bed, and a transformation would take place. The man began talking, saying over and over again, 'What a pretty dog—is a pretty dog.' The whole time he was talking to Flapper, he would stroke his face, pull his ears, and Flapper just let him."

To learn to sing together more melodiously, perhaps couples can gain something by tuning into the special bond between humans and their pets.

Imagine how embarrassing it would be if someone taped the little talks you have with your dog or cat and then played them over the loudspeaker at a large public event! People often lapse into baby talk with their pets. They use sing-song patter, strange sounds, and meaningless questions. They come up with silly words and names for their pets and even their pet's toys—no doubt somewhat perplexing the animal! "Do wou want wou's Mr. Chewy toy? Do wou? Are you mamma's little kitty-cat, angel?" are examples I heard just today from the mouth of a highly respected physician.

We seem quite comfortable singing to our pets, holding them in our laps, rocking them, taking their head and looking them in the eyes, stroking them, and using a childlike lyrical and mellow speech pattern that we seldom use with any humans besides babies. We alter some words and make up others as if tuning into some archetypical vocabulary shared only between humans and the animals they love.

We "pet talk" not only because it soothes our cats or dogs but because it feels soothing and pleasurable to us. But once we tire of pet talk, we usually clear our throat and quickly revert to the less domesticated form of speech we reserve for the more mature humans in our life who apparently are much beyond needing the silly comfort we extend to the family pet.

Strange as it may sound, I suggest that we consider treating our partner like a beloved pet (at least once in a while, when no one is looking or listening). I'm not suggesting that spouses ask each other, "Do wou want to go bye-bye?" But perhaps if we took the same playful and gentle tone when we spoke to the person who matters most in our life, we would find more shared pleasure. If we were comfortable enough with ourselves, we could intentionally engage in what Sigmund Freud called a little "regression in the service of the ego." By that he meant being psychologically strong and confident enough in our adult identity to selectively engage in intentional forays into foolishness.

We don't really have to go so far as speaking to our partner in the silly ways we do our pets, but we could try talking to him or her as if to a fragile, trusting, vulnerable individual—a child, perhaps, as the chapter subtitle suggests—one in need of comfort and stroking. Perhaps if we used the same endearing, joyful, gentle speech that we reserve for our pets, we might find less conflict and insensitivity and more fun and joy in the relationship we say matters most in our life.

Scientists are fond of dismissing peoples' reports of their sometimes magical connections with animals as "only anecdotal." But the Greek root of the word *anecdote* is *anekdotos*, simply meaning "not published." As with most of the Hawaiian anecdotes, lessons, and *mo`olelo* (legends) in this book, these reports of humans and their animals may indeed be unpublished stories. But this does not diminish their importance as sources of learning and reflection.

Listening with *Aloha*

Anyone who has watched a *hula* being danced cannot help but be impressed with its grace and beauty. It is a most pleasing thing to watch and even a little provocative. To Hawaiians, *hula* was holy, an integral part of their spiritual legacy. Its underlying principle remains the reaffirmation of the cherished beliefs and values of Hawai`i and Hawaiians. As you read in chapter 7, *hula* is a form of body prayer that invokes the sacred *mana* or life energy. It is a lovely sight to behold, but its full message cannot be understood and appreciated unless it is also "listened to" with an oceanic sensitivity. The second part of learning to communicate together *kakou*-style is to try to emulate the Hawaiian way of listening to *hula* as taught to me by the generous *hula* dancers and *kumu hula* (*hula* masters) of Hawai`i.

Hula is accompanied by songs and chants that convey the message or *mo`olelo* of the *hula*. As mentioned earlier, the interaction between the chanter or singer and the dancer is fundamental to the dance and what it is intended to convey. *Hula* is easy to see with the eyes, but if you listen with your heart, you may not only hear the words of the *mele* (song) or *oli* (chant) but also be able to sense the very subtle but important signals that constantly flow back and forth between the singer/chanter and the dancer. You may also hear the soft words of the dancers as they say some of the words of the *hula* out loud. This is the intense, emotionally committed listening required in practicing the second art of singing together: listening with *aloha* for the meaning behind the words.

The specific words of the *oli* and *mele* are vitally important to *hula*. They are rich with multiple meanings and are in themselves a form of prayer. Ethnomusicologist Ann Stillman writes, "Verbal communication of the message via the text is the most important aspect of *hula*."[6] She states that the *hula* motions depict key words or ideas of the chant and that the words are the most significant aspect of the dance. But in fact, while a full understanding of the Hawaiian language is essential to a full understanding of the poetry of *hula*, a *kupuna* told me, "The words are of no greater importance than the dance, any more than the night is more important than the day. That again is the *naupaka* principle. It takes both halves to make a whole *hula*."

Likewise, in a *naupaka*-style partnership, as in the *hula*, while words do have immense power, there are other important messages we should listen for when we try to sing the same song together. (Great singers have a good ear.) Although in Hawaii words are considered very powerful, much of the *hula*'s power also comes from and combines with the *mana* or loving energy generated by the dancers, singers, chanters, musicians, and others in the sacred space being created. Learning this second element of communication involves creating not just a place to talk to one another but also a sacred place to listen together.

Resting as One

One way to build such a space—and one of the most neglected sources of joy—is taking the opportunity to sit together and share complete silence. Wanting "a little peace and quiet" is a common pleasure goal stated by most of the couples I have worked with. Not counting hours spent sleeping, how many times a day do you and your partner sit quietly and do absolutely nothing together? Just sitting quietly enhances your shared song—much as a rest enhances a musical score.

In classical music, there is something called the Haydn Hold. Haydn was the master of the rest in musical scores. He often indicated a silent pause with a fermata—a dot under an upside-down semicircle—placed over a rest mark. Such a mark instructs the musician to pause for an indefinite period of time—the "while" discussed in chapter 8—in a state of what might be called active alert rest. Adagio movements often seem restful because they usually have many such rests within them.

Skilled duet singers know how to rest together, so take the time in your relationship simply to rest as one. Doing so may help you listen with *aloha* for the essence of your partner's communications. As Emerson pointed out, who we really are can be drowned out by what we are saying.

No Words for Feelings; No Feeling for Words

Uncovering the deeper meaning of our partner's communications also involves understanding that while we do not always have words to express our emotions, the absence of a word does not mean the absence of the feeling or concept. Before Western contact, Hawaiians had no word for *technology*, yet they clearly had a deep knowledge of various clever and efficient means for dealing with their environment. The ingenious fishponds they constructed to take advantage of the changing tides and of the growth rates of various forms of sea life still stand as testament to Hawaiian technological skill.

We all have feelings that are difficult if not impossible to put into words. We may feel so sad or happy that no words can express the depth and range of our feelings, but we can still communicate them.

Simply by sitting with our partner in the cardio-synchronization way of joining left hand to right, our other hand on our heart, and looking into one another's eyes, we can "hear" all that needs to be said at that moment.

The other side of this communication coin is overcoming the temptation to use words without feeling. There is a clinical condition called *alexithymia*, which refers to those who cannot seem to express their feelings in words. They have feelings but just can't seem to say or share them very easily. Being partners in pleasure involves having meaningful conversations that include making the effort of saying words that convey feeling, rather than just communicating Clint Eastwood–style with a "yup" or a "nope."

Aunty Genoa Keawe, a revered *kupuna*, is one of the most talented singers in Hawai`i. During a performance, she was talking story with the audience between songs and teasing one of the young musicians who was having trouble keeping up with her energy. "If you are going to sing, sing from your heart. Sing with feeling. A song with no feeling is like the night sky with no stars. It feels a little empty and not very interesting or pretty."

A Moving Conversation

The last of the three ideas about how to sing the same song goes beyond speaking and listening with *aloha*; it involves moving with *aloha*. Much of what we say we say with our body, and research shows that moving around while talking can help get the message out.[7]

Thomas Edison once said that the body was merely a vehicle for the brain, but he was wrong. The body and brain are not separate. Our movements are not just a mechanical reflex to the brain's instructions any more than *hula* is just a body being dragged along by the head. In her book *Spirit in Action* Irene Lamberti writes, "Through conscious physical movement ...we can learn to unite body, mind, and spirit. ... Moving our bodies provides Spirit with an important avenue to our hearts."[8] Partners in pleasure don't just talk and listen to one another; they also express their feelings with their body movements.

I noticed one of the oldest couples in Ka Ha Naupaka communicating together in a buffet line. Eating is always a part of Hawaiian gatherings, an important aspect of the communication ritual. As with all of the Hawaiian ways of coming together, eating is never rushed or loud and is done with a deep sense of respect for the source of the food, for those with whom we are eating, and for our ancestors. A Hawaiian diet focuses as much on how and with whom we eat as on what we eat. Eating together is an excellent time for singing the same song so long as that song is one of *aloha*. The *kupuna* couple's bodies engaged in a wordless conversation as they moved through the line. The wife touched her husband's shoulder, and he automatically reached for a roll and put it on her plate. He lifted one of his shoulders, and his wife stepped in to retrieve the eating utensils they had forgotten. As she moved back, she dropped the roll off her plate and it landed with a splash in the soup. She tilted her head to one side and held one hand up in the air as her husband did the same. They laughed together and the husband tilted his head to one side as if to tell his wife to get the waiter's attention. They moved on through the line, found their table, and entered together into their pre-meal *pule* or prayer. As far as I could tell, they had not said a single word to one another until they began their *pule*, and even that was started by an exchange of glances. Their mouths had been silent, but their bodies had said a mouthful.

As partners in pleasure, try paying more attention to your own unique body talk. Most couples have it, but it becomes so subtle that they forget to use it when words fail to express their feelings or needs.[9] Once in a while try speaking together using only facial and body cues, and you will probably discover that you are pretty good at it. This form of "couples charades" can help partners avoid the dangerous buzz words that often lead to hurt feelings and conflict.

Showing Thank You

In the original Hawaiian language, there was no word for "thank you."[10] While the word *mahalo* is often used today to express appreciation, it actually means to honor someone as well as all of their ancestors and your own, and to acknowledge doing what is *pono* or right. As in most Polynesian cultures, the humility and grace with which you receive a gift or kind gesture is supposed to say it all and render a spoken "thank you" unnecessary and even a little contrived.

Learning to sing the same song together is learning to constantly show appreciation not just with verbal compliments and thank you's, but by modeling sincere gratitude with body and face. Stopping, taking your partner's hand for a while, and flashing a little smile is an excellent way to show thank you.

The Capacity to Confide

Throughout this book, I have asked you to sit down with your partner and discuss the various tests and assignments. There is a larger reason for doing this than merely learning the material. One of the greatest advantages to becoming partners in pleasure is the luxury of having someone with whom we can share anything and everything.

The Hawaiian phrase for confiding is *"Ho`ike i ka mana`o huna."* It literally means to share a secret from deep inside. A *kupuna* said, "One of the most *aloha* things you can do for someone is to confide in them. You are giving them the gift of your trust and inviting them to feel free and safe to share their secrets. When you are *kakou*, you can both confide because there is no danger of the *`o wau* not listening or caring."

Psychologist James Pennebaker of Southern Methodist University has studied the physical and emotional benefits of confiding our deepest thoughts and feelings. Dr. Pennebaker reports that when lie-detector tests are given to guilty people, the lie-detector technician is often able to elicit a confession. Once the person has confessed and is headed for jail, a second lie-detector test is often given to verify the first. During the second test, the guilty person is generally much more relaxed, despite the fact that he or she is headed for jail. Pennebaker says this is an example of the power of revealing those things that trouble us.[11]

It takes a lot of psychological, emotional, spiritual, and even physical energy to hold back our most pressing thoughts and feelings, particularly traumatic ones.[12] As a *kupuna* said, "If I didn't have my husband to confide in, I would keep recycling the same anger, sadness, or hurt inside me. Our body is always remaking itself with billions and billions of new cells. I don't want my new body to have the old bad stuff in it. We help each other stay new."

The Same Song Test

In my book *The Pleasure Prescription*, which introduces the magic of *aloha* as a source of personal pleasure, I wrote about the Hawaiian tradition of talking story. This refers to the practice of just talking things over without any particular goal or problem-solving in mind. It is a way of sharing feelings, memories, and associations. Learning to sing the same song requires taking time to talk story together, free of issues to be confronted or family problems to be resolved. Talk story about the three components of singing together—melody, meaning, and movement—as they apply to your relationship.

To help with this process, here's another test used in the Ka Ha Naupaka groups. As with the other tests presented in this book, each partner should score him/herself individually, and then score his/her partner. Then the pair should get together and score their relationship. Afterward, talk (sing?) about the items together as you practice some of the suggestions presented in this chapter. As always, your post-test discussion—or shall I say duet—is more important than your scores.

The Same Song Test

$$0 - 1 - 2 - 3 - 4 - 5 - 6 - 7 - 8 - 9 - 10$$

NOT AT ALL — — — OFTEN — — — ALWAYS

Do you each:

1. speak as politely to one another as you do to strangers?

2. say "please" and "thank you"?

3. compliment the other?

4. speak in glowing terms about your partner to other people?

5. find one another's voice pleasant and pleasing?

6. avoid being sarcastic and cynical?

7. avoid sulking and carrying a grudge?

8. feel listened to and understood?

9. avoid being critical of one another?

10. avoid angry words, put-downs, and ruminating over negatives?

Total _____

The higher your score, the more likely it is that you are already singing the same song.

Maukaukau—Get Ready

The Hawaiian word *maukaukau* means "ready". If you listen very carefully, you will hear the chanter slap the *ipu* and pound it on the mat as she or he asks gently, "*Maukaukau?*" The chanter is asking if the dancer is ready to *hula*—not only physically but on a spiritual, emotional, and mental level. If he or she is, the answer is `ae, yes, and the *hula* is free to begin with due respect and honor.

Doing the *hula* when one is not *maukaukau* leads at best to a meaningless, hollow performance that is little more than a folk dance. It is very tiring and doesn't seem to say much. Being ready to *hula* means having prepared oneself by connecting totally with and honoring the `aina (the land), the *aumakua* and Ke Akua (the gods and God), and the `ohana (extended family).

To learn to sing the same song requires a similar preparation and dedication. If you are *maukaukau* together, what you say and hear can be filled with the same *aloha* or love that audiences feel when the *hula* dancer communicates with them beyond words.

Chapter Ten

Becoming One Body

Paired Pleasure Prescription Seven: Hold each other each time as if it were the last time.

Ua kohu ke kaunu ana i Waialoha

Lovemaking at Waialoha is suitable.[1]

Refers to making a good match and encouraging the course of true love.

Is This About Sex?

When groups ask me to talk to their organizations on the theme of "partners in pleasure," they sometimes ask, "We want to hear about your research, but it isn't just about sex, is it? We wouldn't want to offend our audience." I can easily answer "Of course not" to their question because, as you have read, becoming partners in pleasure is about much, much more than physical connection—and no human interaction is ever "just" about sex.

My work as director of professional education at the Kinsey Institute for Research in Sex, Gender, and Reproduction; my training at the Masters and Johnson Institute for Reproductive Biology; and my work as founder and clinical director of the Sexual Dysfunction Clinic at Sinai Hospital of Detroit taught me long ago that nothing is ever just about sex. Physical intimacy with another person is, whether both partners are fully aware of it or not, a profoundly connective act that involves a union of our physical, emotional, mental, and spiritual beings. Try as we might to ignore the implications of physical closeness, "casual sex" is impossible because our bodies do not work separately from the rest of who and how we are. Our bodies cannot make love without us.

Learning the seventh paired pleasure prescription requires remembering that the body, brain, and heart are one inseparable system. Your brain may think you are just having a "quick snack," but the rest of your body knows only that you are eating. Your body does not have different eating modes for casual or serious eating, and the same goes for sex. When we are sexually intimate with someone, our heart, body, and spirit join with another complete human system whether the often hurried and selfish brain knows or wants to know it or not.

Stuck in Sexual Adolescence

Our culture seems stuck in its sexual adolescence. Sexual titillation is everywhere; movies contain preadolescent sexual silliness; sexual innuendo and explicit language fill the airwaves; and pornography flashes across television and computer monitors every second of the day. Logging on to lewdness has become a major national hobby and megaindustry, and explicit sex Web sites are among the most popular on the Internet. But when it comes to serious, direct, open, comfortable talk about body-to-body intimacy, we act shocked and offended.

Our fascination with anything dealing with sex is matched in intensity only by our discomfort. A lingering teenage silliness about sex and an accompanying guilt still find their way into our intimate adult relationships, often preventing them from being the source of healthy pleasure and joy they could be. Instead of dealing with important and potentially confusing questions—such as the difference between "making love" and "having sex"—honestly and straightforwardly in our culture, such matters become the stuff of sensational talk shows.

This paired pleasure prescription is about rediscovering the joy of enlightened physical intimacy between two persons already in love; however, it is not a means to find it or test for it. It is not a set of directions or another sex manual. It is a sharing of the healthy openness about sexual intimacy that is so well known to the elder members of Ka Ha Naupaka.

Fulfilling *Naupaka*'s Yearning

If we can get past our insecurity and immaturity about the topic of sexual intimacy, it can become one of the most important means through which the *kakou* or "we" of a couple is physically actualized. As one *kupuna* put it, "It can be a way that the mountain and seaside *naupaka* plants become one again." In the context of the *naupaka* principle, sexuality is not limited to just the act of sex. It refers to joining the essences of our maleness and femaleness by sharing the *naupaka* gifts you have read about: giving sufficient time and focused attention to our relationship to allow it to blossom into one whole body that includes heart and soul.

Spiritual teacher Irene Lamberti writes, "Sexuality is not limited to the act of sex. It is one part of our being that influences how we see the world and how we act in the world, how we connect with others, and how we express our spirituality."[2] In this context, sexuality becomes an expression of our innate *naupaka* yearning for union and for the physical experience of *kakou*. It becomes our body-to-body way of experiencing the non-two of partners in pleasure rather than individuals giving and seeking physical gratification.

Naupaka physical yearning is not just a craving for another person's body but a longing to feel whole by merging with our other half. It is an awareness that who we are does not stop at our skin. When we are overwhelmed with great joy or deep sorrow, we seem to automatically seek contact with another body. We need to fall into the arms of another being who understands beyond words what it means to be a human trying to learn from the series of spiritual challenges we all face. As Sir James Jeans wrote, "In the deeper reality beyond space and time, we may all be members of one body."

Sensual Rain: Hawaiian Lessons of Sexual Intimacy

The Hawaiian word *le`a* has two meanings: joy and orgasm. Hawaiians did not separate the two. Very few dictionaries contain poetic definitions, but the *Hawaiian Dictionary* by brilliant Hawaiian scholar Mary Kawena Pukui is an exception. It defines *le`a* as "sexual gratification, orgasm, joy, pleasure, happiness, merriment, delighted, happy, pleased."[3] This wonderful set of words is also a profile of a pleasure partnership.

Pukui's definition reflects the pre-Western-contact Hawaiian view of sexual intimacy and the orientation of the seventh pleasure prescription. This orientation is described by Pukui as "Lightened with merriment. Lifted beyond body sensation with the quality of joy."[4] Until Western sailors, saddled with beliefs about "guilty" pleasure, walked off their tall ships and onto the shores of paradise, and until taught to think otherwise by the missionaries, Hawaiians suffered little from the guilt, embarrassment, anxiety, and childish immaturity that often characterizes Western sexuality. Body-to-body intimacy was seen by Hawaiians as a loving, happy, natural, and wonderful way to share one of life's greatest privileges: the opportunity to unite physically with another to become as one in pleasure.

Have you ever felt a gentle rainy mist on your face, or smelled and even felt the freshly ionized air after a rain shower? Have you ever taken a deep breath to inhale this air? Such is the sensual joy referred to by Pukui. As you may have gathered from this book, the Hawaiian *naupaka* lessons always contain many levels of meaning; the word *le`a* is also used to express the unique feeling of comfort we experience from a refreshing, cool mist or wind. Many *mele* or Hawaiian songs speak of the sensual nature of the rain that represents the intimate and fruitful joining of Wakea (Father Sky) with Papa (Mother Earth). They sing of the sensuous wetness left on the flowers, an erotic symbol of the sexual arousal of two bodies in a loving embrace.

To learn the prescription of becoming one body, here are some lessons from Ka Ha Naupaka about sexuality. They require again that you go out of your continental mind and embrace the oceanic view of sexual intimacy—the idea of joining with rather than doing to or for. A *kupuna* told me, "If you want to really understand our idea of two bodies becoming one in joy, you have to know the word *hua`i*. It means to disclose, share, reveal, and just pour forth all that you are in your body, mind, and spirit. Our Hawaiian word for sexual climax is *huahua`i*. When you double up a word like *hua`i* in our language, it means to really, really do what the word says. The joy of sex for Hawaiians is to pour forth your entire being and be like the rain together. It is sharing the sacred *ha* or breath, the *ka ha naupaka*—the breath of *naupaka*. This is how the *naupaka* flower on the mountain and at the sea become one."

Anticipatory Pleasure

Original Hawaiians knew well the delights of anticipatory pleasure. In our modern world, "do it now" seems to be the sexual credo. The English word *foreplay* reveals this ready-set-go orientation: the "play" happens before the "real thing." For Hawaiians, anticipation was enjoyable in and of itself. Their sexual intimacy was free from the goal of climax and involved enjoying the acts of touching, holding, and caressing in their own right. A *kupuna* told me, "*Honi* is what we are doing when we touch noses side-to-side and breathe in one another's breath. *Honi* is Hawaiian kissing, in which we become of one breath, and it is very loving and sensual to us. We love to just *honi* and *kilipue* [hug ardently]."

Another *kupuna* described the traditional sex secrets of her `ohana. She said, "People think we Hawaiians just grabbed each other and ran off into the forest. That is not right. We loved to play at sex. The *ali`i* [royalty] had a game where a person would slide a small coconut shell cut in half to hit a target in front of the person you were interested in. If you hit the target, you could *honi* the person.[5] Common people had their own game called *`ume* [to attract or entice]. They all sat around together in a big circle and the game leader would touch a certain man and woman with his wooden stick and they could then go off together. Everyone knew ahead of time who they wanted to be with and told the game leader and everyone laughed as he teased and played with the group. The anticipation was the real fun."

Once talking story starts with *kupuna*, it really gets going, particularly when the topic is sexual intimacy. Their comfort with and joy in the topic is so obvious that it is easy to understand why the sailors misinterpreted this healthy view of sex as wantonness. They saw the games described above, but did not understand the loving and respectful rules and codes upon which they were based. Even today, Hawaiian comfort with sexuality is more than a little disconcerting to those non-Hawaiians who may not be so at ease with the topic.

Another *kupuna* added her family story of sexual play for its own sake and for the shared joy it can bring. She said, "The *kane* [man] would go and find just a little powder or pollen from the *hinano*, the male blossom of the pandanus tree. He would put some pollen on his fingertip and blow it very gently onto the *`i`o`i`o* [clitoris] of his lover." The *kupuna* winked at her husband and they laughed together as he added without embarrassment, "It was our secret and my lover knew its power."

To become partners in pleasure along the lines of the seventh prescription, your relationship might want to take some clues from these Hawaiian ways of enjoying anticipation, teasing, and fun in sexual intimacy. A little less foreplay and a little more playing together might add a new dose of delight to your sexual intimacy.

Pleasurable Places

Not only anticipation but place mattered in Hawaiian lovemaking. Another *kupuna* said, "We *wahine* also had our ways, you know. We would perfume our sleep mats at night to encourage our lover. We would sometimes eat things that we knew would smell very good when we would sweat, and in this way we made our own natural body perfume."[6]

The "anointed bed" was a way in which Hawaiians created a pleasurable place to love. Care was taken to make and prepare the ideal mat for love. A *kupuna* told me, "All the different things that go into thinking about making love is what is really enjoyable. We would think and plan and talk about it for hours and days. We would not just turn off the television and start up."

Spontaneity

Anointed beds and long anticipation, however, were not the only Hawaiian methods of lovemaking—the unplanned sensual moment could be their way of love too. While they treasured setting the mood and thinking about the joys of anticipated lovemaking, they were comfortable enough with their own sexuality not to be bound by this.

Hawaiians made themselves available to their lover. Sexual intimacy was so much a part of their life and was seen as so natural that they could allow mood and opportunity to guide some of their interactions. Being free of clock time and having worked hard early in the morning to rest during the time of hot sun, they could indulge in gentle trade-breeze afternoons under palm trees at the beach—sort of a Polynesian version of the lunch-hour motel room. Being free of linear clock time also allowed them to avoid the modern concerns about "taking too long" or "coming too fast."

Hawaiian Sex Education

Beneath their joyful anticipation, free-play orientation, and openness to following their sexual desires lay the indigenous Hawaiians' clear and full understanding of sexuality. They came to their lovemaking with an open and comfortable knowledge derived from early and thorough sex education from parents and grandparents. Just as modern parents take their children to soccer and Little League and talk freely about these activities as a family, Hawaiians spoke and taught openly and explicitly about sex.

Hawaiian sex education was clear, specific, and accurate, but never without the loving emphasis on the unity of two spirits. Rather than a mechanically oriented "how to do it" education, it was based on know-ing about your body and your partner's body and about how bodies respond in sex. It emphasized the view that our body is not just our own; it is a sacred trust shared with the `ohana (family) and aumakua (ancestors), whom it represents. It taught that when we touch one another, we are touching everyone for whom we have respect and responsibility. A kupuna said, "We were taught that Ke Akua gave us all one thing—our body. It is a sacred trust. We are to honor it and cher-ish and never hurt it or another body. We were told how to touch and hold as means of respecting bodies, not just how to turn them on."

No Rules

A kupuna said, "Except for ali`i [royalty], whose kapu [cultural rules] must always be honored, there was no manual of sexual postures or rules of sexual intimacy for Hawaiians. There was no one way to have sex and of course no concern for a 'missionary position,' because we Hawaiians were never too sure that missionaries ever really had joyful sex." She paused and began to laugh. "Now that I think of it, maybe that is what the missionary position is. It's taking the position that there should not be too much joy in sex."

As you can tell from the openness and relaxed humor of the kupuna quoted above, Hawaiian interest in sexual intimacy does not diminish with age.

Another kupuna said, "We members of Ka Ha Naupaka have nearly two thousand years of marriage between all of us couples if you add them all up. We talk freely of our sexuality into our later years, but we do not mean to offend. The impotent man or frigid woman just were not known to us, no matter our age. As long as we are breathing, we can continue to share the sacred breath. Our Viagra is the gentle breeze and sweet smells of Hawai`i. Why do you think le`a is the same word for orgasm and for joy?"

Sacred Fun

Despite the frankness, openness, and just plain good fun that charac-terized traditional Hawaiian sexuality, sex remained a sacred act. As you have read, Hawaiian spirituality is as happy as it is profound, and the same holds true for sexuality. The sexual organs were seen as sacred because they were associated with the birth of descendants and were where the connection with ancestors was continued. Another *kupuna* pointed out, "Oh, yes, the genitals and sex are sacred, but we still make jokes. You see how we joke about the genitals in some of our *hula*, but we mean no disrespect in our laughter. We Hawaiians make jokes about everything and anything because laugher happens when you are *kakou* and *lokahi* [sharing] the feeling of that connection. *Aka* [laughter] is a way we sing together."

Sex Secrets of the Poor and Unknown

Hawaiians may not have been rich and famous, but what they lacked in money and the outside world's awareness of and sensitivity to their wisdom they more than made up for in their poetic and symbolic way of finding meaning in nature. The Hawaiian language is full of *kaona*: hidden meanings. In learning the sixth paired pleasure prescription about communicating by singing the same song, you read about the importance of listening for the many meanings of words—their *kaona*—in order to really share.

After the missionaries came, *kaona* became even more fun for Hawaiians. They found it irresistible to make sexual innuendoes as ways of teasing or tricking the more uptight *haole* (the breathless ones from the West). A *kupuna* told me, "Watch out now. We Hawaiians can be a tricky bunch. We see sex as a very spiritual thing, but we know it can also be very funny. My ancestors used to fool the missionaries and visitors by saying the word *mea* [thing] when they were really talking about the female genitalia. The would also say *poheo* [knob] when they were really talking about the head of the penis. You could talk about the *poheo* being in the *mea*, and the non-Hawaiians never knew why we were laughing so hard."

Another *kupuna* said, "When we sing of the mist and spraying rain, pollen, and gentle blossoms, Westerners always think we are singing about a beautiful place or thing. Sometimes we are, sometimes we aren't. Most of the time we are singing about both things at the same time. Sometimes we are telling a sex story or joke." Pukui warned, "When the Hawaiians all start giggling, then you know it means something else."[7]

Good Sex Is Good for You

To become partners in pleasure, consider including the Hawaiian orientation to sexual intimacy in your approach to lovemaking. If you do, your sex life will not be the only thing to benefit from this ancient wisdom of love; so will your overall sense of well-being, your feelings of connection with your partner—and quite possibly your physical health.

Drs. Robert Ornstein and David Sobel write that pleasing sex "puts a spring in your step, a sparkle in your eye, and a glow in your skin. Like a full belly, when your sexual appetite is satisfied, the world seems like a more wonderful place."[8] But besides helping you feel good, loving intimacy has positive influences on your entire body system. Research shows that fulfilling sex can help reduce the impact of stress and ward off some of its physical side effects, such as fatigue, agitation, and headaches.[9]

Because of these positive effects, the sexual excuse "not tonight dear, I have a headache" might be changed to the sexual invitation "please tonight dear, I have a migraine." In a survey of persons who experienced migraines, one of four sufferers reported that orgasm helped soothe the pain.[10] They also reported that the stronger the orgasm, the greater the relief. Even though a severe headache is a turnoff, partners in pleasure might consider getting turned on as one way to deal with their headaches.

Getting Close

Because loving sex helps us feel the *kakou* experience, and because researchers know that feelings of connection translate to a more balanced immune system and a generally healthy body, making the kind of healthy love described in this chapter is also making a healthy life.

As you have read, *kupuna* can be as rascally as they are wise. One *kupuna* said, "Sex is a wonderful thing. We should never be ashamed to let everyone know we are sexual beings. At our age, it is even better than ever because we know how to do it right. We know that it is the *naupaka* principle in action." She took her husband's hand as she began to laugh. "It's when you become of one body, like both halves of the *naupaka* flower, and you might say 'coming together'—if you get my meaning."

"Coming together"—in the *kakou* sense of the phrase—might be described as one of the benefits of sexual intimacy. We don't only have sex *because* we feel close; when we have it, we *become* closer. This is true not only emotionally and spiritually but also physically. A "bio-bonding" takes place in sex because of a unique kind of hormonal synchronization that occurs between intimate partners.

Testosterone is the primary sex-arousal hormone for both men and women. Testosterone levels are usually lower in women than in men, but they are at their highest around the middle of a woman's menstrual cycle, when ovulation is taking place. This serves nature's procreative plan because it leads to women being more sexually aroused at the time when they would be most likely to conceive. But testosterone not only increases sex drive; it also helps men and women bond as a couple.[11] Research shows that the testosterone levels of partners in a lasting, pleasurable relationship tend to fall into synch. Over time and much as women living together experience a synchronization of their menstrual periods, loving partners' hormonal systems begin to parallel one another. We literally, at least in terms of the sex hormones, become one body.

A persistent myth maintains that the longer two people are together, the less they desire sex with each other. Hormonal synchronization and other research proves this wrong. Happily married men and women actually report having more frequent and satisfying sex than unmarried couples living together.[12] As loving partners satisfy what the *kupuna* call their "*naupaka* yearning for union," sexual intimacy becomes increasingly significant over time.

More than Skin Deep

In discussing the deepened connection that occurs between two people who are learning to become one body, it is important to remember that although most people may think about the genital contact implied in the phrase "having sex," in fact there is much more contact going on. Sexual intimacy is skin talk through which two bodies communicate pleasure to one another. It is also a way of expressing feelings that seem beyond words. A *kupuna* said, "When we say the words 'just hold me,' we are speaking as *naupaka*. We are expressing our need to be comforted by merging with our other half. Making love is a form of mutual healing that goes beyond words."

The "C^2" Index

There seems to be a "C^2" (contented couple) index in relationships.[13] This index is determined by counting your frequency of "connecting" (the number of times you make love joyfully together, including just holding and caressing one another with no genital contact) and subtracting the number of "conflicts" you experience in your relationship during that same time period. For example, if you experience conflicts 10 times per month but feel joyfully sexually connected 12 times per month, your C^2 index would be +2. The higher the C^2 index, the happier and more pleasured the partnership. While trying to "out-sex" the number of fights you have won't work, being aware of this index might help you both keep an eye on this paired pleasure prescription.[14]

A Two-Faced Partnership

To further help couples learn the symbolism behind becoming one body, I developed the Two-Faced Test.

Researchers have used drawings representing human facial expressions to study individual happiness.[15] They present a face with a big smile, a neutral face, and a face with a frown. They ask respondents to pick the face that comes closest to expressing how they feel as a whole right now. Nine out of ten persons pick the faces toward the happy side of the scale.

In my work with couples, I wanted to go beyond the individual definition of joy to assess the state of *kakou* or partner pleasure. I designed the *naupaka*-style faces below: two half-faces that can be combined into one shared expression. While many combinations were possible, I wanted a simple grading system. I devised six combinations from which couples could select, as follows:

A+ Two very big smiles

A   Two smiles

B   One smile combined with one neutral line

C   Two neutral lines

D   One smile combined with one frown

E   Two frowns

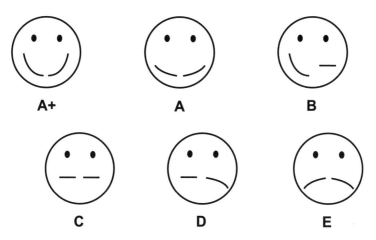

A+   A   B

C   D   E

Couples were asked to pick which combination seemed to best reflect their "state of the union," particularly as related to their sexual and sensual relationship. Each partner was also asked to reflect on which *naupaka* half-face they contributed to the total. (I used a variation on this test with some Hawaiian *kupuna*. I asked them to draw two halves of the *naupaka* flower, each in a varying state of health, from very bright and blossoming to wilting and weak.)

Where would you and your partner fall on this scale? Remember to focus on what *you* are contributing to the face more than what you think your partner is contributing. What *naupaka* half are you bringing to the whole?

A variation on this test calls for each partner to draw three half-faces: a smile, a neutral face, and a frown. Each partner should select one of the three pieces, without seeing what the other has selected. On the count of three, each should place his/her half-face next to the other's half.

The result is a more spontaneous indication of the emotional state each partner is bringing to the relationship at this moment. From here, take the opportunity to discuss lovingly and gently what aspects of the paired pleasure prescriptions might be of help, if desirable, in changing the face of your relationship.

The One Body Test

Here is a test to promote talking story between you and your partner about the issues raised in this chapter. Score it in the same five ways you have scored the other tests. Then take the time and give the attention to discussing the sensual and sexual aspects of your partnership.

You may notice that not all of the questions are overtly related to sex, but remember the *naupaka* idea of sexuality discussed at the beginning of the chapter. Sexuality is the totality of your maleness and femaleness (your alpha and beta characteristics), including how you think, feel, believe, and act.

The One Body Test

$$0 - 1 - 2 - 3 - 4 - 5 - 6 - 7 - 8 - 9 - 10$$

NOT AT ALL — — — OFTEN — — — ALWAYS

1. Do you agree that it is easy to sleep together (not fighting over the blanket, bothering the partner, snoring, etc.)?

2. Do you share the same tastes in food, equally value what you both consider to be a healthy diet, and share many slow, enjoyable meals together?

3. Are you in agreement on the issues of drinking alcohol and smoking?

4. Is your relationship free of annoying habits by one or the other partner?

5. Do you both attend equally to your physical appearance and bodily hygiene?

6. Do people say you're beginning to look like one another?

7. Is your lovemaking a way of connecting more than of releasing tension?

8. Do you share the same sense of humor about sex and sexual matters?

9. Are you equally committed to physical fitness, and do you
   share the same views as to body weight and shape?

10. Do you both monitor the sensual aspects of your relationship,
    see what needs to be done to help that aspect of your relation-
    ship grow, and take responsibility for its "C^2" (contented cou-
    ple) index?

Total ____

The higher your score, the more likely it is that you are on the way to
becoming one body.

Flying Together

Becoming one body is remembering the importance of mutual, caring
touch in your relationship. It means truly being *partners* in pleasure in
that you both assume responsibility for the sensual pleasure of your
relationship. It means caring and learning about one another's bodies;
creating sensual places and times and erotically anticipatory joy; and
embracing an open, happy, nondemanding pleasure orientation with
regard to the meaning and frequency of sexual connection.

It also requires remembering philosopher Uciano de Crescenzo's
statement about intimate connection: "It is important to remember
that we are, each of us, angels with only one wing. And we can only fly
embracing each other." The sexual intimacy of the kind described in
this chapter provides spiritual shelter for those in a *naupaka* relationship
because it inoculates them against one of the deadliest diseases of civi-
lization—feeling alone. Author Anthony Welsh wrote, "It is not the
threat of death, illness, hardship, or poverty that crushes the human
spirit; it is the fear of being alone and unloved in the universe." As you
will read in the next chapter about connection that crosses time and
space, once you have joined minds, hearts, souls, and bodies, you need
never feel alone again.

Chapter Eleven

Sharing a Sixth Sense

Paired Pleasure Prescription Eight:
"Psi" together

I ho`okahi kahi ke aloha

Be one in love. [1]

Refers to a connection between lovers that transcends
time and space.

Lincoln's "Wonderful Things"

Abraham Lincoln was a strong believer in what researchers now call psi (pronounced "sigh"), a sense of timeless connection with everything and everyone beyond the usual range of our five basic senses.[2] He told his close friend and biographer, Ward H. Lamon, that he somehow sensed he would be elected to a second term but that he would die before the end of it. When the newspaper, *The Cleveland Plain Dealer,* published this story, Lincoln was asked if the account was true. He replied, "The only falsehood in the statement is that the half of it has not been told. This article does not begin to tell the wonderful things I have witnessed."

As difficult as it may be for one or both of the brains in your relationship—particularly the more alpha brain—to accept, your hearts will be warmed by reading about what Lincoln called the wonderful things that give proof that you and your partner can be connected anywhere, anytime, and forever across time and space.[3] You will read about the immortality of your relationship, a profound connection supported by the research on various aspects of psychic phenomena, represented by the Greek letter Ψ, or psi.

What you are about to read may seem like sorcery. It is an enchanted way of thinking, a concept of life that is first and foremost organic and holistic, filled with meaning and a level of interconnectedness that goes far beyond the usual rational view of boundaries and limits. It is a view of the universe that some philosophers call "naturalistic panpsychism."[4]

Naturalistic panpsychism is the idea, long embraced by Hawaiians and other indigenous peoples, that the universe is actually awareness itself, what philosopher Michael Lockwood calls a living, remembering, conscious "what it's likeness" that is built into every cell in our body and every atom in the cosmos. We are "aware" of things like electrons, trees, and love because that is what *they* are—awareness.

In the context of this universal awareness resonating in every stone and star, partners in pleasure are two persons who decide to give the time and attention to becoming totally "aware of their awareness" of one another and to match their daily behaviors to that awareness. They decide to psi together as a way of extending their level of awareness beyond the daily nonmagical—to go beyond "that's all there is" to "there is only all."

It's Magic

In Part One you read about the magic of the *menehune*, the mysterious little people of Hawaiian legend who represent the power of the "little things." You read that the magic of lasting and joyful love is created by caring about and attending to the everyday. Psi phenomena also tend to be little things, happenings that we become more aware of when we are fully engaged in sharing daily life with another. They are the little surprises and strange synchronicities that keep popping up in our relationship when we have the time and pay the attention to experience them.

These psi surprises, which reflect our connectedness, probably are happening around us most of the time, dancing just beyond the artificial boundaries of self established by our continental brain. Sometimes it is the phone ringing at just the moment you were thinking about your partner. Other times it is the sense of dread you feel just when your loved one is suffering or needing you in a moment of crisis. For those who have lost a partner, it may be the sudden passing thought, image, or almost-heard words of a departed lover—apparent evidence that they are still with us. These "wonderful things" that most lovers have experienced imply, despite the doubts and mockery of cynics, that communication of some kind and on some level is always going on within and around us.

Dreaming the Same Dream

In addition to discussing how to become more open to these seemingly magic little things—these spontaneous phenomena—the eighth paired pleasure prescription also describes an intentional technique for psychically connecting with your partner: dream telepathy. This is a method of literally learning to dream the same dream while sleeping side by side.

Research shows that about half of all spontaneous psychic or mental-telepathy experiences occur in the dream state.[5] A total of 450 dream-telepathy sessions were reported on between 1966 and 1973. The results of all the experiments combined showed an overall success rate of 63 percent for sending dreams to another person. This means that in more than six out of ten tries, dream telepathy worked. The 95-percent statistical confidence reported from these studies clearly rules out chance.[6]

If dreaming the same dream sounds like just a romantic illusion, it is only because the idea that our consciousness can be connected with another person's pushes the continental brain beyond its rational limits.

A Sweet Connection

Drs. Gary Schwartz and Linda Russek are pioneers in the careful, scientific, and creative approach to learning more about what they call the living energy universe.[7] They reverse what might be considered the question of a lifetime (or death time): "Is their life after death?" Instead, they ask, "Is there death [in the sense of total disappearance of our identity] after we physically die?" As psi researchers and partners in pleasure themselves, their answer is an unequivocal no.

Interconnectedness, like memories, lasts forever. Despite the illusion of a boundary between being alive and then dissolving into nothingness, in our heart most of us sense that we are psi partners for infinity. Learning to appreciate and take joy now in that reassuring fact is the objective of this final prescription.

Consider what happens when you stir a teaspoonful of sugar into a glass of water.[8] After a few moments, it will seem as if the sugar has disappeared or dissolved into nothingness—has "died," if you will. But if you were to take a sip of the water, the sugar's essence could still be tasted.

The sugar's "death" is clearly evident to the brain's eye. It was there and now it is gone. But the water has been changed—made sweet—by the sugar's essence, and thus the sugar is still "alive" in the sense that its essence and influence have not ended. If you were to use only one of your five senses—your eyesight—to look for it, the sugar would seem nonexistent. You have to use another sense and taste the water to discover that the sugar is not really gone at all; it is still present in "ghost" or essence form. But because of the union of sugar and water, its form— and also that of the water—has been changed forever.

Now consider what would happen if you were to let the glass of sugar-water (what one *kupuna* calls *waugar*) sit for several hours. When you returned, you would see additional evidence of the permanence of the sugar. As the water evaporated—as it changed its form to merge with the air around it—the sugar crystals "magically" would reappear, but in a new form, one containing an "imprint" of their merging with the water. Before, you couldn't see or touch them, for they seemed gone forever, but in fact they were there all along.

Drs. Schwartz and Russek describe the implications of the sugar-water analogy on connection and infinite memory. They write, "Wouldn't it be wonderful if our loved ones, as expressed in their living info-energy systems, maintained their integrity and identity as they extended into space and became an integral part of the fabric of eternal life? Like the light of distant stars, their 'dissolving' souls were still unique and whole, entangled with us dynamically and eternally? This is a sweet vision indeed."[9]

A *kahuna* shared the following wisdom about learning to tap into this eternal flow: "Whenever people say to me, 'Life is difficult,' I always answer, 'And exactly what are you comparing it to?' When they say life is pointless, I tell them that their existence is point enough. You must always put your local pain in the perspective of the cosmic joy of *aloha*, of loving forever. We are like the sugar in the water, connected far beyond the limits of our body's senses. When a man came from France to me for healing, he described Hawai`i as being *doceur*. He told me the word means a sweetness, tenderness, and gentleness of manner. We must remember to be like that. We must be sweet like the sugarcane, for that is when the wonderful things you call psi happen."

Scientific Confirmation

No less a scientist than Albert Einstein described a "ghostly" connection that exists across time and space. He was responding to a finding that shocked the scientific world. In 1964, physicist J. S. Bell proved that when one member of any quantum pair—two electrons spinning in space—is interfered with, its partner is also altered at exactly the same time.[10] Einstein and others were perplexed by this seemingly impossible faster-than-time phenomenon. But Bell's Theorem remains a cosmic fact of life: once connected, always connected—everywhere and forever. Change the spin of one electron of a pair, no matter where that electron may be, and its partner changes its spin at precisely the same instant, no matter where it is.

So astonishing was Bell's Theorem that several attempts have been undertaken to disprove it. All have failed. The principle that scientists now call "action at distance" is a fact of quantum science. Physicist Nick Herbert wrote of this amazing principle, "No local [time-, space-, or boundary-restricted] reality can explain the type of world we live in."[11]

Bell's Theorem is the two-thousand-year-old Hawaiian *naupaka* principle in action, visible to the continental mind. It teaches that local reality—the limitation imposed by time and space—is insufficient to explain our loving connection. It shows from a scientific point of view how we are *kakou* forever. The cosmos keeps giving us little clues and hints about this fact of life, the little wonderful psi things that happen to lovers every day.

Oceanic Sorcery

An ancient Polynesian sorcery exists, called *hana aloha*. It means "love magic," and this prescription applies some of the wisdom and lessons of *hana aloha* to strengthening your *naupaka* relationship.

In *hana aloha*, all of the various components of psi were employed by *kahuna*. These included telepathy (the exchange of information between two minds without use of the five physical senses), clairvoyance (the receiving of information from a distance, again beyond the five senses), psychokinesis (sometimes called telekinesis; so-called mind-over-matter phenomena, in which the mind interacts with and alters the action of objects), and precognition (so-called premonitions or "presponding" to a person or event before they are present or occur).

In learning to share a sixth sense, you have to be willing to drop your "psi shyness." I hope you and your partner will consider that two thousand years of ancient Hawaiian *hana aloha*—as supported by two hundred years of careful scientific research conducted by more than seventy respected scientists—proves that we can, to varying degrees and in various ways, blend our consciousness together in a psi partnership.[12]

Love Energy: An Example of *Hana Aloha*

The Polynesian psi of *hana aloha* is reflected in many Hawaiian *mo`olelo* (legends) that teach of its immense power to induce connections across time and space. Here is one example as told to me by a *kupuna* in Ka Ha Naupaka. It is based on a long-told Hawaiian story of *hana aloha* as practiced by a *kahuna* on the island of Maui: "A man went to a *kahuna* to ask him to practice his *hana aloha* as a way to bring his lover back to him. The *kahuna* sent the man to stand with his back to the wind while holding a flower in his hand at a spot where his lover might pass by. He was to *kahu* [spit] on the flower and say the *hana aloha* words `*Nau no`oe e hele a`e*—you [the lover] come to seek me of your own accord!' When the 'love target' came near the flower where the man had dropped it, an intense love *mana* or energy overcame her, and she immediately went in search of the man who had dropped the now magic flower."

Imbuing objects with "love energy" may sound impossible, but this phenomenon is described in a scientific context by Dr. Robert Jahn, director of the Princeton Engineering Anomalies Research (PEAR) program, where millions of research trials have been conducted on the psi process of psychokinesis, or consciously "connecting with" and influencing an object. Two decades of research at the PEAR laboratory have shown that the performance of machines can be altered when research subjects focus their intent on the machine.[13] For example, men and women sitting in front of machines that were generating random numbers could, by gently focusing their attention on the machine, influence the numbers generated in the direction of their intention. PEAR subjects were also able to influence the swinging of a pendulum of a clock located in a vacuum; the beating of a drum attached to a random number machine; and the course of a tiny frog-shaped computer randomly moving about on a table until mentally "called" by the subject.

Jahn writes, "The most common subjective report of our most successful human/machine experimental operators is some sense of 'resonance' with the device—some sacrifice of personal identity in the interaction—a 'merging' or bond with the apparatus. As one operator put it, 'I simply fall in love with the machine.' And indeed, the term 'love,' in connoting the very special resonance between two partners, is an apt metaphor."[14]

Beyond Paranormality

The first person to be awarded a doctoral degree in "paranormal psychology" was Dr. Jeffrey Mishlove. He is a careful researcher and cautious psychologist who now writes, "I am refraining from using that term [*parapsychology*] . . . along with the related term *paranormal*. Such terms may have caused damage to a field whose subject matter is, in my view, properly conceived of as normal and psychological."[15]

Likewise, when I use the words *sixth sense*, I am referring to all five of our basic senses added together to equal a subtle but powerful "extra" sense. This combining of our senses is focused by a consciousness aware that it is not alone, that it is a co-consciousness always connected with the consciousness of others and particularly of our lover. The "wonderful things" of psi phenomena tend to happen when we use the power of all our senses to honor our *naupaka* yearning to consciously connect with another person irrespective of time or place—when we are being less self-conscious and more co-conscious. There is much to be learned about this consciousness-blending and how we can become more sensitive to a connection that most of us seem to experience.

We humans do have a tendency, as author and self-proclaimed debunker Michael Shemer points out, to believe in some pretty strange things.[16] Careful research has shown, however, that we need not believe in the supernatural or in pseudoscience to form a psi partnership. We can do so by learning more about a phenomena I have noticed in my years of work with couples: their natural ability to "prespond" or "preact"—to have loving hunches about each other.

A Life-Saving Hunch

Have you ever "had a hunch"? Have you ever been walking along and suddenly "had a bad feeling" that something was going to happen, stopped at the curb, and watched as a car that might have killed you sped through a red light? Having a hunch is being aware of something without knowing how you became aware of it.

It has been documented many times that Lincoln foresaw his own assassination. He saw himself dead on a catafalque surrounded by soldiers in the East Room of the White House. Even more relevant to the *naupaka* principle is a similar story of what Julia Grant foresaw concerning her husband, Ulysses S. Grant. Something on a psi level led to a hunch that saved the general's life.

Mrs. Grant told her husband that she felt a great sense of urgency to leave Washington and return to their home in New Jersey. Something kept nagging at her that they were in jeopardy. General Grant had just accepted General Robert E. Lee's unconditional surrender and was honored along with his wife with an invitation to accompany President Lincoln to Ford's Theater.

Mrs. Grant's bad feelings grew so intense on the day they were to attend the theater that she sent word to her husband several times, imploring him for the sake of their love to leave with her immediately. The general finally and very reluctantly gave in to his wife's "sense," and they quickly left Washington. As they were approaching Philadelphia on their journey home, they received the news that President Lincoln had been assassinated. They learned later that they had been scheduled to sit with the president in his box and that General Grant was on John Wilkes Booth's hit list.[17] Something about Julia Grant's *kakou* sense saved her husband's life.

Preactive Partners

Branislaw Malinowski writes, "Science is founded on the conviction that experience, effort, and reason are valid; magic on the belief that hope cannot fail or desire divide."[18] Most of us "hope" we can connect with our partners profoundly and beyond time and space, but I have observed this connection with hundreds of couples in my own research and with my wife, Celest.[19] I have noticed a unique intimacy intuition that exists between couples about what is happening to one another no matter where they may be and before events happen.

Although thousands of stories about couples' hunches exist, I decided to study the phenomenon to see if it could be verified other than by anecdote. In searching for prior studies of presentiment, I found work showing that people's nervous systems became activated in anticipation of seeing shocking pictures, such as erotic photos or autopsies, even when they had no idea that such pictures were going to be flashed before them.[20] When the subject was exposed randomly to either calm-inducing or emotion-eliciting pictures, her "orienting response" (physiological alert state, including sweating, dilation of the pupil, change in heart rate, etc.) occurred in anticipation of what the next picture would be. The surprising finding was that her response was more intense just before an emotionally disturbing picture was shown, even though she could not possibly have known the nature of the next picture. That is, she displayed a kind of preaction or presentiment.

For my study, I collected twenty cases from the couples coming to my clinic for marital therapy. While this was not a true random sample, I took the couples without regard to diagnosis, age, etc. I asked the spouses to sit in two separate videotape rooms. We attached measuring devices to each partner that detected skin conductance and heart-rate changes. We then showed the "responder" spouse random pictures of flowers or erotica. The other spouse was asked to just read a book while his/her partner was being "tested for response time as a part of therapy."

Because our instruments were crude and the sample not random, the results are open to criticism on many counts. However, it was interesting to note that fourteen of twenty partners showed physiological changes *even before* their partner—the "responder" spouse—was exposed to the next random picture. In each of the fourteen cases, the "presponse" was quickest and most intense when the image was an emotional instead of a calming one.

The "presponding" spouse was not merely tuning into his or her spouse's reactions, because according to our timing devices, the "responder" spouse had not yet reacted. (Perhaps less surprisingly, all of the "responders" also showed physical reactions prior to the next picture; however, and interestingly, in the "responders," we were unable to differentiate between the response to calming or emotional pictures in terms of the intensity of the physiological changes.)

An interesting side note to this informal psi study was that the fourteen couples in whom presentiments or "sent hunches" were detected all successfully completed their marital therapy program and, at five-year follow-up, still reported satisfaction with their relationship. The other six couples—those in whom no psi connection could be recorded in terms of our physiological study—dropped out of therapy; four of them divorced (we could not get information on the other two).

It seems possible that couples who psi together stay together. They seem to share a sixth sense—that is, an ability to blend their consciousness into one co-consciousness. My wife and I experienced this psi-ing together when I was dying of cancer. Celest would "just sense" that something was about to go wrong with my medications or with some hospital procedure; she would rush to the hospital just in time to protect me from iatrogenic (treatment-caused) damage.

Love Lessons from Psychic Spies

The Central Intelligence Agency conducted several psi experiments during the Cold War. Recent documents released under the Freedom of Information Act reveal how "remote viewers" were able to consciously connect with distant places and activities in precise detail.[21] This work can provide guidelines for how loving couples might enhance their own psi partnership.

Some of the CIA's psychic spies, viewers, or operators were more successful than others at employing their abilities. Based in part on the experiences of the super psychic sleuths who tended to be on target in their sixth-sense work, I have compiled the following list of conditions and traits for partners in pleasure to emulate in learning to share a sixth sense.[22] It is interesting to note how these parallel the paired pleasure prescriptions.

1. *Discover a mutual vision*: Persons who are "on the same wavelength" seem most able to connect on a psi level. In the CIA work, remote viewers who were open to and excited about the possibilities of psi phenomena tended to be the most successful, accurate, and reliable in their psychic experiences. As one *kupuna* put it, "Only those who see the invisible can do what may seem impossible."

2. *Be of one mind*: Russel Targ, who worked with the government programs on psychic spying, writes, "Psi is a partnership, not a master/slave relationship."[23] Try to be psi *partners* rather than one "psychic" trying to convince or dominate an unwilling participant.

3. *Connect heart to heart*: The best psi spies seemed emotionally

compatible—one might say working not only side by side but heart to heart. Psi events such as couple preactions are more likely to occur if you are practicing the cardio-synchronization technique on a regular basis.

4. *Pray from the same soul*: Many of the feelings of spiritual awe that accompany miracles are related to psi experiences. Leading psi researcher Dean Radin writes, "From a parapsychological point of view, the great religious scriptures are encyclopedic repositories of stories about psi effects—telepathy, clairvoyance, precognition, mental healing, and mind-matter interactions."[24]

5. *Dance to the same beat*: Slow down. Psi experiences tend to be subtle and slight in their manifestations, so an easier, less rushed, patient pace seems to establish an ecology conducive to the appearance of these wonderful things. Those psychic spies who did not rush one another and who proceeded with persistent patience were the most accurate in their remote viewing and hunches.

6. *Sing the same song*: In chapter 9, you read about the power of the word. Don't expect wonderful psi happenings to occur if you speak cynically about them. The successful psychic sleuths were those who spoke together as colleagues with mutual respect and kindness rather than with selfish arrogance and trying to "do it alone."

7. *Become one body*: If the "sixth sense" really comprises all five of our basic senses operating together, then couples who regularly share the *le`a* or sensual joy described in chapter 10 can actually experience a "twelfth sense" composed of the total of their senses joined together by acts of physical intimacy.

Sweet Shared Dreams

Practicing the paired pleasure prescriptions—and being aware of how doing so enhances the profound, timeless connection between you— prepares you for learning dream telepathy. I have saved this remarkable technique until last because establishing a foundation of paired pleasure will undoubtedly open your minds, hearts, souls, and bodies to this magical process.

You read early in the chapter that the success of dream telepathy is documented by careful scientific research. The odds of the results of these studies happening purely by chance are one in seventy-five million![25] Based on research involving clairvoyance, psychokinesis, and telepathy, then, here are the steps to connect and communicate in your dreams.[26]

1. *Practice dream control*: Psychologists know about the process of lucid dreaming. This happens when you actually control what you dream about. Try a little self–dream-control to prepare for shared dream telepathy. Before you go to sleep, select a dream you would like to have. Write it down, read it back to yourself several times, and then turn off the light. Do this several nights in a row. You may find that you are having dreams at least related to the theme of your chosen dream.

2. *Practice dream editing*: Once you have experienced a dream you feel was self-selected at least to some degree, the next step is to try to edit a dream in progress. You can influence your dreams by gently altering what is taking place while the dream is in process. You can be the director of the movie in your mind. Most of my patients have experienced this lucid dreaming several times in their life. One woman said, "I was walking in a beautiful field and saw my deceased father way up on a hill. In my dream I was going to walk on, but I changed it. I decided to walk up to the hill to hug him. I did, and it was wonderful."

3. *Practice dream sending and receiving*: Now you are ready to try sending and receiving dreams between your partner and you.

   Decide which of you will send and which will receive. The sender should select a simple picture of something he or she enjoys, perhaps a picture of a child, flower, or pet. Just be sure the dream sender does not show the picture to the dream receiver. If one of you is skeptical about all of this, the skeptic should be the sender. There is more action or mental effort required in pitching a dream than in catching it, and the skeptic may benefit from having a tangible assignment.

The sender should spend some quiet time alone several times during the day looking at the picture. Think about what the image means to you. If possible, talk to or call the person if you are going to be sending a person's image. If it's a pet, spend some time with the pet. If it's a flower, touch, smell, and hold the flower. The idea is to make as much conscious contact as possible with the image you want to send. You might even try drawing a copy of the picture to fix it in your mind. Remember, the dream receiver should have no idea what the image is.

Pick an evening when you are not going to bed exhausted or sick and are as free from stress, conflict, or next-day worries as possible. The sender should write down a dream about the picture that he or she would like to send via dream telepathy. Again, the receiver should not see the picture or the dream description. The description should be as detailed and specific as possible with regard to every aspect of theme, setting, characters, etc.

On the selected evening, spend some time hugging and holding your partner before you fall asleep. Try to synchronize your breathing by falling into an inhaling and exhaling rhythm that feels comfortable to both of you.

As soon as you wake up in the morning, write down any dreams either of you had. If either of you is awakened in the middle of the night, try to write down the dream that occurred just before awakening. This takes a lot of discipline, because the temptation is to go right back to sleep, but the brain censors our dreams, so the fresher the recollection, the more accurate the dream recall tends to be.

Later in the day, compare dream notes. Together, look at the sender's dream description and picture, and examine the sender's and receiver's dreams. Dreams tend to be poetic and highly symbolic, so look for symbols and images, not just exact pictures. Keep practicing; eventually you will see that dreams can be sent.

Have an open mind in your dream analysis. Dreams are mystical and magical. No one has yet fully understood why we dream or what dreams mean. They can be tricky and extremely subtle in their messages, so look for hidden meanings and feelings in the dreams. The tone and mood of a dream—more than specific images—tend to be what is received first.

Dream Telepathy in Action

Here is an example from my clinic of one couple's dream telepathy. It illustrates the symbolic nature of the dreamers' communication.

Husband (dream sender): "I didn't believe in this hocus-pocus stuff, so I picked a picture of my BMW to send. My wife had never seen the photo, because it was taken in the parking lot at work when I had the car delivered. I looked at the picture for a few days, and I drew a very poor likeness of it. I was caught in a horrendous traffic jam on the way home, so I had plenty of involuntary car-connection time. I even sat a little longer in the car when I got home that night just to fix it in my mind. The dream I wrote down was of my driving my BMW in the Indianapolis 500 and winning."

Wife (dream receiver): "I do believe in sending dreams. I know I can control my own dreams and dream what I want, but I wanted to see if my husband could do it. He went along with it more than I thought he would. When I woke up on the morning after our dream-test night, I just could not think of or remember a dream to write down. My husband laughed and said that proved this stuff was crazy. He didn't show me the picture, and we sort of forgot about the whole thing. I was sure he was going to try to send an image of one of our four kids, but it never came to me.

"The next night, something very bizarre happened. I had a horrendous nightmare that jarred me awake. My husband was on a business trip, but I got up and wrote down my nightmare. It was about my husband being chased around and around in circles by his doctor. The doctor had a long tube in his hand and said he wanted to do a colonoscopy on my husband. My husband kept running and running, yelling, 'No way. I have good BMs. No way.' The doctor said Fred was too pressured by the rat race and had to slow down for the sake of his health. The next scene made me cry; my husband had gotten sick because he wouldn't get the test the doctor wanted. He looked like he was bloated, and he weighed 500 pounds. I was terrified and woke up. The dream seemed scary but silly.

"When I showed my dream to my husband, he seemed nervous. He showed me the picture of his BMW he had tried to send the night of our test. He said his dream was about him going around and around a track of some kind, but he had fallen out of his car and was running with his fuel line in his hand. He lost the race because the fuel line had disconnected. We thought the racing around in circles, the fuel-line/tube thing, the 500 pounds and the Indianapolis 500, and even the 'BM' in BMW might be signs that a little bit of his dream had filtered through to me. Maybe we're reaching too far, but it was strange that I didn't get it until the next night. It sure has been a trip at least discussing this together."

This couple's dream-telepathy experiment resembles most of those in my clinic sample. Bits and pieces of the sender's dream seem to get though to the receiver, and, because dreams are timeless, many couples report a gap in the sending and receiving times. The essence of the theme of the dream—more than just the images—seems to come through strongest. In the case of this couple, the themes of rushing and racing through life and trying to "win" at the expense of health seemed to be the message sent and received. Even if it was not, talking about this issue seemed beneficial to them.

The dream-sending experiment reported here does not prove that dreams can be sent. Skeptics will say that the couple and I are making a mountain out of a molehill and are going too far in our interpretation. They may be right. Perhaps dream sending is impossible, although I doubt it. Even if it is impossible to send and receive dreams, it really does not matter to the task of forming a partnership in pleasure. The real benefit of trying to communicate through our dreams (that is, of realizing the possibility of a couple connection beyond time and space) is in the journey rather than in the destination.

And even if the whole idea is silly, taking the time together to do something out of the ordinary and to have fun conducting a couple's parapsychological experiment, whether it succeeds or not, is worth doing as another way to share a little joy.

The Sixth Sense Test

By now you know how to take and score the pleasure-prescription tests. You are aware of the importance of discussing the items. For this test, however, you might try a little psi-ing. Pick an item and try to telepathically communicate about it during the day. Even if one or both of you fail to retain any conscious memory of the "discussion," don't discount the benefits of playing together with a new idea.

The Sixth Sense Test

$$0 - 1 - 2 - 3 - 4 - 5 - 6 - 7 - 8 - 9 - 10$$

NOT AT ALL — — — OFTEN — — — ALWAYS

1. Do you experience "hunches" about something that might happen to one or both of you before any indication is visibly present?

2. Do you agree and are you both sensitive to the idea that you can "send thoughts" to one another?

3. Can you literally feel one another's gaze ?

4. Can you "just look" at each other and know what the other is thinking? Can you recognize "the look" your partner gives you?

5. Have you sensed that either of you is going to call by phone just before the call comes in?

6. Have you "felt" what your partner is experiencing, even when she or he is out of town?

7. Can you "preact" to one another by anticipating what your partner needs or wants?

8. Do you feel that you know what your partner really needs, even if he or she is not clear about such feelings himself or herself?

9. Do you make wishes together, or engage in private, superstitious couple rituals?

10. Are you equally "sixth sensitive" and open to those things and events that cannot be seen or touched (accepting of psi or psychic phenomenon)?

Total _____

The higher your score, the more likely it is that you already are psi-ing together.

Love Is a Wonderful Thing

An old Hawaiian phrase says, "*Makani ka`ili aloha o Kipahulu*"—translated literally as "the love-snatching wind of Kipahulu."[27] It refers to the mysterious psi connection that can be established between two lovers. The *mo`olelo* (legend) to which the phrase refers is of a woman of Kipahulu, Maui, who was tempted away from her husband by a man from O`ahu. A *kupuna* described the legend this way:

> Her husband agonized over losing her and grieved daily for the other half of his *naupaka* flower. He decided to consult a *kahuna* skilled in *hana aloha* sorcery, the love magic of Hawai`i. The *kahuna* told the man to find a container with a lid, and to speak his wish for *lokahi* (reconnection) with his lover into the container. The man expressed his *aloha* from his *pu`uwai* (heart) and told of his love for his wife. Then the *kahuna* uttered an incantation into the container, closed the lid, and hurled it into the sea. The wife was fishing one morning at Kalie on the island of O`ahu. She saw a container floating on a wave and waded out to pick it up. She opened it, whereupon a great loving and yearning for her *naupaka* half possessed her to return home again, where her heart belonged. She walked until she found a canoe, and then she paddled across the sea to become *kakou* again with her husband on Maui.

This last prescription, and much of what you have read in the eight prescriptions of paired pleasure, no doubt seems quite mysterious. A lover's wish sent psychically to recover his love may seem like the stuff of legend alone. The ideas you have just read—that we can share the same vision, be of one mind, connect hearts, live our prayers together, select the pace at which we will live and love, use words that have the power to protect our love, join as one body, and be psi partners forever—are oceanic concepts that challenge the doubting continental mind. They all teach of love as a wonderful thing, to use Abraham Lincoln's phrase. They are as much art as science, but as Einstein said, "The most beautiful experience we can have is the mysterious. It is the fundamental emotion which stands at the cradle of true art and true science."

Chapter Twelve

Sailing Through Life Together

`O ke aloha ka mea i ho`ola ai

Compassion is the healer.[1]

Refers to sharing the sacred breath of life and the power of *aloha* as the essence of healing and coping with life's crises.

Feeling Passion, Choosing Compassion

The proverb at the start of this chapter speaks of compassion as the healer. Feeling passion is automatic, but being compassionate is a choice.

If we say we feel passion for our partner, we are probably referring to the intense romantic, sensual, and sexual feelings that seem to happen to us when we are very attracted to someone. Feeling passionate is easy because we are genetically predisposed for it. It is our biological imperative to mate and to make copies of ourselves, and the drive to do so is elicited by all kinds of subtle cues unique to each culture. As our relationship grows, our passion may broaden to include more intense emotional feelings, but we have to give much time and attention to our partnership for it to become a *compassionate* one.

The word *passion* literally means "to suffer." We use it when we feel so intensely emotionally aroused by another person that it seems almost to hurt. The word has become synonymous with the suffering of Jesus during the period from the Last Supper to his agony on the cross. In its romantic meaning, passion is a sweet suffering, and most of us want to suffer the passion of deep love.

Compassion literally means "to suffer with." It refers to sharing the physical, emotional, and spiritual dimensions of the losses and crises in life.[2] To be partners in pleasure, you have to be willing to be partners in suffering. As a *kupuna* put it, "*Maui ola* means breath of life. Compassion means sharing *maui ola* with someone you love. When you share the sacred breath, you share the whole breath, the bad and the sweet. You can't share part of a breath. To share joy, you must share grief. That's the *naupaka* rule."

Now that you have read about the eight paired pleasure prescriptions, this last chapter helps you apply what you have learned to make your relationship not only passionate but deeply compassionate, so that you and your partner may become a unit that grows together, becomes stronger, and even increases its pleasure despite the suffering that is the price we pay for the gift of life.

Three Ways to Feel Great When Things Are Terrible

While psychologists and the lay public know that negative feelings accompany stress, there is now evidence to show that positive feelings also may come with bad times.[3] As I touched on in chapter 2, although we all feel anxiety and despair when we encounter stress, we can also experience a sense of challenge and mastery that leads to feelings of eagerness, excitement, and confidence. When we solve a problem or reduce our stress, we often feel happiness and pride and a calming sense of relief at the successful resolution.[4, 5]

Having negative feelings does not preclude you from having positive ones at the same time. While this may seem impossible, researchers have shown that people under severe stress—such as those diagnosed with AIDS or other serious illnesses—feel anxious but often also challenged and alert.[6]

Here are three ways, supported by research, that a partnership in pleasure might help you to feel great even when things seem to be going terribly:

1. *Mutual positive reappraisal*: Try applying the eight paired pleasure prescriptions to reframing what is going on in your life. One *kupuna* said, "His heart attack devastated us at first. We felt lost. I was scared to death I would lose him, and he was just plain scared of death. We talked for hours in the hospital and looked together for the rainbow after the rain. We came up with the idea that, while this was very serious, it really reminded us about the two *naupaka* gifts of time and attention. We did the cardio-synchronization ceremony many times, and we used the heart attack to focus on being more heart to heart together."

   Positive reappraisal means seeking together to look at a problem in a new light. It involves a mutual decision to relinquish previous goals and alter personal expectations in order to establish a new shared perspective, an amending of the couple's mission statement.

2. *Shared goal-directed and problem-solving behaviors*: When crisis strikes, we can sink or swim. Couples who choose to swim together seem to fall into a solve mode in which they mutually seek ways to deal with their problem. The key to finding any pleasure through the pain is to define the stressor as mutually experienced rather than seeing it as one person suffering and the other helping. The question becomes less "how can I help you?" than "now what can we do?" Instead of complaining and ruminating about a problem, partners in pleasure focus on what needs to be done to solve it. Doing so involves mutual information-seeking, planning together, and looking for and acquiring resources.[7] A *kupuna* said, "Working through this thing with my mother and her Alzheimer's was very, very rough for us, but it was *we* doing it, and that drew us together even more. In a strange way, it was something entirely new for us to do together that really mattered."

3. *Mutually infusing ordinary events with positive meaning*: When I was dying of cancer, I learned the value of celebrating the ordinary rather than looking ahead for the extraordinary. Doing jigsaw puzzles with my wife, watching a silly television program together that we would never have watched before, and counting how many lightning flashes we could see from my hospital-room window were just some of the simple but comforting activities we shared. When you expect to die, one of things you can do is lower your expectation of what constitutes a pleasurable life and seek joy and meaning in the mundane.

We also learned to look for, if not silver linings, at least anything other than dark ones. While my doctors dismissed the clinical significance of my being able to breathe for just a few minutes without an oxygen mask, for my wife and me it became a cause for major celebration, leading to hours of discussion that things might finally be turning around in the course of my illness. An advantage to being partners in pleasure is that you each have someone willing to search for meaning in the simplest of life events and to support your necessary delusions and hopeful denial.

Situational Significance

By "positive meaning" I am referring here to a situational meaning as opposed to a global meaning. Situational meaning is the evaluation of the significance attached to a stressful event or life occurrence. It is how the two of you decide to interpret what is happening here and now ("Breathing with the oxygen mask for one minute is a good sign today"). Global meaning, by contrast, is a more abstract, general meaning related to our fundamental assumptions and beliefs about life and its purpose.

To understand the kind of situational meaning that can help us find some joy even during terrible times, researchers posed the following question to caregivers of AIDS patients: "Describe something that you did or something that happened to you that made you feel good and that was meaningful to you and helped you get through the day."[8] Persons who were able to provide answers to this question tended to cope better with their stress than those who could not find a little relief in any of the events of their day.

I suggest you ask the question a little differently as partners in pleasure. I suggest you ask, "What has happened to our relationship today that has made us feel good together, was at least a little meaningful for both of us, and helped us to be more *kakou*?" Remember, I'm not talking here about looking for a life-altering event. A shared time during the day when you seemed to experience a sixth-sense connection might be enough to enhance the ordinary with some jointly discovered meaning.

Frequent "benefit reminding" between partners is an important adaptive tool in a fast-paced world that can contain many quick and surprising setbacks. It is one of the perks that comes with a commitment to a partnership in pleasure.[9]

A Higher Monogamy

Author George Leonard wrote about what he called high monogamy, in which both partners put their marriage first in all regards.[10] A partnership in pleasure is similar to high monogamy in that it transforms the partners into more than two single-minded people. They mark off their life passages not through their own "midlife crises" but through the development of their relationship. They see their relationship as a kind of growing child for whose welfare they are equally responsible.

Deciding to form a partnership in pleasure is one of the most significant choices we make. It colors all that we do and say and influences every decision we make—our purpose, thinking, emotions, spirit, time, words, sensuality, and consciousness. It dictates where and how we focus our attention. It is a way of life and of seeing life through the lens of the eight paired pleasure prescriptions and the issues they address.

Here is a review of the prescriptions as they relate to the key areas of living:

▼ Discovering a mutual vision—PURPOSE: *Kakou* changes your definitions of both success and happiness to those of "our" success and happiness; it ultimately shapes your answers to key questions such as: What is the most important thing to do, when should I do it, and with whom?

▼ Thinking with one mind—THINKING: *Kakou* shapes your reflections about what is on your mind, how you think about life, and how you make decisions and judgments; they become based on "us" rather than "me."

▼ Connecting heart to heart—EMOTIONS: *Kakou* determines your definition of what constitutes true love; it literally connects you heart to heart with another person in a shared daily feeling ecology.

▼ Praying from the same soul—SPIRIT: *Kakou* determines that you pray as one and decide together to lead a life that is a prayer in action.

▼ Dancing to the same beat—TIME: *Kakou* determines that your time and attention are couple-focused, and that time is interpreted, valued, and spent as two rather than one.

▼ Singing the same song—WORDS: *Kakou* changes your way of speaking. It causes you to laugh, talk, and cry from the perspective of what is happening to "us" rather than to "me."

▼ Becoming one body—SENSUALITY: *Kakou* determines your view and fantasies of what constitutes pleasing and fulfilling sexuality by replacing "my" sex life with "our" sensual and intimate life.

▼ Sharing a sixth sense—CONSCIOUSNESS: *Kakou* is not only *on* our mind; it *becomes* our mind. It is a non-two thinking between two people that opens up the possibility of psi-ing together.

Split but Never Separated

Aunty Betty held the *ipu* as if it were her child. It had once been cracked by a customs agent during one of Aunty's many world trips to teach the lessons of *naupaka*. The agent was certain there was some illegal substance inside the polished and decorated gourd, so to Aunty's horror he smashed it open. Once he glanced inside the *ipu*, he thought nothing was in there, but he was terribly wrong. The *ipu* contained centuries of *mana*, the loving energy of Aunty's ancestors and `ohana. Aunty was heartbroken. She and her `ohana worked for weeks restoring the *ipu*. They offered *pule* (prayers) for its healing.

On this day, Aunty lifted the mended *ipu* with pride so everyone could see the stitched line where it had cracked in half, now highlighted in dark paint. She pointed to the crack and told Ka Ha Naupaka the story of her *ipu*'s crisis and the reuniting of its two halves.

She told of the special significance of the *ipu*, the bottle-shaped gourd that Hawaiians have long used as receptacles to hold water, *poi*, and other valuable materials. They serve as drums for *hula* and for other sacred ceremonies. Aunty's *ipu* was beautifully decorated with Hawaiian patterns burned around its neck. There were symbols that represented the various meanings of *aloha*: patience, unity, pleasantness, humility, and tenderness. The *ipu* had been in her `ohana for generations and was treated not as an inanimate object but as a living, feeling, and revered member of the family.

"We do not seek to hide the wound," she said as she gently stroked the *ipu*. "We have healed it now, and its two halves are again one, but we painted over where the wound was so it will stand as a reminder that nothing can break apart *kakou*. It was hurt, but not destroyed. Like our precious *naupaka*, its halves are forever one. Nothing can destroy that. *Kakou* is forever."

Aunty slowly removed the lid from the *ipu*. She looked around, her eyes inviting the *kupuna* to chant softly with her. "When we remove the lid from the *ipu*, we remember that all that is said and felt will enter the *ipu*. When the lid is off, we must honor the sharing of the sacred breath of life and the power of our words. We must remember *kakou*. We choose our words very carefully, because our ancestors will hear them and judge us. We must think of what is going into the *ipu* and ask if we are speaking from our heart and with the spirit of Hawai`i: *ha* for the breath that we all breathe together; *wai* for the water and the `aina (land) that sustains us and which we must sustain; and *i* for the spirit of *aloha*, the love that binds us like the *naupaka* across time and space forever."

For the rest of the meeting, the *ipu* sat as a reminder of *aloha*. Everyone, even the hotel service staff, was constantly aware that the *ipu* was open and that great care must be taken to see that only *aloha* filled the air and that the breath we shared was pure and free of selfishness, arrogance, negativity, hostility, and animosity toward anyone.

Making Your Own *Ipu*

We have explored how pleasure in the *naupaka* sense arises from looking at life from the perspective of *kakou*, cherishing every breath together as one breath shared between two lovers. You have read about the eight paired pleasure prescriptions, the oceanic way of thinking associated with the *naupaka* principles, and the immense power of *kakou*—a non-two orientation to life ever vigilant to our half-ness. As a symbol to help you remember what we have explored, I suggest that you make your own *ipu* as a couple. Much as a revered elder might sit at the head of the table, Ka Ha Naupaka couples' *ipu* always sit in places of honor in their homes. They serve as constant reminders of *kakou* and *aloha*.

In Hawai`i, we spend days selecting the right gourd. Actually, we spend days trying to open our hearts so that the right gourd can find us. As we sort through piles of mud-stained gourds, one always seems to call out to us. We clean and stroke it for hours, and then carve it, decorate it, and *pule* over it until we feel we have helped the *ipu* become *kakou* with us. As Tutu Mama, the revered Hawaiian matriarch whom you have read about, said, "You do not make or create your *ipu*; you open your heart and allow it to form and develop itself and to join with you forever."

You can find your own form of *ipu*. If you can't come to Hawai`i to make one, you can make or select any object you feel represents something special to your relationship. Be sure the *ipu* has a top that you can remove and replace.

Be sure also that the *ipu* belongs to both of you. Some couples in my seminars make two *ipu*, each representing one of the half-flowers of the *naupaka*. Others work together to make one *ipu*, representing their unity. What matters is that you decide together what will represent the ideas you have read about in this book—and that your *ipu* is *kakou* and not `o wau.

Partner Protocol

In Hawai`i, protocol is very important, and so is ceremony. In fact, ceremony in Hawai`i is a form of body prayer Doing things the right way over and over again is a necessary part of daily living, loving, and working. This ritualistic nature of life is how we bring the past to the present and show our ancestors that we are aware of their presence in all we do.

The word *ritual* comes from an Indo-European root that means "to fit together."[11] It originally referred to such things as art, weaving, arithmetic, or anything that tended to draw things together to create order. As you journeyed through the paired pleasure prescriptions, you encountered many exercises that the continental brain may have called gimmicks or tests. But the oceanic mind recognized them as ceremonies or rituals intended to help you "fit together" the two halves of your brain, or the two partners in a relationship—like two halves of the *naupaka* reunited again.

Other than the marriage ceremony, modern couples seldom practice regular rituals that celebrate and confirm their partnership. The eight prescriptions and all of the exercises and tests associated with them are offered as modern forms of partner protocol, ways to stay aware of the miracle of being partners in pleasure. Having your own couple's *ipu* can help you incorporate that loving protocol into your daily life. If you have children, there are few better ways to give them the gift they need most in their lives: a consistent sign of two persons showing their commitment to loving together forever.

The process of selecting and making an *ipu* can be a ceremony of love that couples incorporate into a renewal of their marriage vows. I recently attended a "renewal of commitment to *kakou*" ceremony on the beach at sunset. As lovely Hawaiian music played and everyone prayed, the couple turned to hold up the *ipu* they had made. The wife said to the group, "Thirty years ago, we gave each other rings. Now, we're sharing a symbol we made together." The husband said, "As we are 'ours,' so is the *ipu* 'ours.' It is like our life together in *kakou*."

Things That Remind

Mea ho`omana`o refers in Hawaiian to "things that remind." It literally means "to bring forth a thought or idea." Your *ipu* can be your *naupaka mea ho`omana`o*, a shared reminder of the pleasure of seeing life through four eyes, with one heart and a shared soul.

One couple on the mainland who attended a *naupaka* seminar selected as their *ipu* a wicker basket with a top attached. It was a family heirloom originally used by the wife's great-grandmother as a picnic basket, and it had been in their attic collecting dust for years. The couple repaired it, painted it, and engraved on it dates that were significant in their relationship. Inside they placed a brief summary of each paired pleasure prescription, to pull out from time to time as a *naupaka* reminder. They also added other reminders as they were inspired to do so. I suggest you create your own *mea ho`omana`o* together.

Describing the role of the *ipu* in their daily life, the wife said, "We have it right in the middle of our kitchen table. It's not very big, but it's right there to remind us about *kakou*. We even carved the word *naupaka* into the top. When we sit down to eat, we open the top to remind us about being two halves in constant need of each other. We pull out one of the *naupaka* messages every so often."

The husband added, "When we're in some kind of snit or conflict or under stress, one of us usually goes and gets the *ipu* basket. That's our signal to try one of the prescriptions like cardio-synchronization. We've put most of these exercises in the *ipu* and pull one out when we need it."

Partnership Passages

Many books about happiness and health focus on passages or developmental stages through which individuals pass on their way to self-fulfillment and well-being. The *kakou* view of a pleasure partnership is concerned with "partnership passages," the stages and developmental tasks couples experience on their way to shared pleasure. Consider how what you have learned about the *kakou* view of loving and living as *naupaka* halves might apply to the following eight stages of a life together.

To help you remember them, the key words describing each stage begin with the letter *C* (for couple). With each, I have included a message from paradise: notes from couples who have come to Hawai`i to learn about the *naupaka* principle.

1.   Partnership Passage One: Commitment

The first couple development task is to define the relationship's view of commitment. You have read about the difference between passion and compassion—about the relatively easy passionate beginning of a relationship and the more difficult challenge of a compassionate decision to remain within it forever.

Couple's note: "It was love at first sight for us, and we really fell into it. Then we learned that we had to stop falling and start walking together. Our commitment is to our relationship overall, and that has meant each of us saying no to individual opportunities that have come up that we both decided would rob us of the two *naupaka* gifts, our time with and attention to one another."

2.   Partnership Passage Two: Compatibility

You have read about the alpha and beta styles of thinking that often characterize partners. Once the decision to commit has been made, the next challenge is not only to tolerate but to benefit from the unique styles of living, working, and making love that each partner brings to the relationship.

Couple's note: "We went through what we expect is pretty common in couples married for a while: we seemed out of sexual synch. One of us wanted to make love when the other was tired, and we became concerned that we were not sexually compatible. Every night became a test, and we wondered who wanted to do what to whom, when, and for how long. Then we just focused on being one body. We agreed to just hold each other without any obligation or pressure for sex and let arousal happen to us together instead of trying to arouse each other. We decided to stop thinking about having sex and to let sex have us in the sense that it would sort of happen to both of us."

3.   Partnership Passage Three: Challenge

After committing to one another and allowing compatibility to develop, the next partner passage relates to balancing career or work with relationship time and investment.

Couple's note: "The challenge was in our goals. We didn't really think you could have a truly great marriage and have both people be hugely successful individually. We were right. Our definition of success was related to promotions at work, money, and prestige. We needed a new mutual definition of success and really worked on our couple's mission statement. It was not easy, and it's still in progress, but at least we're taking the *kakou* view of success rather than the 'mine' and 'yours' orientation that was stressing us."

4.   Partnership Passage Four: Children

Next comes one of the most important passages of all, the mutual decisions about whether to have children and about how invested in children the relationship (not one partner) will be, in both word and deed.

Couple's note: "Kids—that was our most difficult problem. We had to learn to think about what our relationship was going to give to the world in a broader framework. Kids were one way, but there are many ways to share and give back to the world. We eventually decided we wanted to have children, but when you asked us why, we never really thought about that. We had to consider whether we would just have them or really commit together to truly raise them. We went over and over the guidelines about homemaking and decided we were asking the wrong question. The issue became not whether we would have kids but whether we were both willing to give up some of our individual goals to allow our children to fully have us."

5. Partnership Passage Five: Caring

Whatever the decision regarding children, the issue of assisting parents is the next passage for partners. Determining how much time and attention, how much obligation, who should do what how often, and how much money should be spent on helping parents is an ongoing, challenging developmental task for relationships.

Couple's note: "Parenting our parents was beginning to be the big issue that we got in trouble over. We had to separate guilty obligation from caring love. When Dave's grandfather lost control of his bowels, we really had to deal with the issue. Then we noticed that each of us had spent a lot of time changing our new babies' diapers and never complained about it. When Gramps became incontinent, we decided that he had a hell of a lot more seniority and had given much more to us than our babies had at that time, and that we should take the same caring approach to changing his diaper as we did with our babies."

6. Partnership Passage Six: Coherence

The next stage in *kakou* development is finding a sense of shared meaning in life. This is a mutual search for the global kind of meaning mentioned earlier: a shared perspective on religion, spirituality, and what happens after physical death.

Couple's note: "We had gone to church together every Sunday since the day we were married, but we never really talked about issues like reincarnation, life after death, what heaven is and is not, and what we called the 'spiritual specifics.' Now we talk at length about these things. Right now our topic of conversation is trying to come up with a common and mutually comfortable and meaningful way of explaining the terrible things that keep happening in the world."

7.   Partnership Passage Seven: Control

As time passes and the issue of growing old together becomes more of a reality, the developmental task becomes one of accepting the natural deterioration that accompanies getting older and dealing with how aging affects each partner's body and health differently. This stage requires the couple skills not only of achieving a sense of control together over the relationship's destiny as it is influenced by aging, but also of mutually knowing when to give up and accept those aspects of life that are beyond our control.

Couple's note: "It happened when we were looking at our wedding pictures. We laughed, but we were really moved. We look so old now. We have gone on a million diets and bought enough exercise machines and health-club memberships to serve an army, but we see now that fearing aging and fighting against it to stay young forever only set us up for failure. We know that no one is free of the fact that, from the time you are born, gravity is tugging and pulling you back into the ground. We talk a lot about how much we are willing to do in terms of diet, exercise, and other health issues as opposed to just enjoying life together. We got hold of your book *The Pleasure Prescription* that talks about health terrorism and the importance of enjoying life rather than trying to outrun or under-eat death."

8.   Partnership Passage Eight: Connection

Accepting the fact that physical partnership is as mortal as love is immortal is the last stage of couple development. Here, the *naupaka* principle can bring comfort because it teaches that time and space do not limit a strong *kakou* relationship. Discussing and dealing with the issue of partner loss and surviving the loneliness of losing a partner are very difficult, but embracing the idea that we are, like sugar and water, together forever despite our physical transformation into other forms of energy offers consolation. The two *naupaka* flowers are never truly separated by the distance between mountain and sea.

A widow's note: "We had talked about which one of us would go first. When he died, I wasn't ready at all. When I wrote to you to ask if you took single people into the *naupaka* seminars, you said no. I laughed when you added that you took people who were currently physically separated but willing to acknowledge a connection beyond the physical that could never be ended. When you asked if our relationship was over, I thought you were nuts. I told you my husband was dead, but you said you didn't ask that. You wanted to know if our relationship was dead, and I knew it wasn't. When I came and shared with the other *naupaka* couples, I could sense the same infinite love that my husband and I still have. That's the advantage of the *naupaka* idea. There are no boundaries, and that includes the one we fear the most—the boundary between life and death."

Memories are forever, and as with sugar and water, all systems are connected forever. Author Virginia Peterson captures the idea of this partnership passage when she writes, "However often marriage is dissolved, it remains indissoluble. Real divorce of heart and nerve and fiber does not exist, since there is no divorce from memory."[12]

Going *Holoholo* Together

The Hawaiian word *holoholo* means to sail. In its most basic sense, a partnership in pleasure is an enjoyable way of navigating the calms and storms of life together and enjoying the voyage. When Hawaiians say they are "going *holoholo*," they mean they are just kicking back and going through life easily and gently, and that is what it feels like to be in a pleasure partnership.

Any couple can be happy when things are going great. The true test of a partnership in pleasure comes when the gale blows and the storms and stresses associated with life's passages rage. As Shakespeare pointed out, all ships seem to handle well when the seas are not stormy. The skill of a sailor is tested when the seas rise up, and the same is true of partners in pleasure. They know that life is not a matter of being given all the breaks but of being able to find joy and happiness even during the bad breaks.

Author Anne Morrow Lindbergh captured the essence of a partnership in pleasure when she wrote, "The best marriages, like the best lives, were both happy and unhappy. There was even a kind of necessary tension, a certain tautness between the partners that gave the marriage strength, like the tautness of a full sail. You went forward with it."[13] Partners in pleasure sail forward together under a taut sail, powered by *aloha*, steadied by a shared soul.

Epilogue

The Six Most Important Words — and a Love Song

A *Makana* (Gift) from Tutu Mama and Ka Ha Naupaka

Throughout the pages of this book, you have come across the wisdom of Tutu Mama Ellis, the ninety-six-year-old native-Hawaiian matriarch. Her proverb at the end of her daughter Aunty Betty's foreword—*Hauoli ke like na mea male* (Happy is a marriage, shared)—set the tone for all you have read in these pages. As her *haumana* (student), I most humbly share with you the wonderful gift Tutu shared with me for this book, her words of *aloha* from Hawai`i that teach the lessons of the *mo`olelo* of the *naupaka*. She offers them with the wish that your relationship will find loving pleasure forever, and I present her words here exactly as they were given to me.

This epilogue ends with the words to "The Song of the *Naupaka*." It is sung by Ka Ha Naupaka at their meetings, and they share it here as their *makana* to you and their invitation to know in your heart the enduring grace of *aloha*, of *naupaka* love.

Tutu's Words of *Aloha*

The *kaona* (hidden meaning) of these words lies in the embracement of *kakou* (we) and the dismissal of *oukou* (you). They are words of *aloha* for you to share together in your daily life as *naupaka* connected forever.

The six most important words . . .

I admit I made a mistake.

The five most important words . . .

You did a good job.

The four most important words . . .

What is your opinion?

The three most import words . . .

If you please . . .

The two most important words . . .

Thank you!

The most important word . . . **We!**

The least important word . . . **I.**

The Song of the *Naupaka*

O `oe ku`u lei o naupaka

You are my lei, o naupaka

Ke onaona a kealoha

The sweet fragrance of love

Hau`oli mau kaua

Happy forever we will be

I na pue ala onaona

My sweet fragrant blossom

A pili mau loa kealoha

Forever close, my love

He pua no `oe ho`opai ae ke kehau

Indeed you are my flower freshly scented with dew

Kou maka palupalu mau momi a lohilohi

Your eyes soft, like pearls shining

Maliu mai e ku`u pua

Come to me, my flower

Na`u e inu e kou nani

That I may drink of your beauty

Pulama a malama o naupaka

To hold, to cherish, o naupaka

Hawaiian Glossary

Notes

Bibliography

Index

Hawaiian Pronunciation Guide and Glossary

Following are some of the Hawaiian words used throughout the text. The definitions are based on the *Hawaiian Dictionary,* by M. K. Pukui and S. H. Elbert (Honolulu, HI: University of Hawai`i Press, 1986), and are given enhanced meaning from my "talking story" with the Ka Ha Naupaka group and other *kupuna* (elders), *kahuna* (healers), and *kumu* (teachers). Hawaiian words have many meanings, and the context in which they appear often determines their definition.

Pronouncing Hawaiian Words

The Hawaiian language has the shortest alphabet in the world—twelve letters. In simplified form, here is a guide to pronouncing Hawaiian words.

Vowels

a like *a* in above

e like *e* in bet

i like *y* in city

o like *o* in sole

u like *oo* in moon

Unlike in English, there are no silent vowels; all vowels are pronounced. For example, whereas, according to the rules of English pronunciation, the word *hale* might rhyme with *mail,* in Hawaiian it sounds more like *hol-lay.*

Consonants and Diacritical Marks

p, k about the same as in English but with less aspiration and emphasis

h, l, m, n   about as in English

w   when it appears after *i* and *e,* usually like *v;* after *u* and *o,* usually like *w;* initially and after *a,* like *v* or *w*

`    a glottal stop (`okina); similar to the sound between *ohs* in the English "oh-oh"

-    a macron *(kahako)* over any vowel prolongs the sound of the vowel. To simplify the reading and pronunciation of the many Hawaiian words and phrases in the chapters, I have left off the macrons. This is a Hawaiian spelling error, but I hope it will encourage the reader to make the effort to begin to learn to pronounce the words. My apologies to my teachers for this simplification.

Hawaiian Words and Phrases in the Text

`A`a a no`on`ono `ole* — Selfish disregard for others

`Ae* — Yes

`Aha Kuka* — A mutual consultation, to talk it over together

`Aha Mele* — Lecture/concert

Ahonui — Persistent patience

`Aina* — Land, the earth, the source

Aka — Laughter

Akahai — Gentle tenderness and kindness

Ali`i — Hawaiian royalty

Alo — To give, share

Aloha — Literally means "sharing the sacred breath of life"; also means love, hello, and good-bye.

`*A`ole*` — No

`*A`ole Pilikia*` — No problem

Au`a holomau — Selfish success

Aumakua — Deified ancestors

`*Eha Koni*` — Heartache

Ha — The sacred breath of life

Ha`aha`a — Humble modesty

Haipule — Humility, deference, and reverence, as to the gods or God

Hale — House, home

Hana Aloha — Love magic or sorcery

Haole — Refers to a white person or to adopting the ways of a white person; also refers to someone who seems "breathless," hurried, and more taking than giving of the sacred breath (the opposite of *aloha* or sharing of the breath)

Haumana — Student

He Kakalaioa — An unpleasant person

Hinano — Male blossom of the pandanus tree, sometimes seen as an aphrodisiac or erotic stimulant

Hi`u — Tail

Holoholo — To sail, to walk, to go forth for pleasure

Honi — Hawaiian kissing, done by placing noses side by side and inhaling the breath of the partner

Ho`olu — Please

Ho`opa`i — Punishment by the gods

Ho`waiwa — Prosperity

Huahua`i — Sexual climax

Hua`i — Disclose, share

Ihi — Respect

`*I`o`i`o*` — Clitoris

Ka Ha Naupaka — Literally, "the breath of the naupaka," referring to an enduring aloha that transcends time and space; also the name of the group of married Hawaiian couples who provided their wisdom and love for this book

Kahuna — Expert in any field, particularly as qualified by lineage, spiritual experience, and training; also sometimes refers to a healer or priest

Kai — Sea

Kakou — Us, we, or all of us together

Kaku — Spirit

Kane — Man, male

Kaona — Hidden meaning of a word or phrase

Kapu — Taboo, forbidden, prohibition, cultural rule

Kaukau — A more spontaneous, casual kind of prayer, as if talking with the *aumakua* or ancestors

Ke Akua — God, the Higher Power

Keiki — Child, children

Kilipue — Hug ardently

Kilu — Small coconut shell cut in half and used in old Hawaiian games

Kulia Kakou — To try together

Kulikuli — Quiet (or "be quiet")

Kumu — Teacher

Kupuna — Hawaiian elder

Lani — Heaven

Laumana — Student

Le`a — Joy; also sexual pleasure and orgasm

Leo Nui — Loud-voiced

Lokahi — Unity and harmony; also, tied fast together

Mahalo — Thank you, but also, to give respect and appreciation to the ancestors and for honoring pono

Maha`oi — Selfish arrogance, presumptiveness

Mahele — To share

Makana — Gift

Makua — Parents

Mana — Subtle, invisible energy

Mana`o — Wisdom, knowledge

Manawa — Hawaiian concept of time, the here and now

Manawa ole — Enjoy life right here and right now

Maukaukau — Ready!

Mea — Thing; sometimes refers to the female genitalia

Mea ho`oman`o — Thing(s) to remember, reminder

Mele — Song, sing

Menehune — The mythical "little people" of early Hawai`i

Mo`olelo — Legend

Nani — Beautiful

Naupaka — The mountain and seaside half-flower that is a symbol of enduring love across space and time

Naupaka Kahakai — The *naupaka* half-flower of the sea; represents the female lover

Naupaka Kuahiwi — The *naupaka* half-flower of the mountains; represents the male lover

Noho malie — Keep still, be quiet

`Ohana — Family

Okole — Buttocks

`Olelo No`eau — Hawaiian proverb or saying

Oli — Chant

`Olu`olu — Pleasantly agreeable

Ono — Delicious, tasty; sometimes refers to savoring or relishing something

Oukou — You

`O Wau — I

Pa`a* — Like many Hawaiian words, *pa`a has many meanings, depending on the context or qualifying words around it. As I have used it, it means grounded, solid, adhering, durable, firm, and permanent.

Pahu — Drum

Papa — Mother Earth

Papale — Hat

Poheo — Knob; sometimes refers to the head of the penis

Poi — The Hawaiian staff of life, made from cooked taro corms that have been pounded and thinned with water; *poi* represents the living *`aina.*

Pono — The natural order of things, that which is righteous, proper, the way things are supposed to be

Po`o — Head

Pule — Prayer

Pu`uwai — Literally "lump of water," it means heart.

Tutu — Term of endearment for grandmother

`Ume — Attract, entice

Waena — Middle

Wahine — Woman

Wakea — Father Sky

Notes

Introduction

1. M. K. Pukui, `Olelo No`Eau: Hawaiian Proverbs and Poetical Sayings, no. 245 (Honolulu, HI: Bishop Museum Press, 1983), 29.

2. The concept of rock versus water logic was first presented and discussed by Edward de Bono in his book *I Am Right—You Are Wrong: From Rock Logic to Water Logic* (New York: Viking Press, 1991).

3. J. Leo, "The Sleeper Effect," *U.S. News and World Report*, 2 October 2000, 18.

4. P. Amato and A. Booth, *A Generation at Risk.* (Boston, MA: Harvard University Press, 2000).

5. J. Wallerstein, *The Unexpected Legacy of Divorce* (New York: Hyperion, 2000).

6. As reported by P. Amato and A. Booth, *A Generation at Risk.*

7. L. Waite, *The Case for Marriage* (New York: Doubleday, 2000).

Chapter 1

1. Psychologist Carl Jung wrote that love is like a chemical interaction. When two people join in true love, both are transformed by the joining.

2. For a discussion of the immune- and health-enhancing aspects of intimacy and connection, see H. Dreher, *The Immune Power Personality* (New York: Dutton, 1995).

3. See the work of J. W. Pennebaker, *Opening Up: The Healing Power of Confiding in Others* (New York: William Morrow, 1990).

4. For one research example of the health benefits of love or "affiliative trust" (shared love and trust), see J. R. McKay, "Assessing Aspects of Object Relations Associated with Immune Function: Development of the Affiliative Trust-Mistrust Coding System," *Psychological Assessment* 3:4 (1991): 641–47.

5. For one example of the health benefits of "self-complexity" and the availability of many roles, see P. W. Linville, "Self-Complexity and Affective Extremity: Don't Put All of Your Eggs in One Cognitive Basket," *Social Cognition* 3:1 (1985): 94–120.

6. For research on the "helper's high" of helping another person find a degree of joy in her life, see A. Luks, *The Healing Power of Doing Good* (New York: Fawcett Columbine, 1992).

7. E. Diener et al., "Subjective Well-Being: Three Decades of Progress," *Psychological Bulletin* 125 (1999): 276–302.

8. As qtd. in T. Moore's *Soul Mates* (New York: HarperPerennial, 1987), 56.

9. For a pioneering discussion of well-being and relationships, see J. Shapiro and D. H. Shapiro, "Well-Being and Relationship," in *Beyond Health and Normality*, edited by R. Walsh and D. H. Shapiro (New York: Van Nostrand Reinhold Company, 1983), 207–14.

Chapter 2

1. M. K. Pukui, `Olelo No`Eau: Hawaiian Proverbs and Poetical Sayings*, no. 1852 (Honolulu, HI: Bishop Museum Press, 1983), 200.

2. The concept of SOC—sense of coherence—as a major health factor was developed by psychologist Aaron Antonovsky; see *Unraveling the Mystery of Health: How People Manage Stress and Stay Well* (San Francisco, CA: Jossey-Bass, 1987).

3. For a discussion of stress and heart disease and managing stress, see Paul E. Bracke and Carl E. Thoresen, "Reducing Type-A Behavior Patterns: A Structured-Group Approach," in *Heart and Mind: The Practice of Cardiac Psychology*, edited by Robert Allan and Stephen Scheidt (Washington, DC: American Psychological Association, 1996).

4. For example, see Marianne Delon, "The Patient in the CCU Waiting Room: In-Hospital Treatment of the Cardiac Spouse, in *Heart and Mind: The Practice of Cardiac Psychology*, edited by Robert Allan and Steven Scheidt (Washington, DC: American Psychological Association, 1996), 421–31.

5. R. F. DeBusk, "Sexual Activity Triggering Myocardial Infarction: One Less Thing to Worry About," *Journal of the American Medical Association* 275:3 (1996): 1447–48.

6. A study published in the *Journal of the American Medical Association* showed a relationship between lack of sexual intimacy in the days and months prior to heart attack and the occurrence of heart attack (J. E. Muller et al, "Triggering Myocardial Infarction by Sexual Activity: Low Absolute Risk and Prevention by Regular Physical Exertion?" *Journal of the American Medical Association* 275:6 [1996]: 1405–9). See also David Sobel and Robert Ornstein, "Sexual Activity and Heart Attack: Not to Worry," *Mind/Body Health Newsletter* 5 (1996): 2–3.

7. D. Ornish, *Love and Survival: The Scientific Basis for the Healing Power of Intimacy* (New York: HarperPerennial, 1999), 14.

8. For a brief and fascinating discussion of the power of prayer, see Larry Dossey, *Prayer Is Good Medicine* (San Francisco, CA: HarperSanFrancisco, 1996).

9. For example, see Fred Sicher, Elisabeth Targ, Dan Moore, and Helene Smith, "A Randomized Double-Blind Study of the Effect of Distant Healing in a Population with Advanced AIDS," *Western Journal of Medicine* 169 (December 1998): 356–63.

10. Norman Cousins's book *Head First: The Biology of Hope and the Healing Power of the Human Spirit* (New York: Dutton, 1989) presents several studies that document the power of laughter and humor to promote healing and maintain health.

11. As qtd. in Joan Borysenko and Miroslav Borysenko, *The Power of the Mind to Heal* (Carson, CA: Hay House, 1994), ix.

Chapter 3

1. M. K. Pukui, `Olelo No`Eau: Hawaiian Proverbs and Poetical Sayings*, no. 1068 (Honolulu, HI: Bishop Museum Press, 1983), 114.

2. S. Covey, *The 7 Habits of Highly Effective People* (New York: Simon and Schuster, 1989), 106.

3. These terms are used by author Guy Glaxton, *Hare Brain, Tortoise Mind*, (London: Ecco Press, 1997) to describe findings from cognitive science about the differences between a fast versus a more intuitive thinking process.

4. For an example of dream telepathy, see J. B. Rhine, *Extra-Sensory Perception* (Boston, MA: Bruce Humphries, 1964).

Chapter 4

1. M. K. Pukui and S. H. Elbert, *Hawaiian Dictionary* (Honolulu, HI: University of Hawai`i Press, 1986), 372.

2. J. Gottman, *Why Marriages Succeed and Fail . . . and How You Can Make Yours Last* (New York: Simon and Schuster, 1994), 14–15.

3. Pukui and Elbert, *Hawaiian Dictionary*, 4th ed., 338.

4. There are many kinds of *lei*. I was given the honor of receiving a *lei hulu*, a deep-red feather *lei* that will last forever if I care for it and respect it.

5. For more about Erikson's views of human development and the importance of intimacy, see E. H. Erikson, *Childhood and Society* (New York: W. W. Norton, 1950).

6. See J. L. A. Horna, "The Dual Pattern of Marital Conflict," paper presented to the Eleventh World Congress of Sociology, New Delhi, India, 1986.

7. R. W. Weiss, *Staying the Course* (New York: Free Press, 1990), 286.

8. L. G. Russek and G. E. Schwartz, "Narrative Descriptions of Parental Love and Caring Predict Health Status in Midlife: A 35-Year Follow-Up of the Harvard Mastery of Stress Study," *Alternative Therapies* 2:6 (1996): 55–62.

9. A persuasive and data-based criticism of men's failure to help out around the house is presented by Anne Machung, *Second Shift: Working Parents and the Revolution at Home* (New York: Viking, 1989).

10. These are often referred to by researchers as husbands specializing in "instrumental" or executional "get-it-done, fix-it, honey-to-do-list" tasks, whereas wives specialize in so-called "expressive" tasks such as keeping the home going by balancing the food, the spending, and the daily details. See T. Parsons and R. F. Bales, *Family, Socialization, and Interaction Process* (Glencoe, IL: Free Press, 1955). See also D. Gutmann, *Reclaimed Powers* (New York: Basic Books, 1987).

11. S. Lindner, *The Harried Leisure Class* (New York: Columbia University Press, 1971).

12. As qtd. in S. Covey, *The 7 Habits of Highly Effective People* (New York: Simon and Schuster, 1989), 106.

13. Covey, *The 7 Habits of Highly Effective People*, 18.

14. This story and myth was taught to me by my *kumu* or teacher Frank Kawaikapuokalani Hewett, the cultural director at the Waimanalo Health Center on the island of O`ahu.

15. For an example of "middle way" thinking, see Mahasi Sayadaw, *The Progress of Insight* (San Francisco, CA: Buddhist Publication Society, 1973).

16. J. Kornfield, "Higher Consciousness: An Inside View," in *Beyond Health and Normality*, edited by R. Walsh and D. Shapiro (New York: Van Nostrand Reinhold Company, 1983), 333.

Chapter 5

1. M. K. Pukui, `Olelo No`Eau: Hawaiian Proverbs and Poetical Sayings*, no. 376 (Honolulu, HI: Bishop Museum Press, 1983), 46.

2. For a discussion of the differences between male and female thinking styles, see A. Moir and D. Jessel, *Brain Sex: The Real Differences Between Men and Women* (New York: Lyle Stuart, 1991).

3. Moir and Jessel, *Brain Sex*, 8. See also Richard Restak, *The Brain Has a Mind of Its Own: Insights from a Practicing Neurologist* (New York: Harmony Books, 1991).

4. J. Durden-Smith and D. De Simone, *Sex and the Brain* (Lancaster, England: MTP Press, 1980).

5. As qtd. In Durden-Smith and De Simone, *Sex and the Brain*, 20.

6. J. Archer, "Biological Explanations of Psychological Sex Differences" in *Exploring Sex Differences*, edited by B. Lloyd and J. Archer (London: Academic Press, 1987), 241–65.

7. In the adrenogenital syndrome, the girl can have underdeveloped male external genitalia along with a normal set of internal, female reproductive apparatus. Surgery can correct the unnecessary boyish parts, but it cannot reverse the brain's hormonal programming. In most cases of a "alpha female," however, there is no physical abnormality, only a male way of thinking. This may be due to hormonal changes in the mother's body affecting the developing fetus; and the same is true for a "beta male."

8. Issues related to this point are discussed in C. Gouchie and D. Kimura, "The Relation Between Testosterone Levels and Cognitive Ability Patterns," *Research Bulletin 690* (London, Canada: Department of Psychology, University of Western Ontario, May 1990).

9. Similar cases and issues are discussed by A. A. Ehrhardt and H. F. L. Meyer-Bahlburg, "Effects of Prenatal Sex Hormones on Gender-Related Behavior," *Science* 211:4 (20 March 1981), 1312–18.

10. Edward de Bono, *I Am Right—You Are Wrong: From Rock Logic to Water Logic* (New York: Viking Press, 1991), 8.

11. I found a little book of funny statements about the interaction between men and women that contains most of my patients' statements. I recommend it to you as a fun way to promote your oceanic thinking. The book, by Diana Jordan and Paul Seaburn, is titled *A Wife's Little Instruction Book: Your Survival Guide to Marriage Without Bloodshed* (New York: Avon Books, 1994).

12. G. Jampolsky and D. Cirincione, *Change Your Mind, Change Your Life* (New York: Bantam Books, 1994).

13. See G. Jampolsky, *Love Is Letting Go of Fear* (Berkeley, CA: Ten Speed Press, 1979).

Chapter 6

1. M. K. Pukui, `Olelo No`Eau: Hawaiian Proverbs and Poetical Sayings*, no. 418 (Honolulu, HI: Bishop Museum Press, 1983), 52.

2. My book *The Heart's Code: Tapping the Wisdom and Power of Our Heart Energy* presents research supporting the fact that the heart is a sentient organ with its own unique energy that connects with other hearts (New York: Broadway Books, 1998).

3. The pioneers of this field are Gary Schwartz and Linda Russek; see their article "Energy Cardiology: A Dynamical Energy Systems Approach for Integrating Conventional and Alternative Medicine," *Advances: The Journal of Mind-Body Health* 12 (1996): 4–45.

4. This point is developed by physicist Ken Wilber in his classic book related to the *kakou* and `o wau* issue; see K.Wiber, *No Boundary: Eastern and Western Approaches to Personal Growth* (Boston, MA: New Science Library, 1979), 17–19.

5. These figures are reported in S. Schiefelbein, "Powerful River," in *The Incredible Machine*, edited by R. Poole (Washington, DC: The National Geographic Society, 1986).

6. For a thorough, interesting, and practical discussion of the unique role of the heart, see D. Childre and H. Martin, *The HeartMath Solution* (San Francisco, CA: HarperSanFrancisco, 1999).

7. T. S. Wiley and B. Formby, *Lights Out: Sleep, Sugar, and Survival* (New York: Pocket Books, 2000).

8. J. Armour and J. Ardell, eds., *Neurocardiology* (New York: Oxford University Press, 1984).

9. H. Benson, *Timeless Healing: The Power and Biology of Belief* (New York: Scribner, 1996).

10. J. Lacey and B. Lacey, "Some Autonomic-Central Nervous System Interrelationships," in *Physiological Correlates of Emotion*, edited by P. Black (New York: Academic Press, 1970), 205–27.

11. As defined in *The Random House College Dictionary* (New York: Random House, 1995).

12. G. Schwartz and L. Russek, *The Living Energy Universe: A Fundamental Discovery That Transforms Science and Medicine* (Charlottesville, VA: Hampton Roads Publishing Company, 1999).

13. P. Pearsall, G. E. R. Schwartz, and L. G .S. Russek, "Changes in Heart Transplant Recipients That Parallel the Personalities of Their Donors," *Journal of Integrative Medicine* (January 2000).

14. C. Sylvia and W. Novak, *Change of Heart* (New York: Little Brown, 1997).

15. Sylvia and Novak, *Change of Heart*, 136.

16. D. Ornish, *Love and Survival: The Scientific Basis for the Healing Power of Intimacy* (New York: HarperPerennial, 1998), 11.

17. These three components of love were identified and researched by R. J. Sternberg, "A Triangular Theory of Love," *Psychological Review* 93 (1986): 119–35.

18. For research on entrainment, see S. H. Strogatz and I. Stewart, "Coupled Oscillators and Biological Synchronization," *Scientific American* 269:6 (December 1993): 102–9.

19. This happens when the heart finishes one full "pumping cycle" every ten seconds. See R. McCraty, W. A. Tiller, and M. Atkinson, "Head-Heart Entrainment: A Preliminary Survey," in *Proceedings of the Brain-Mind Applied Neurophysiology EEG Neurofeedback Meeting* (Key West, FL: 1996).

20. J. Quinn, "Building a Body of Knowledge: Research on Therapeutic Touch 1974–1986," *Journal of Holistic Nursing* 6:1 (1988): 37–45.

21. R. McCraty et al., "The Electricity of Touch: Detection and Measurement of Cardiac Energy Exchange Between People," in *Brain and Values: Is a Biological Science of Values Possible?* edited by K. Pribram (Mahway, NJ: Lawrence Erlbaum Associates, 1998), 359–79.

22. L. G. Russek and G. E. Schwartz, "Interpersonal Heart-Brain Registration and the Perception of Parental Love: A 42-Year Follow-Up of the Harvard Mastery of Stress Study," *Subtle Energies* 5:3 (1994): 195–208.

23. Reported to me in personal conversation with Dr. Gary Schwartz.

24. J. C. Pearce, *Evolution's End: Claiming the Potential of Our Intelligence* (San Francisco, CA: HarperSanFrancisco, 1992), 104–5.

Chapter 7

1. Kumu Kawaikapuokalani Hewett.

2. Joel Goldsmith, *Consciousness Unfolding* (New York: Citadel Press/Carol Publishing Group, 1994), 172.

3. Sri Nisargadatta Maharaj, in *I Am That: Talks with Sri Nisargadatta Maharaj*, edited by Sudhakar Diskshit (Durham, NC: The Acorn Press, 1973), 8.

4. Larry Dossey, *Prayer Is Good Medicine* (San Francisco, CA: HarperSanFrancisco, 1996).

5. Goldsmith, *Consciousness Unfolding*.

6. Joseph Campbell and Bill Moyers, *The Power of Myth* (New York: Doubleday, 1988).

7. A. Schopenhauer, *The World as Will and Representation* (1818; New York: Smith Peter, 1969).

8. G. Easterbrook, *Beside Still Waters: Searching for Meaning in an Age of Doubt* (New York: William Morrow, 1998), 41.

9. The Hawaiian values reflected in prayer are described in G. H. S. Kanahele *Ku Kanaka—Stand Tall: A Search for Hawaiian Values* (Honolulu, HI: University of Hawai`i Press, 1986), 124.

10. Kanahele, *Ku Kanaka—Stand Tall*, 127.

11. Gen. 6.5–7, New Revised Standard Version.

12. H. Benson, *Timeless Healing: The Power and Biology of Belief* (New York: Scribner, 1996).

13. The concept of a Spiritual Quotient or spiritual intelligence as related to the unified neural structures in the brain itself is introduced by D. Zohar and I. Marshall, *SQ: Connecting with Our Spiritual Intelligence* (New York: Bloomsbury Publishing, 2000).

14. This story is reported in V. S. Ramachandrun and S. Blakeslee, *Phantoms in the Brain: Probing the Mysteries of the Human Mind* (New York: William Morrow, 1998), 175.

15. Ramachandrun and Blakeslee, *Phantoms in the Brain*.

16. Peggy Ann Wright, "The Interconnectivity of Mind, Brain, and Behavior in Altered States of Consciousness: Focus on Shamanism," *Alternative Therapies* 1:3 (1995): 50–55.

17. Reported in *Sunday Times* London (November 1997), 2.

18. More likely, it is not a "spot" or "module" but rather a complex, interactive weaving of neurons that reacts to so-called spiritual stimulation.

19. 1 John 4.16. New Revised Standard Version.

Chapter 8

1. M. K. Pukui, `Olelo No`Eau: Hawaiian Proverbs and Poetical Sayings, no. 2718 (Honolulu, HI: Bishop Museum Press, 1983), 298.

2. Alan W. Watts, *The Way of Zen* (New York: Pantheon Books, 1957).

3. Steven Bertman, *Hyperculture: The Human Cost of Speed* (Westport, CT: Praeger, 1998), 56.

4. Louis Harris, *Inside America* (New York: Random House, 1987), 9–10.

5. Survey conducted by Princeton Survey Research Associates, Inc., in *American Demographics*, September 1994, pp. 14–15. The tabulations of publications related to stress and time are based on a review of *The Readers' Guide to Periodical Literature* and *Books in Print*.

6. In his book *Beside Still Waters* (New York: William Morrow, 1998), author Greg Easterbrook writes that nature is not always based on a competitive kill-or-be-killed orientation. The example of the maple tree and goldenrod and other examples of nature's cooperativeness can be found in T. Dawson, "Hydraulic Life and Water Use in Plants," *Oceologia* (spring 1993).

7. Easterbrook, *Beside Still Waters*, 80.

8. This data is from Honolulu divorce attorney Brad Coates, "Some Sad and Surprising Divorce Statistics," *East Honolulu Newspaper* (December 1999): 14.

9. For a clear discussion of the physiological and cardiovascular aspects of "overcare," see D. Childre and H. Martin, *The HeartMath Solution* (San Francisco, CA: HarperSanFrancisco, 1999), 165–71.

10. Childre and Martin, *The HeartMath Solution*, 165.

11. As qtd. in H. Dreher, *The Immune Power Personality* (New York: Dutton, 1995).

12. From Howard Pyle, *The Merry Adventures of Robin Hood* (New York: Penguin, 1991).

13. The pioneering research on the importance of a sensitive assertiveness was conducted by George F. Solomon, "Emotional and Personality Factors in the Onset and Course of Autoimmune Disease, Particularly Rheumatoid Arthritis," in *Psychoneuroimmunology*, edited by R. Ader (New York: Academic Press, 1981).

14. G. F. Solomon et al., "An Intensive Psychoimmunologic Study of Long-Surviving Persons with AIDS," *Annals of the New York Academy of Science* 496 (1987): 647–55.

15. This concept is discussed by B. Azar, "A New Stress Paradigm for Women," *Monitor on Psychology* 31:7 (July/August 2000): 42–43.

16. This theory is proposed by University of California psychologist Shelley Taylor and five of her colleagues. It is introduced in the journal *Psychological Review* (in press).

17. T. S. Wiley and B. Formby, *Lights Out: Sleep, Sugar, and Survival* (New York: Pocket Books, 2000). This book presents the research about the importance of nine hours of sleep in darkness and its relationship to our general health, hormonal balance, and cardiovascular system.

Chapter 9

1. M. K. Pukui, `Olelo No`Eau: Hawaiian Proverbs and Poetical Sayings*, no. 1191 (Honolulu, HI: Bishop Museum Press, 1983), 129.

2. L. Dossey, "The Healing Power of Pets: A Look at Animal-Assisted Therapy," *Alternative Therapies* 3:4 (1997): 8–15.

3. L. A. Hart, "Dogs as Human Companions: A Review of the Relationship," in *The Domestic Dog*, edited by J. Serpell (London: Cambridge University Press, 1996).

4. E. B. Karsh and D. C. Turner, "The Human-Cat Relationship," in *The Domestic Cat*, edited by D. C. Turner and P. Bateson (London: Cambridge University Press, 1989).

5. This story is reported in J. M. Masson, *Dogs Never Lie About Love* (New York: Random House, 1997), 185.

6. A. Stillman, "The Communication of Contemporary Hawaiian Cultural Values in *Lua`au Hula*," unpublished paper.

7. Henry Dreher's book *The Immune Power Personality* (New York: Dutton, 1995) introduces the results of collaboration between psychologist James Pennebaker and dance therapist Anne M. Krantz, Ph.D. They have examined the ways in which movement can serve as a means of "confiding" traumatic events and feelings. See particularly pp. 115–16 and pp. 123–24.

8. I. Lamberti, *Spirit in Action* (New York: Ballantine Wellspring, 2000), 4.

9. A. Krantz, "Dancing Out Trauma: The Effect of Physiological Expression on Health" (unpublished manuscript).

10. This is documented by the research of Hawaiian scholar George Hu`eu Sanford Kanahele, *Ku Kanaka—Stand Tall: A Search for Hawaiian Values* (Honolulu, HI: University of Hawaii Press, 1986).

11. J. W. Pennebaker, *Opening Up: The Healing Power of Confiding in Others* (New York: William Morrow, 1990). Also see Henry Dreher, *The Immune Power Personality*, which contains the research behind several helpful ways to benefit from the healing power of confiding and describes guidelines for spoken and written confessions.

12. J. W. Pennebaker and S. Beall, "Confronting a Traumatic Event: Toward an Understanding of Inhibition and Disease," *Journal of Abnormal Psychology* 95 (1986): 274–81.

Chapter 10

1. M. K. Pukui, `Olelo No `Eau: Hawaiian Proverbs and Poetical Sayings* (Honolulu, HI: Bishop Museum Press, 1983), 115.

2. Irene Lamberti, *Spirit in Action* (New York: Ballantine Wellspring, 2000), 73.

3. M. K. Pukui and S. H. Elbert, *Hawaiian Dictionary*, 4th ed. (Honolulu, HI: University of Hawai`i Press, 1971), 183.

4. M. K. Pukui, E. W. Haertig, and C. A. Lee, *Nana I Ke Kumu (Look to the Source)*, vol. 2 (Honolulu, HI: University of Hawai`i Press, 1970), 81.

5. This is described in A. Fornander, *A Collection of Hawaiian Antiquities and Folklore* (Honolulu, HI: University of Hawai`i Press, 1970), 216–17.

6. A. Fornander, *A Collection of Hawaiian Antiquities and Folklore* (Honolulu, HI: Bishop Museum Press, 1917), 80.

7. M. K. Pukui, `Olelo No `Eau: Hawaiian Proverbs and Poetical Sayings* (Honolulu, HI: Bishop Museum Press, 1983), 86.

8. R. Ornstein and D. Sobel, *Healthy Pleasures* (New York: Addison-Wesley, 1989), 77.

9. J. W. Howard and R. M. Dawes, "Linear Prediction of Marital Happiness." *Personality and Social Psychology Bulletin* 2 (1996): 479–80.

10. J. Couch, "Relief of Migraine Headache with Sexual Orgasm," *Headache* 30 (April 1990): 19.

11. D. Hales and R. Hales, "The Bonding Hormone," *American Health* (November/December 1982): 37–44.

12. B. Zilbergeld, "Married Women Can Have the Best Sex Lives," *Redbook* (April 1988): 108–9.

13. In their book *Healthy Pleasures*, Drs. Ornstein and Sobel proposed an "F" index to summarize data from studies showing the importance of sex in reducing stress and conflict in a marriage. Their formula was the frequency of fornication minus the number of fights.

14. Zilbergeld, "Married Women Can Have the Best Sex Lives," 108–9.

15. F. M. Andrews and S. B. Withey, *Social Indicators of Well-Being: Americans' Perceptions of Life Quality* (New York: Plenum Publishing Corp., 1976), 207, 306.

Chapter 11

1. M. K. Pukui, `Olelo No `Eau: Hawaiian Proverbs and Poetical Sayings (Honolulu, HI: Bishop Museum Press, 1983), 127.

2. "Psychic Powers," in Mysteries of the Unknown, edited by Time-Life Books (Richmond, VA: Time-Life Books, 1987), 17.

3. Some researchers are using the term anomalous cognition to describe psi occurrences, meaning "an as yet not fully understood way the mind works."

4. The philosopher most associated with this concept is Michael Lockwood; see his Mind, Brain, and the Quantum: The Compound "I" (New York: Basil Blackwell, 1979).

5. J. Prasad and I. Stevenson, "A Survey of Spontaneous Psychical Experiences in School Children of Uttar Pradesh, India," International Journal of Parapsychology 10:2 (1968): 241–61. See also J. B. Rhine, Extra-Sensory Perception (Boston, MA: Bruce Humphries, 1964).

6. These results are described in detail in Dean Radin's classic book about psi titled The Conscious Universe: The Scientific Truth of Psychic Phenomena (San Francisco, CA: HarperSanFrancisco, 1997), 68–73.

7. G. Schwartz and L. Russek, The Living Energy Universe: A Fundamental Discovery That Transforms Science and Medicine (Charlottesville, VA: Hampton Roads Publishing Company, 1999).

8. For this analogy I am indebted to Drs. Schwartz and Russek (The Living Energy Universe, 162–63), who present it as a "home research project" of sorts for readers to try.

9. Schwartz and Russek, The Living Energy Universe, 164.

10. J. S. Bell, Speakable and Unspeakable in Quantum Mechanics (Cambridge, England: Cambridge University Press, 1987).

11. N. Herbert, Quantum Reality (New York: Anchor Books, 1987), 245.

12. The best source for a careful summary of this evidence is Dean Radin, The Conscious Universe. I doubt that any serious scientist could come away from reading Radin's book without accepting that, to various degrees and in many manifestations, psi is real. Studies about psi connections are no longer designed to see if psi exists; they are conducted to learn more about how such connections work and what they mean. The relevance of psi to the eighth pleasure prescription is that it suggests a new "old" way to love one another beyond the five senses.

13. R. G. Jahn and B. J. Dunne, Margins of Reality: The Role of Consciousness in the Physical World (New York: Harcourt Brace Jovanovich, 1987).

14. R. G. Jahn, "Report on the Academy of Consciousness Studies." Journal of Scientific Exploration 9:3 (1995): 402.

15. J. Mishlove, *Roots of Consciousness: The Classic Encyclopedia of Consciousness Studies Revised and Expanded* (Tulsa, OK: Council Oaks Books, Rives Edition, 1993).

16. For an interesting discussion of skepticism and a careful assessment of outrageous claims, see M. Chermer, *Why People Believe Weird Things* (New York: W. H. Freeman, 1997).

17. Chermer, *Why People Believe Weird Things*, 17–18. This story is also recounted by Dean Radin in *The Conscious Universe*, 112–13.

18. As qtd. in Chermer, *Why People Believe Weird Things*, 11.

19. For an excellent and beautifully illustrated presentation of psi research, see Jean Millay, *Multidimensional Mind: Remote Viewing in Hyperspace* (Berkeley, CA: North Atlantic Books, 1999).

20. R. L. McCarthy, "Present and Future Safety Challenges of Computer Control," *Computer Assurance: Compass 1988,* IEEE Catalog No. 88 CH 2628-6 (New York: IEEE), 1–7.

21. For a discussion of this work, see Russel Targ and Jan Katra, *Miracles of Mind* (Novato, CA: New World Library, 1998).

22. See J. Schnabel, *Remote Viewers: The Secret History of America's Psychic Spies* (New York: Dell Books, 1997).

23. Schnabel, *Remote Viewers*, 81.

24. Schnabel, *Remote Viewers*, 295.

25. Radin, *The Conscious Universe*, 73. These odds are based on combining the results of all similar studies on dream telepathy through a statistical technique called meta-analysis. Of course, unpublished studies may exist that fail to show that it is possible to send our dreams (scientists call this the "file drawer" problem). Other factors may also exist that lower these odds, but any reasonable scientist can conclude from the research that in some way, to some extent, we can connect across time and space in our dreams.

26. These steps are modified from and based on the research reported in M. Ullman, S. Krippner, and A. Vaughan, *Dream Telepathy* (New York: Macmillan, 1973). The steps involve my own applications of their research as employed in my clinic at Sinai Hospital of Detroit, MI.

27. M. K. Pukui, `Olelo No`Eau: Hawaiian Proverbs and Poetical Sayings*, no. 1463 (Honolulu, HI: Bishop Museum Press, 1983), 1458.

Chapter 12

1. Kumu Kawaikapuokalani Hewett.

2. I introduced this idea as related to couples in my book *The Ten Laws of Lasting Love* (New York: Simon and Schuster, 1993), 87.

3. For research related to the idea of "positive emotions" as the other side of coping, see Susan Folkman and Judith Tedlie Moskowitz, "Positive Affect and the Other Side of Coping," *American Psychologist* 55:6 (June 2000): 647–54.

4. See Steven Folkman and Richard S. Lazarus, "If It Changes It Must Be a Process: Study of Emotion and Coping During Three Stages of a Couple Examination," *Journal of Personality and Social Psychology* 48:1 (1985): 150–70.

5. For research on the sense of relief and control following a health crisis, see Stephen E. Taylor et al., "Self-Generated Feeling of Control and Adjustment to Physical Illness," *Journal of Social Issues* 47 (1991): 91–109.

6. S. Folkman et al., "Stress and Coping in Caregiving Partners of Men with AIDS," *Psychiatric Clinics of North America* 17:1 (1994): 35–55.

7. See Richard Lazarus and Stephen Folkman, *Stress, Appraisal, and Coping* (New York: Springer, 1991).

8. Of 1,794 persons, 99.5 percent answered with a positive experience. See S. Folkman, "Positive Psychological States and Coping with Severe Stress," *Social Science and Medicine* 45 (1997): 1207–21.

9. We can construct benefits from adversity, and having someone to share in doing so makes it happen more easily and often. For research support of this idea, see George Affleck and Harold Tennen, "Construing Benefits from Adversity: Adaptational Significance and Dispositional Underpinnings," *Journal of Personality* 64:4 (December 1996): 899–922.

10. G. Leonard, "The End of Sex," in *The Fireside Treasury of Light*, edited by M. O. Kelly (New York: Simon and Schuster, 1990).

11. This concept is developed in A. Combs and M. Hollad, *Synchronicity: Science, Myth, and the Trickster* (New York: Paragon House, 1990), 137–38.

12. V. Peterson, qtd. in "Sunbeams," *The Sun* 291 (March 2000): 48.

13. A. M. Lindbergh, qtd. in "Sunbeams," *The Sun* 291 (March 2000): 48.

Bibliography

Affleck, G., and H. Tennen. "Construing Benefits from Adversity: Adaptational Significance and Dispositional Underpinnings." *Journal of Personality* 64, no. 4 (December 1996): 899–922.

Alper, M. *The "God" Part of the Brain: A Scientific Interpretation of Human Spirituality and God.* New York: Rogue Press, 1998.

Amato, P., and A. Booth. *A Generation at Risk.* Boston, MA: Harvard University Press, 2000.

Andrews, F. M., and S. B. Withey. *Social Indicators of Well-Being: Americans' Perceptions of Life Quality.* New York: Plenum Publishing Corp., 1976.

Antonovsky, A. *Unraveling the Mystery of Health: How People Manage Stress and Stay Well.* San Francisco, CA: Jossey-Bass, 1987.

Archer, J. "Biological Explanations of Psychological Sex Differences." In *Exploring Sex Differences,* edited by B. Lloyd and J. Archer, 241–65. London: Academic Press, 1987.

Armour, J., and J. Ardell, eds. *Neurocardiology.* New York: Oxford University Press, 1994.

Azar, B. "A New Stress Paradigm for Women." *Monitor on Psychology* 31, no. 7 (July/August 2000): 42–43.

Bell, J. S. *Speakable and Unspeakable in Quantum Mechanics: Collected Papers on Quantum Mechanics.* Cambridge, England: Cambridge University Press, 1987.

Bennett, W. J. *The Index of Leading Cultural Indicators: American Society at the End of the Twentieth Century.* New York: Simon and Schuster, 1994.

Benson, H. *Timeless Healing: The Power and Biology of Belief.* New York: Scribner, 1996.

Bertman, S. *Hyperculture: The Human Cost of Speed.* Westport, CT: Praeger, 1998.

Borysenko, J., and M. Borysenko. *The Power of the Mind to Heal.* Carson, CA: Hay House, 1994.

Botwin, M. D., et al. "Personality and Mate Preferences: Five Factors in Mate Selection and Marital Satisfaction." *Journal of Personality* 65, no. 1 (March 1997): 107–36.

Bracke, P. E., and C. E. Thoresen. "Reducing Type-A Behavior Patterns: A Structured-Group Approach." In *Heart and Mind: The Practice of Cardiac Psychology*, edited by R. Allan and S. Scheidt. Washington, DC: American Psychological Association, 1996.

Buss, D. M. "The Evolution of Happiness." *American Psychologist* 55, no. 1 (January 2000): 15–23.

Campbell, J., and B. Moyers. *The Power of Myth.* New York: Doubleday, 1988.

Chermer, M. *Why People Believe Weird Things: Pseudoscience, Superstition, and Other Confusions of Our Time.* New York: W. H. Freeman, 1997.

Childre, D., and H. Martin. *The HeartMath Solution.* San Francisco, CA: HarperSanFrancisco, 1999.

Coates, B. "Some Sad and Surprising Divorce Statistics." *East Honolulu Newspaper*, December 1999, p. 14.

Collier, J. L. *The Rise of Selfishness in America.* New York: Oxford University Press, 1991.

Combs, A., and M. Hollad. *Synchronicity: Science, Myth, and the Trickster.* New York: Paragon House, 1990.

Couch, J. "Relief of Migraine Headache with Sexual Orgasm." *Headache* 30 (April 1990): 19.

Cousins, N. *Head First: The Biology of Hope and the Healing Power of the Human Spirit.* New York: Dutton, 1989.

Covey, S. *The 7 Habits of Highly Effective People: Powerful Lessons in Personal Change.* New York: Simon and Schuster, 1989.

Csikszentmihalyi, M. *The Evolving Self: A Psychology for the Third Millennium.* New York: HarperPerennial Library, 1993.

———. "If We Are So Rich, Why Aren't We Happy?" *American Psychologist* 54, no. 10 (October 1999): 821–27.

Dawson, T. "Hydraulic Life and Water Use in Plants." *Oceologia* (spring 1993).

Dayton Daily News. 27 March 1996.

de Bono, E. *I Am Right—You Are Wrong: From Rock Logic to Water Logic.* New York: Viking Press, 1991.

DeBusk, R. F. "Sexual Activity Triggering Myocardial Infarction: One Less Thing to Worry About." *Journal of the American Medical Association* 275, no. 3 (1996): 1447–48.

Delon, M. "The Patient in the CCU Waiting Room: In-Hospital Treatment of the Cardiac Spouse." In *Heart and Mind: The Practice of Cardiac Psychology*, edited by R. Allan and S. Scheidt. Washington, DC: American Psychological Association, 1996.

Diener, E., et al. "Subjective Well-Being: Three Decades of Progress." *Psychological Bulletin* 125 (1999): 276–302.

Dossey, L. "The Evil Eye." *Alternative Therapies* 4, no. 1 (January 1998): 9–18.

———. "The Healing Power of Pets: A Look at Animal-Assisted Therapy." *Alternative Therapies* 3, no. 4 (1997): 8–15.

———. *Prayer Is Good Medicine.* San Francisco, CA: HarperSanFrancisco, 1996.

Dreher, H. *The Immune Power Personality: Seven Traits You Can Develop to Stay Healthy.* New York: Dutton, 1995.

Dunbar, R. I. M. "Coevolution of Neocortical Size, Group Size, and Language in Humans." Behavioral and Brain Science 16, no. 4 (1993): 681–694.

Durden-Smith, J., and D. De Simone. *Sex and the Brain.* Lancaster, England: MTP Press, 1980.

Easterbrook, G. *Beside Still Waters: Searching for Meaning in an Age of Doubt.* New York: William Morrow, 1998.

Ehrhardt, A. A., and H. F. L. Meyer-Bahlburg. "Effects of Prenatal Sex Hormones on Gender-Related Behavior." *Science* 211, no. 4 (20 March 1981): 1312–18.

Eisler, R. T. *Sacred Pleasure: Sex, Myths, and the Politics of the Body—New Paths to Power and Love.* San Francisco, CA: HarperSanFrancisco, 1996.

Erikson, E. H. *Childhood and Society.* New York: W. W. Norton, 1950.

Ferrini, Paul. "The Door to the House of Love." *Miracles Magazine* 1 (autumn 1991): 53.

Fisher, H. E. *Anatomy of Love.* New York: W. W. Norton, 1992.

Folkman, S. "Positive Psychological States and Coping with Severe Stress." *Social Science and Medicine* 45 (1997): 1207–21.

Folkman, S., et al. "Stress and Coping in Caregiving Partners of Men with AIDS." *Psychiatric Clinics of North America* 17, no. 1 (1994): 35–55.

Folkman, S., and R. S. Lazarus. "If It Changes It Must Be a Process: Study of Emotion and Coping During Three Stages of a Couple Examination." *Journal of Personality and Social Psychology* 48, no. 1 (1985): 150–70.

Folkman, S., and J. T. Moskowitz. "Positive Affect and the Other Side of Coping." *American Psychologist* 55, no. 6 (June 2000): 647–54.

Fornander, A. *A Collection of Hawaiian Antiquities and Folklore.* Honolulu, HI: Bishop Museum Press, 1917.

———. *A Collection of Hawaiian Antiquities and Folklore.* Honolulu, HI: University of Hawai`i Press, 1970.

Friedman, H. S., et al. "Psychosocial and Behavioral Predictors of Longevity." *American Psychologist* 50, no. 2 (1995): 69–78.

Friedman, M., and D. Ulmer. *Treating Type-A Behavior and Your Heart.* New York: Knopf, 1984.

Genesis. New Revised Standard Version.

Glaxton, G. *Hare Brain, Tortoise Mind.* London: Ecco Press, 1997.

Goldsmith, J. *Consciousness Unfolding.* New York: Citadel Press/Carol Publishing Group, 1994.

Gottman, J. *Why Marriages Succeed and Fail . . . and How You Can Make Yours Last.* New York: Simon and Schuster, 1994.

Gouchie, C., and D. Kimura. "The Relation Between Testosterone Levels and Cognitive Ability Patterns." *Research Bulletin 690.* London, Canada: Department of Psychology, University of Western Ontario, May 1990.

Gutmann, D. *Reclaimed Powers.* New York: Basic Books, 1987.

Hales, D., and R. Hales. "The Bonding Hormone." *American Health* (November/December 1982): 37–44.

Harris, L. *Inside America.* New York: Random House, 1987.

Hart, L. A. "Dogs as Human Companions: A Review of the Relationship." In *The Domestic Dog*, edited by J. Serpell. London: Cambridge University Press, 1996.

Herbert, N. *Quantum Reality.* New York: Anchor Books, 1987.

Horna, J. L. A. "The Dual Pattern of Marital Conflict." Paper presented to the Eleventh World Congress of Sociology. New Delhi, India, 1986.

Howard, J. W., and R. M. Dawes. "Linear Prediction of Marital Happiness." *Personality and Social Psychology Bulletin* 2 (1996): 479–80.

Jahn, R. G. "Information, Consciousness, and Health." *Alternative Therapies* 2, no. 3 (1996): 32–36.

———. "Report on the Academy of Consciousness Studies." *Journal of Scientific Exploration* 9, no. 3 (1995): 402.

———. "Science and the Subjective." In *Technical Notes*. Princeton, NJ: Princeton University Press, 1997.

Jahn, R. G., and B. J. Dunne. *Margins of Reality: The Role of Consciousness in the Physical World*. New York: Harcourt Brace Jovanovich, 1987.

Jampolsky, G. *Love Is Letting Go of Fear*. Berkeley, CA: Ten Speed Press, 1979.

Jampolsky, G., and D. Cirincione. *Change Your Mind, Change Your Life*. New York: Bantam Books, 1994.

1 John. New Revised Standard Version.

Jordan, D., and P. Seaburn. *A Wife's Little Instruction Book: Your Survival Guide to Marriage Without Bloodshed*. New York: Avon Books, 1994.

Kaminer, W. *I'm Dysfunctional, You're Dysfunctional*. New York: Addison-Wesley, 1992.

Kanahele, G. H. S. *Ku Kanaka—Stand Tall: A Search for Hawaiian Values*. Honolulu, HI: University of Hawai`i Press, 1986.

Karsh, E. B., and D. C. Turner. "The Human-Cat Relationship." In *The Domestic Cat*, edited by D. C. Turner and P. Bateson. London: Cambridge University Press, 1989.

King, L. A., and S. J. Broyles. "Wishes, Gender, Personality, and Well-Being." *Journal of Personality* 65, no. 1 (March 1997): 49–76.

Kornfield, J. "Higher Consciousness: An Inside View." In *Beyond Health and Normality*, edited by R. Walsh and D. Shapiro, 320–33. New York: Van Nostrand Reinhold Company, 1983.

Krantz, A. "Dancing Out Trauma: The Effect of Physiological Expression." In press.

Lacey, J., and B. Lacey. "Some Autonomic-Central Nervous System Interrelationships." In *Physiological Correlates of Emotion*, edited by P. Black, 205–27. New York: Academic Press, 1970.

Lamberti, I. *Spirit in Action: Moving Meditations for Peace, Insight, and Personal Power*. New York: Ballantine Wellspring, 2000.

Lazarus, R., and S. Folkman. *Stress, Appraisal, and Coping*. New York: Springer, 1991.

Leo, J. "The Sleeper Effect." *U.S. News and World Report*, 2 October 2000, 18.

Leonard, G. "The End of Sex." In *The Fireside Treasury of Light*, edited by M. O. Kelly. New York: Simon and Schuster, 1990.

Lindbergh, A. M. Quote in "Sunbeams." *The Sun* 291 (March 2000): 48.

Lindner, S. *The Harried Leisure Class.* New York: Columbia University Press, 1971.

Linville, P. W. "Self-Complexity and Affective Extremity: Don't Put All of Your Eggs in One Cognitive Basket." *Social Cognition* 3, no. 1 (1985): 94–120.

Littiere, A. L. "Toward a Philosophy of Science in Women's Health Research." *Journal of Scientific Exploration* 2, no. 2 (1990): 250–60.

Lockwood, M. *Mind, Brain, and the Quantum: The Compound "I."* New York: Basil Blackwell, 1979.

Luks, A. *The Healing Power of Doing Good.* New York: Fawcett Columbine, 1992.

Machung, A. *Second Shift: Working Parents and the Revolution at Home.* New York: Viking, 1989.

Maharaj, S. N. *I Am That: Talks with Sri Nisargadatta Maharaj,* edited by Sudhakar Diskshit. Durham, NC: Acorn Press, 1973.

Margenau, H. *Open Vistas: Philosophical Perspectives of Modern Science.* New Haven, CT: Yale University Press, 1964.

Masson, J. M. *Dogs Never Lie About Love.* New York: Random House, 1997.

McCarthy, R. L. "Present and Future Safety Challenges of Computer Control." *Computer Assurance: Compass 1988.* IEEE Catalog No. 88 CH 2628-6. New York: IEEE, 1–7.

McCraty, R., et al. "The Electricity of Touch: Detection and Measurement of Cardiac Energy Exchange Between People." In *Brain and Values: Is a Biological Science of Values Possible?* edited by K. Pribram, 359–79. Mahway, NJ: Lawrence Erlbaum Associates, 1998.

McCraty, R., et al. "Head-Heart Entrainment: A Preliminary Survey." In *Proceedings of the Brain-Mind Applied Neurophysiology EEG Neurofeedback Meeting.* Key West, FL: 1996.

McKay, J. R. "Assessing Aspects of Object Relations Associated with Immune Function: Development of the Affilliative Trust-Mistrust Coding System." *Psychological Assessment* 3, no. 4 (1991): 641–47.

Meyers, D. G. "The Funds, Friends, and Faith of Happy People." *American Psychologist* 55, no. 1 (January 2000): 56–67.

———. *The Pursuit of Happiness.* New York: William Morrow, 1992.

Millay, J. *Multidimensional Mind: Remote Viewing in Hyperspace.* Berkeley, CA: North Atlantic Books, 1999.

Mishlove, J. *Roots of Consciousness: The Classic Encyclopedia of Consciousness Studies Revised and Expanded.* Tulsa, OK: Council Oaks Books, Rives Edition, 1993.

Moir, A., and D. Jessel. *Brain Sex: The Real Differences Between Men and Women.* New York: Lyle Stuart, 1991.

Moore, T. *The Re-Enchantment of Everyday Life.* San Francisco, CA: HarperSanFrancisco, 1996.

———. *Soul Mates: Honoring the Mysteries of Love and Relationship.* New York: HarperPerennial, 1987.

Morowitz, H. J. *Cosmic Joy and Local Pain: Musings of a Mystic Scientist.* New York: Charles Scribner's Sons, 1959.

Muller, J. E., et al. "Triggering Myocardial Infarction by Sexual Activity: Low Absolute Risk and Prevention by Regular Physical Exertion?" *Journal of the American Medical Association* 275, no. 6 (1996): 1405–9.

"Nouveau Riche Less Charitable," *Honolulu Advertiser*, 24 July 2000, B6.

O'Neill, G., and N. O'Neill. *Open Marriage: A New Life Style for Couples.* New York: M. Evans & Co., 1972.

Ornish, D. *Love and Survival: The Scientific Basis for the Healing Power of Intimacy.* New York: HarperPerennial, 1999.

Ornstein, R., and D. Sobel. *Healthy Pleasures.* New York: Addison-Wesley, 1989.

Parsons, T., and R. F. Bales. *Family, Socialization, and Interaction Process.* Glencoe, IL: Free Press, 1955.

Pearce, J. C. *Evolution's End: Claiming the Potential of Our Intelligence.* San Francisco, CA: HarperSanFrancisco, 1992.

Pearsall, P. *The Heart's Code: Tapping the Wisdom and Power of Our Heart Energy.* New York: Broadway Books, 1998.

———. *The Pleasure Prescription: To Love, To Work, To Play—Life in the Balance.* Alameda, CA: Hunter House, 1996.

———. *The Ten Laws of Lasting Love.* New York: Simon and Schuster, 1993.

———. *Wishing Well: Making Your Every Wish Come True.* New York: Hyperion, 2000.

Pearsall, P., G. E. R. Schwartz, and L. G. S. Russek. "Changes in Heart Transplant Recipients That Parallel the Personalities of Their Donors." *Journal of Integrative Medicine* (January 2000).

Peck, M. S. *The Road Less Traveled.* New York: Simon and Schuster, 1978.

Pennebaker, J. W. *Opening Up: The Healing Power of Confiding in Others.* New York: William Morrow, 1990.

Pennebaker, J. W., and S. Beall. "Confronting a Traumatic Event: Toward an Understanding of Inhibition and Disease." *Journal of Abnormal Psychology* 95 (1986): 274–81.

Peterson, K. S. *U.S.A. Today*, 18 July 2000, 1–2.

Peterson, V. Quote in "Sunbeams." *The Sun* 291 (March 2000): 48.

Powell, J. *Happiness Is an Inside Job*. Valencia, CA: Tabor Publishing, 1989.

Prasad, J., and I. Stevenson. "A Survey of Spontaneous Psychical Experiences in School Children of Uttar Pradesh, India." *International Journal of Parapsychology* 10, no. 2 (1968): 241–61.

Princeton Survey Research Associates, Inc. *American Demographics* (September 1994): 14–15.

"Psychic Powers." In *Mysteries of the Unknown*, 17. Richmond, VA: Time-Life Books, 1987.

Pukui, M. K. `Olelo No`Eau: Hawaiian Proverbs and Poetical Sayings*. Honolulu, HI: Bishop Museum Press, 1983.

Pukui, M. K., and S. H. Elbert. *Hawaiian Dictionary*. 4th ed. Honolulu, HI: University of Hawai`i Press, 1971.

———. *Hawaiian Dictionary*. Revised and enlarged ed. Honolulu, HI: University of Hawai`i Press, 1986.

Pukui, M. K., E. W. Haertig, and C. A. Lee. *Nana I Ke Kumu (Look to the Source)*. Vol. 2. Honolulu, HI: University of Hawai`i Press, 1970.

Quinn, J. "Building a Body of Knowledge: Research on Therapeutic Touch 1974–1986." *Journal of Holistic Nursing* 6, no. 1 (1988): 37–45.

Radin, D. *The Conscious Universe: The Scientific Truth of Psychic Phenomena*. San Francisco, CA: HarperSanFrancisco, 1997.

Ramachandrun, V. S., and S. Blakeslee. *Phantoms in the Brain: Probing the Mysteries of the Human Mind*. New York: William Morrow, 1998.

Random House College Dictionary. New York: Random House, 1995.

Restak, R. *The Brain Has a Mind of Its Own: Insights from a Practicing Neurologist*. New York: Harmony Books, 1991.

Rhine, J. B. *Extra-Sensory Perception*. Boston, MA: Bruce Humphries, 1964.

Roberts, S. *Who We Are: A Portrait of America Based on the Latest U.S. Census*. New York: Times Books, 1993.

Russek, L. G., and G. E. Schwartz. "Interpersonal Heart-Brain Registration and the Perception of Parental Love: A 42-Year Follow-Up of the Harvard Mastery of Stress Study." *Subtle Energies* 5, no. 3 (1994): 195–208.

———. "Narrative Descriptions of Parental Love and Caring Predict Health Status in Midlife: A 35-Year Follow-Up of the Harvard Mastery of Stress Study." *Alternative Therapies* 2, no. 6 (1996): 55–62.

Sayadaw, M. *The Progress of Insight: A Treatise on Satipatthana Meditation*. San Francisco, CA: Buddhist Publication Society, 1973.

Schiefelbein, S. "Powerful River." In *The Incredible Machine*, edited by R. Poole. Washington, DC: The National Geographic Society, 1986.

Schnabel, J. *Remote Viewers: The Secret History of America's Psychic Spies.* New York: Dell Books, 1997.

Schopenhauer, A. *The World as Will and Representation.* Orig. pub. 1818. New York: Smith Peter, 1969.

Schwartz, B. "Self-Determination: The Tyranny of Freedom." *American Psychologist* 55, no. 1 (January 2000): 79–88.

Schwartz, G., and L. Russek. "Energy Cardiology: A Dynamical Energy Systems Approach for Integrating Conventional and Alternative Medicine." *Advances: The Journal of Mind-Body Health* 12 (1996): 4–45.

———. *The Living Energy Universe: A Fundamental Discovery That Transforms Science and Medicine.* Charlottesville, VA: Hampton Roads Publishing Company, 1999.

Seligman, M. E. P., and M. Csikzentmihalyi. "Positive Psychology: An Introduction." *American Psychologist* 55, no. 1 (January 2000): 5–14.

Shapiro, J., and D. H. Shapiro. "Well-Being and Relationship." In *Beyond Health and Normality*, edited by R. Walsh and D. H. Shapiro, 207–14. New York: Van Nostrand Reinhold Company, 1983.

Sheldrake, R. *Dogs That Know When Their Owners Are Coming Home.* New York: Crown Publishers, 1999.

Sicher, F., et al. "A Randomized Double-Blind Study of the Effect of Distant Healing in a Population with Advanced AIDS." *Western Journal of Medicine* 169 (December 1998): 356–63.

Sobel, D. "Healthy Pleasures." Presentation to the National Wellness Conference, Stevens Point, WI, 18 July 2000.

Sobel, D., and R. Ornstein. "Sexual Activity and Heart Attack: Not to Worry." *Mind/Body Health Newsletter* 5 (1996): 2–3.

Solomon, G. F. "Emotional and Personality Factors in the Onset and Course of Autoimmune Disease, Particularly Rheumatoid Arthritis." In *Psychoneuroimmunology*, edited by R. Ader. New York: Academic Press, 1981.

Solomon, G. F., et al. "An Intensive Psychoimmunologic Study of Long-Surviving Persons with AIDS." *Annals of the New York Academy of Science* 496 (1987): 647–55.

Statistical Abstract of the United States. Washington, DC: U.S. Department of Commerce, 1989, 53.

Sternberg, R. J. "A Triangular Theory of Love." *Psychological Review* 93 (1986): 119–35.

Stevenson, R. L. *Travels with a Donkey in the Cevennes.* Everyman's Classic Edition. London: J. M. Dent and Sons, 1984.

Stillman, A. "The Communication of Contemporary Hawaiian Cultural Values in *Lua`au Hula.*" Unpublished paper.

Strogatz, S. H., and I. Stewart. "Coupled Oscillators and Biological Synchronization." *Scientific American* 269, no. 6 (December 1993): 102–9.

The Sunday Times (London). November 1997, 2.

Sylvia, C., and W. Novak. *Change of Heart.* New York: Little Brown, 1997.

Targ, R., and J. Katra. *Miracles of Mind: Exploring Nonlocal Consciousness and Spiritual Healing.* Novato, CA: New World Library, 1998.

Taylor, S. E., et al. "Self-Generated Feeling of Control and Adjustment to Physical Illness." *Journal of Social Issues* 47 (1991): 91–109.

Traill, D. A. *Schliemann of Troy.* New York: St. Martin's Press, 1996.

Ullman, M., S. Krippner, and A. Vaughan. *Dream Telepathy: Experiments in Nocturnal ESP.* New York: Macmillan, 1973.

Waite, L. *The Case for Marriage.* New York: Doubleday, 2000.

Wallerstein, J. *The Unexpected Legacy of Divorce.* New York: Hyperion, 2000.

Watts, A. W. *The Way of Zen.* New York: Pantheon Books, 1957.

Webster's Third New International Dictionary. Springfield, MD: Merriam Webster, 1993.

Weiss, R. W. *Staying the Course.* New York: Free Press, 1990.

Wilber, K. *No Boundary: Eastern and Western Approaches to Personal Growth.* Boston, MA: New Science Library, 1979.

Wiley, T. S., and B. Formby. *Lights Out: Sleep, Sugar, and Survival.* New York: Pocket Books, 2000.

Wiseman, R., and M. J. Schlitz. "Experimenter Effects and the Remote Detection of Staring." *Proceedings of Presented Papers*, edited by E. C. May. Thirty-Ninth Annual Parapsychological Association Convention. Fairhaven, MA: Parapsychological Association, 1996.

Wright, P. A. "The Interconnectivity of Mind, Brain, and Behavior in Altered States of Consciousness: Focus on Shamanism." *Alternative Therapies* 1, no. 3 (1995): 50–55.

Zilbergeld, B. "Married Women Can Have the Best Sex Lives." *Redbook* (April 1988): 108–9.

Zohar, D., and I. Marshall. *SQ: Connecting with Our Spiritual Intelligence.* New York: Bloomsbury Publishing, 2000.

Index

TO CONTACT THE AUTHOR

Dr. Paul Ka`ikena Pearsall is one of the world's most-requested lecturers. He gives presentations to business, educational, medical, and lay audiences and is often asked to present his `aha mele`—unique Hawaiian-style edu-concerts—including *halau* (dancers) and musicians that illustrate the application of ancient Hawaiian principles, such as those discussed in this book, to modern living, working, and loving. To contact him to schedule an appearance, please write to his offices at:

Dr. Paul Ka`ikena Pearsall
Founder and CEO, Ho`ala Hou
6910 Kalanianaole Highway
Honolulu, Hawai`i 96825

THE PLEASURE PRESCRIPTION
To Love, to Work, to Play—Life in the Balance

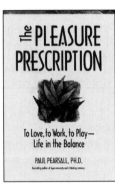

After the author appeared on "The Montel Williams Show" in December 1996, *The Pleasure Prescription* rocketed to the top of the bestseller lists. Its message of finding and giving pleasure by reducing stress and cultivating harmony appealed to readers everywhere. On air, Dr. Pearsall explained why: "Balanced pleasure is the natural way to physical and mental health and the best remedy for the toxic success syndrome that is squeezing the joy out of Western culture."

In this book, Paul Pearsall uncovers the connections between the latest research in physical and emotional health research and the Oceanic Way—the beliefs, customs, and practices of the 2,000-year-old Polynesian cultures. The Oceanic Way is based on enjoying or relishing life and connecting deeply with others, with one's traditions, and with this land, the earth. Balance, happiness, and health come from practicing the five qualities of *aloha:* patience, connection, pleasantness, modesty, and tenderness.

Dr. Pearsall gives simple tests to find areas of particular stress and unhappiness in our lives and offers practical suggestions for dealing with our real, everyday challenges: in relationships, on the job, as parents, and in caring for our community and planet. Dr. Pearsall assures us that we know more than we think we know about what is good and healthy for us.

Today, *The Pleasure Prescription* continues to bring joy and inspiration to thousands of readers all over the world and a new vision of life lived in balance. There is something about its message that appeals to our sense of humanity and to another, almost-forgotten concept: our sense of honor. Dr. Pearsall has shared with us the secrets of a new "way" that is centuries old.

Paperback $13.95 ... Hardcover $23.95 ... 288 pp.... 6 x 9

WRITE YOUR OWN PLEASURE PRESCRIPTION:
60 Ways to Create Balance & Joy in Your Life

A companion volume to *The Pleasure Prescription,* the beautifully designed *Write Your Own Pleasure Prescription* is full of ideas for bringing the spirit of *aloha*—the ability and willingness to fully connect with oneself and others—to everyday life, whether you live in Polynesia or in Pittsburgh.

Would those who know you best say you are a total pleasure to live, love, work, and play with? In this practical guide to slowing down and enjoying small pleasures, Dr. Paul Pearsall gives 60 new ideas for bringing joy and balance back into your life. There are

▼ 15 specific pleasure prescriptions for more healthy and fulfilling loving and sensuality

▼ 15 specific pleasure prescriptions for more fulfilling, productive, joyful working

▼ 15 specific pleasure prescriptions for healthier, happier, relaxing, and more constructive playing

▼ 15 specific pleasure prescriptions for times of loss, illness, and hardship

From learning how to "go with how it goes" at work (pleasure prescription #18) to "just say maybe" (pleasure prescription #26), "pay back your love debts" (pleasure prescription #14) to "do your best to stop global whining" (pleasure prescription #44), these fun, profound, and caring suggestions give us the ability to shift our lives so that we feel the joy that can be a part of each day.

After offering dozens of ideas, Dr. Pearsall describes how everyone can write their own pleasure prescriptions, perfectly suited to their lives. The book also includes three "Learning Supplements," including a "dictionary of delight," a glossary of new "pleasure words," and 2,000-year-old healing proverbs and sayings from Hawai`i.

Paperback $12.95 ... 224 pp. ... 6 x 9

To order see last page or call (800) 266-5592

ORDER FORM

NAME

ADDRESS

CITY/STATE   ZIP/POSTCODE

PHONE   COUNTRY (outside of U.S.)

TITLE	QTY	PRICE	TOTAL
Partners in Pleasure (paper)		@ $14.95	

Prices subject to change without notice

Please list other titles below:

		@ $	
		@ $	
		@ $	
		@ $	
		@ $	
		@ $	
		@ $	
		@ $	

Check here to receive our book catalog ❑   free

Shipping Costs		
First book: $3.00 by bookpost, $4.50 by UPS, Priority Mail, or to ship outside the U.S. Each additional book: $1.00 For rush orders and bulk shipments call us at (800) 266-5592	TOTAL	_____
	Less discount @ ____%	(_____)
	TOTAL COST OF BOOKS	_____
	Calif. residents add sales tax	_____
	Shipping & handling	_____
	TOTAL ENCLOSED	_____
	Please pay in U.S. funds only	

❑ Check ❑ Money Order ❑ Visa ❑ MasterCard ❑ Discover

Card #_____ Exp. date _____

Signature_____

Complete and mail to:

Hunter House Inc., Publishers

PO Box 2914, Alameda CA 94501-0914
Phone (510) 865-5282 Fax (510) 865-4295
Orders: (800) 266-5592 or **www.hunterhouse.com**
email: ordering@hunterhouse.com

PIP- 3/2001